TEXTILES AND CLOTHING
*c.*1150–*c.*1450

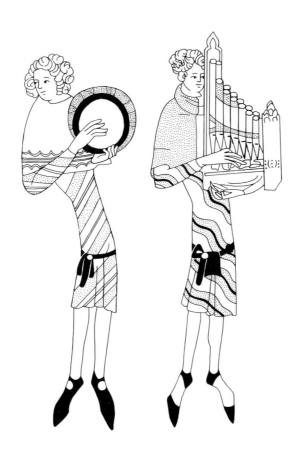

Acknowledgements for grants

The publication of this book has been assisted by grants from the following organisations, which are gratefully acknowledged:

The Marc Fitch Fund
The Pasold Research Fund
The Museum of London
The bequest of John Nevinson to the London
    and Middlesex Archaeological Society
Friends of Fashion

Front cover Linen clothing from the *Tacuinum Sanitatis In Medicina, c.* 1390–1407. (Österreichische Nationalbibliothek, Vienna, Cod.ser.nov.2644, f.105v)

Half-title Minstrels wearing bias-cut tunics made from cloth patterned with weft-faced bands, *c.*1340 (after *The Romance of Alexander*, MS Bodl 264, f.127v)

Title page Gawain and a lady wearing tunics with buttoned sleeves cut straight at the wrist, early 14th-century (after BL Add MS 10294, f.56)

MUSEUM OF LONDON

MEDIEVAL FINDS FROM EXCAVATIONS IN LONDON:4

TEXTILES AND CLOTHING

c.1150–c.1450

Elisabeth Crowfoot, Frances Pritchard and Kay Staniland

Photography by Edwin Baker

Illustrations by Christina Unwin

THE BOYDELL PRESS

First published 1992
Her Majesty's Stationery Office

New edition 2001
The Boydell Press, Woodbridge

ISBN 0 85115 840 4

A Museum of London Publication
Museum of London, London Wall,
London EC2Y 5HN
www.museumoflondon.org.uk

The Boydell Press is an imprint of Boydell & Brewer Ltd
PO Box 9, Woodbridge, Suffolk IP12 3DF, UK
and of Boydell & Brewer Inc.
PO Box 41026, Rochester, NY 14604-4126, USA
www.boydell.co.uk

A catalogue record for this book is available
from the British Library

Library of Congress Cataloging-in-Publication Data applied for

This publication is printed on acid-free paper

Printed in Great Britain by
St Edmundsbury Press Limited, Bury St Edmunds, Suffolk

Contents

Introduction to second edition

Frances Pritchard

One of the most unexpected gains from the rescue excavations undertaken in the City of London during the 1970s and early 1980s was the quantity of medieval textiles retrieved, particularly from sites beside the River Thames. The variety of these textiles remains unsurpassed in Western Europe and the material is as significant for the medieval period as the textiles from Vindolanda, close to Hadrian's Wall, are for the Roman period. Recent archaeological activities in London have yielded nothing comparable and, therefore, the contents of this volume remain as relevant today as when they were first published.

A few developments in the study of medieval textiles have taken place in the decade that has elapsed since the first edition was printed. A valuable new reference book has appeared on the medieval cloth industry, which makes extensive use of information derived from excavated textiles as well as from documentary and visual sources (Cardon 1999). Other research has focussed on patterned silks. One type of silk identified here as probably Spanish (No 398, pp 104–107) is now considered by an eminent textile historian to be of possible French origin – perhaps from the Cevennes region or even Paris (Desrosiers 1999, 105–16). In addition, Iraq, rather than Islamic Spain, has been suggested as the country of manufacture for another distinctive silk (No 459, pp 107–12; Wilckens 1992, 41–42, nos 61 and 62). The date of the grave in Bremen cathedral where the earliest silk of this type was found has also been questioned due to the presence of a gold finger-ring with a 'stirrup-shaped' hoop, which more likely belongs to the 12th than to the 11th century (Hinton 1990, 647).

The book has found a wide international readership among students and scholars interested in the history of dress, urban studies and the material culture of the Middle Ages. It is a great pleasure that it is being republished, together with the rest of the series, to make the information accessible to a new generation.

DESROSIERS, S, 1999 'Draps d'areste (II). Extension de la classification, comparaisons et lieux fabrication', *Soieries médiévales, Techniques & Culture,* **34**, 89–119

CARDON, D, 1999 *La Draperie au Moyen Âge: Essor d'une Grande Industrie Européenne*, Paris

HINTON, D A, 1990 'Metal finger-rings' in Biddle, M (ed), *Object and Economy in Medieval Winchester*, Winchester Studies **7/2**, 646–51

WILCKENS, L von, 1992 *Mittelalterliche Seidenstoffe*, Berlin

Correction

p 133, Fig 100C: for 451 read 449

Acknowledgements

This book would not have been written without the efforts of many field archaeologists, particularly Peter Marsden who conducted excavations at Baynard's Castle. Conservation of the textiles was undertaken by staff of the Guildhall Museum, and its successor the Museum of London, including Helen Ganiaris, Suzanne Keene, Lynn Morrison, Marilee Parrott, Poppy Singer and Kate Starling. Dilys Blum and Poppy Singer advised on a system of storage for the textiles. In addition, practical help has been given over many years by Glynis Edwards of the Ancient Monuments Laboratory.

Other colleagues and former colleagues within the Museum of London who have helped or advised are Jon Bailey, Jenny Bewick, Trevor Hurst, Jan Scrivener and Sue Wookey (Photographic Section); Cathy Collcutt, Barbara Heiberger and Jill Spanner (Costume and Textiles Department); Geoff Egan, Francesca Radcliffe and Alan Vince (Department of Urban Archaeology). Tony Dyson, Francis Grew and Angela Wardle have edited the text and Anne Jenner undertook much of the layout.

Fibres were identified by Harry M Appleyard, Rowena Gale and Michael Ryder. Dye testing was undertaken at Bristol University by Professor M C Whiting and his former students, A Harvey, J Harvey, T Sugiura and M J K Thomas. More recent dye analyses were done by Penelope Walton who also made many helpful suggestions with regard to the textiles. X-ray fluorescence analysis of metal threads was carried out at the Ancient Monuments Laboratory by Justine Bayley and Paul Wilthew.

Most of the excavations and post-excavation processing and analysis were funded by HBMC (England) and its predecessor within the Department of the Environment. The City of London Archaeological Trust Fund and the Museum of London Trust Fund provided the main financial support for the Swan Lane and Billingsgate watching briefs.

The authors have benefited from discussion and correspondence with many individuals. They include Helen Bennett, Patrick Chorley, Geza Féhérvari, Karen Finch, Hero Granger-Taylor, Inga Hägg, Derek Keene, Donald King, Anne Kjellberg, Jerzy Maik, Margareta Nockert, Marianne Straub, Anneliese Streiter, Anne Sutton, Tuuk Stam, Klaus Tidow, Erika Weiland, John Peter Wild and Juan Zozaya. Special thanks are owed to Sandra Vons-Comis for showing us medieval textiles from excavations in The Netherlands, Lisa Monnas who gave considerable help with analysing the silk textiles and offered many valuable comments, and Anna Muthesius who generously shared information concerning medieval silks in continental collections.

Many libraries have provided essential reading resources for this study and we should like to thank the staff of the Conway Library, Guildhall Library, Institute of Archaeology, Institute of Historical Research, London Library, National Art Library, Public Record Office, and Warburg Institute.

The glossary entries are based on definitions from *A Textile Terminology: Warp and Weft* by Dorothy K Burnham, reproduced by kind permission of Routledge.

The publication of the plates has been made possible by grants from The Marc Fitch Fund, The Pasold Research Fund, The Museum of London Publications Committee, Friends of Fashion of the Museum of London and the bequest of John Nevinson to the London and Middlesex Archaeological Society. John Nevinson was the first person to publish an article on the buttons and buttonholes from Baynard's Castle and we are delighted to be the recipients of his beneficence.

Conventions

Numerical references

The numerical references throughout the text fall into three categories:

BC72, TL74, etc.
These codes relate to the sites on which the excavated textiles discussed in this book have been found. The full list of sites, with dates of excavation, is as follows:

BC72	Baynard's House (commonly known as Baynard's Castle), Queen Victoria Street, EC4, 1972
BC75	Baynard's House, Queen Victoria Street, EC4, 1975
BIG82	Billingsgate Lorry Park, Lower Thames Street, EC3, 1982
BWB83	Billingsgate Lorry Park, Lower Thames Street, EC3, 1983 (watching brief)
BYD81	Baynard's Castle/City of London Boys' School, Upper Thames Street, EC4, 1981
CUS73	Custom House, Wool Quay, Lower Thames Street, EC3, 1973
DUK77	2–7 Dukes Place, EC3, 1977
FRE78	New Fresh Wharf, Lower Thames Street, EC3, 1978
Guildhall Car Park Site	Aldermanbury, EC2, 1965
MLK76	1–6 Milk Street, EC2, 1976
Public Cleansing Depot	Upper Thames Street, EC3, 1959
SH74	Seal House, 106–8 Upper Thames Street, EC4, 1974
SWA81	Swan Lane/Upper Thames Street, EC4, 1981
TL74	2–3 Trig Lane, Upper Thames Street, EC4, 1974

Detailed information on the sites is given in the chapter on Excavations.

No 1, No 54, No 159, etc.
The consecutive numbers given to the excavated items discussed in this book, some of which are described in detail in the Selected Catalogues (see below), and all of which are listed in the Concordance (see below).

Fig 1, Fig 73, Fig 183, Table 4, Pl 4A, etc.
References to black and white illustrations, diagrams, tables and colour plates in this book.

Illustrations and bibliographic references

The references No, Fig, Table, Map, Pl relate to this work and are given with an initial capital letter; they are shown first when appearing in conjunction with references to other publications. References to other sources use lower case initials for no, fig, etc.

Selected catalogues

These give full descriptions of selected items, namely wool textiles with woven patterns (but not just colour effects), tapestries, all silk fabrics other than unpatterned cloths in tabby weave, flat tablet-woven braids, purpose-made garters and hairnets. The dates given in these catalogues refer to the date of deposition and not of manufacture.

The selected catalogues (numbered I–XIV) appear at the end of the relevant sections within the main text.

Concordance

This lists in numerical order all the items discussed in this book. It also includes information on the site, the site context, the date, details of fibre/weave/twist of yarn, and, if relevant, gives a reference to Selected Catalogue, Tables, Figures, Plates, dye analysis (see Appendix). Further details regarding identification of the numbered items discussed in this book can be found in the introduction to the concordance.

Abbreviations

acc no	accession number
c	chapter (in Statutes)
c.	circa
Cal Wills	*Calendar of Wills Proved* . . . (see Bibliography)
CCR	*Calendar of Close Rolls* . . . (see Bibliography)
CLR	*Calendar of Liberate Rolls* . . . (see Bibliography)
cm	centimetre
d	diameter
EHD	*English Historical Documents* . . . (see Bibliography)
f.	folio
Fig	Figure, used to denote an illustration/diagram in this book
fn	footnote
h	height
HBMC(E)	Historic Buildings and Monuments Commission (England)
l	length
m	metre
mm	millimetre
MOL	Museum of London

No	Number, used to indicate numbered items in this book
pers comm	personal communication
Pl	Plate, used to denote a colour plate in this book
PRO	Public Record Office, London
S/S, Z/Z	for yarns with a similar direction of twist in both warp and weft (see also Glossary)
w	width
XRF	x-ray fluorescence
Z/S	or mixed spinning, i.e. yarn is Z-twisted in one system (usually the warp) and S-twisted in the other (see also Glossary)

Key for drawings

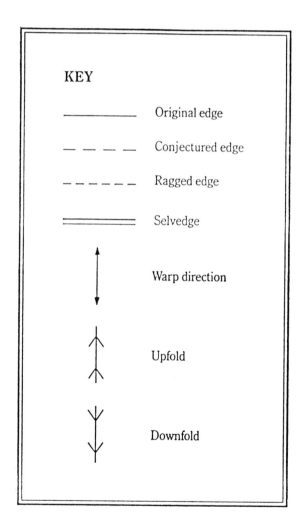

Introduction

Archaeological investigations in the city of London during the 1970s and 1980s have stimulated research into many aspects of urban life. The quantity of everyday objects from the period 1150 to 1450 is particularly impressive and provides information which has never before been available to historians. The timespan was chosen as it coincides with a sequence of riverside rubbish dumping which can be dated very accurately, and from which most of the artefacts described in this series of books were recovered.

Sources

Textiles and clothing are topics which until recently in England have depended largely upon assumptions made from visual sources — such as manuscript illuminations, effigies of stone or wood, monumental brasses, wall and panel paintings — and analyses of written records, supplemented by a few examples of textiles of artistic or historic merit preserved in churches and art collections. While visual and written sources still remain richly rewarding fields of research, the textiles themselves offer tangible proof of what was available, what could be produced and what was worn in medieval London.

This form of evidence is not limited to London. Other English towns, notably Kingston upon Hull (Walton forthcoming), Newcastle (Walton 1988), Southampton (Crowfoot 1975), Winchester (Crowfoot 1990) and York (Walton 1989A), have yielded textiles which fit into the general pattern provided by the more extensive collections from London, and these are complemented by pieces from rural, priory, castle and manor sites (e.g. Crowfoot 1954; Carter & Henshall 1957; Crowfoot 1966; Ford 1983). As a result of this growing quantity of data, a picture is emerging of the type of textiles in everyday use in England during the late medieval period.

Urban excavations elsewhere in northern Europe, usually carried out in rescue circumstances where land is being redeveloped, have also resulted in large numbers of textiles being recovered from medieval deposits. These towns include Novgorod in Russia; Trondheim, Bergen and Oslo in Norway; Wolin, Gdansk and Opole in Poland; Schleswig and Lübeck in West Germany; Amsterdam and Dordrecht in The Netherlands, and Perth in Scotland. Published reports are available for some of these collections (Nahlik 1963; Bergli 1988; Schjølberg 1984; Kjellberg 1979; Kjellberg 1982; Maik 1988; Kaminska & Nahlik 1960; Tidow 1982; Vons-Comis 1982; Bennett 1987), but despite this much of the evidence remains little known to the general public or to dress and economic historians. Textiles from towns in southern Europe have, up to now, been recorded in smaller numbers. Comparative data used to place the London textiles in their European context relies heavily, therefore, upon evidence from northern Europe. They cannot claim to represent a full cross-section of urban society but, nevertheless, they form a valid starting point for investigation.

While town excavations are the largest source of medieval textiles preserved today in England, they are not the only source. Graves and tombs also yield textiles which often have the added fascination of being associated with a known personality. The practice of opening tombs is not a new one. In the middle ages tombs were opened to provide evidence of a body's incorruptibility, and the corpses of saints were sometimes translated from one tomb to another. As a result chroniclers occasionally described textiles removed from tombs or added to them, for example those of St Cuthbert at Durham Cathedral (Battiscombe 1956, 9–14) or of Edward the Confessor at Westminster Abbey (Dodwell 1982, 162–5). Building repairs and restoration have also led to the disturbance and opening of tombs over many centuries; Gervase, a monk at Christ Church, Canterbury, recorded two instances that took place there in the late 12th century after a fire (St John Hope 1891–3, 196), and many are documented from the 19th and 20th centuries. Tombs in England to yield textiles include those of William de Blois (died 1236) and Walter de Cantilupe (died 1266) (Worcester Cathedral: St John Hope 1891–3, 197–200; Christie 1938, 52–4, nos 4–8 and 68–70, nos 33–7; King 1984, 359, no 495); probably Henry de Blois, Bishop of Winchester (died 1171), who was the younger brother of King Stephen and a distinguished patron of the arts (Winchester Cathedral: Joyce 1869, 309; Crowfoot 1990, 477–9, 486–8); Hubert Walter, Archbishop of Canterbury (died 1205), a leading negotiator in the Holy Land during the Third Crusade (Canterbury Cathedral: St John Hope 1891–3; Christie 1938, 59, nos 15–18; Muthesius 1982A, 71–89; King 1984, 358, no 493); Walter de Gray, Archbishop of York (died 1255), who was Chancellor to King John and a regent of England during the minority of Henry III, and Godfrey de Ludham, Archbishop of York (died 1265) (York Minster: King 1971). In addition, the coffin of Edward I in Westminster Abbey was opened in 1774 but records give only the barest account of the king's burial robes and, on this occasion, no fragments of textiles were removed (Ayloffe 1786; Alexander & Binski 1987, 368, nos 382–3).

Textiles from tombs such as these provide a standard against which those from urban excavations can be assessed. Although it is rare for urban refuse to include items of the quality of the burial garments of nobles or bishops, occasionally points of similarity do emerge, especially as the variety of silk cloths excavated from London is greater than that recorded from other towns in northern Europe. Materials used as the ground fabrics for English embroideries also sometimes provide comparisons. A Chinese twill damask from a deposit dating to the second quarter of the 14th century, for example, finds parallels from England only among pieces of *opus anglicanum*. What is absent from these tombs are wool cloths. Here the contribution of London's extensive assemblages, particularly those dating to the 14th century, is of immense importance for they encapsulate the main grades of cloth available at the time and indicate changes in the types of cloth used within a dated framework.

Preservation of the textiles

Unlike pottery, textiles are extremely perishable. Only in the stable conditions of a dry desert or sealed within a layer of permafrost are textiles prevented from decaying. Conditions of burial on sites in London from which textiles have been recovered are by no means identical and never ideal, and the surviving textiles are biased by the types of deposit in which they are preserved. They occur most frequently where anaerobic conditions prevail, along the Thames waterfront, for example, and occasionally in cesspits. These acid conditions have the effect of causing cellulose fibres to break down very rapidly, particularly through fungal attack, and linen is, therefore, poorly represented. Negative evidence in the form of traces of missing sewing threads and facings indicate, however, where these were originally present. Metallic threads have also decayed in the hostile soil conditions leaving behind areas of threadbare patterning (e.g. Pls 15A, 13B). These metal threads are not all of one type and analysis by energy dispersive x-ray fluorescence (XRF) can often determine their original composition despite very little metal remaining visible. Some decay — in particular photochemical degradation — may have taken place, or at least started, before burial. Dyeing practices, particularly the use of certain mordants, are certainly the cause of some threads rotting as, for example, on wool cloths patterned with transverse stripes of different colours, where threads of some dark purple shades are preserved only in part (e.g. Pls 9A, 11A).

A further difficulty is that the humic acids, tannins and iron salts in the soil cause the cloths to become permanently stained various shades of brown, thereby losing the colourfulness and subtlety of the original hues. Wool textiles are more severely affected by this action than those made from silk, where vestiges of colour are more often visible. The reason for this difference has not yet been determined, although the contrasting chemical and physical properties of the fibres would appear to be decisive. Where colour does remain visible on wool fabrics, the textiles have usually been very densely packed together during burial so that, presumably, they have been better protected against soiling.

Fur is also conspicuously absent from the excavated pieces of clothing, thereby detracting from its important practical and sartorial role. No doubt some small scraps were thrown away and have decomposed, leaving no evidence at all for their presence. It should be noted, however, that the conditions prevailing in the dock infill at the East Watergate (BC72) were sufficiently favourable to preserve such delicate items as the feathers of peacocks and other birds. In addition, none of the sewing or stitch holes hint at the former presence of fur linings such as those recorded on garments of prosperous merchant families buried in a cemetery dating to the 9th and 10th centuries at Birka in eastern Sweden (Hägg 1983, 320, figs 17.4a and b). Fur linings are known, nevertheless, to have been worn by the citizens of London for warmth as well as status (Veale 1966, 3–5). The negative evidence is slightly puzzling until one takes into account the activities of the fripperers, secondhand clothing dealers. They formed a thriving community in London in the 13th century and it is probable that their work generally mirrored that of their Parisian counterparts as outlined by Etienne Boileau in 1268 (Depping 1837, 194–204). In Paris the fripperers were the only citizens allowed to deal in secondhand clothing of any kind, a measure intended to control the fraudulent mixture of old and new materials; there were also regulations concerning the sources of their goods, including the removal of clothing from corpses. The names of numerous secondhand clothing dealers are to be found in London documents, although information about their trade remains obscure. A proclamation of 1310 declaring 'that no tailor or fripperer scour furs except at night in the highways of the City, or in some by-way by day under pain of imprisonment, lest the nobility and others be inconvenienced whilst passing' (Sharpe 1902, Letterbook D, f.cviii, 233) provides, however, an insight into the less sociable aspects of their work.

Circumstances of deposition

The place of deposition may occasionally give an indication of the previous ownership of a textile, but it is rarely possible to reconstruct the complete cycle through which a textile would have passed before it was thrown away. This is because textiles had a considerable reuse value. Household linen and furnishings were handed down from one generation to another and, quite apart from the activity of the fripperers, clothing was frequently bequeathed to relatives, friends, apprentices and servants; even such mundane items as hose were sometimes included as bequests (Cal Wills II, 32). Garments, furnishings and napery were also presented to churches to be transformed into vestments. Agnes Pikerell, for example, widow of a London saddler, by her will dated 9 April 1373 left a 'coverlit smalchekerd and her best sheet of cloth of Reynes' to the church of St Vedast for covering the Holy Sepulchre at Easter; and in 1375 Edelena atte Legh, widow of a stockfishmonger, bequeathed her best tablecloth and towel to the high altar of the church of St Michael Crookedlane (Cal Wills II, 154–5, 178).

Two silk cloths from a cesspit at Dukes Place (DUK77) provide the clearest insight into their original use since they can be directly associated with an important ecclesiastical foundation, Holy Trinity Priory, and there is no doubt that they came from worn-out vestments. The quality of one cloth is so outstanding that it seems probable that it was given to the priory by a wealthy and influential patron in the 12th century, some 200 years before it was finally discarded. On another site, that at Milk Street (MLK76), the small cut-up scraps of wool cloth include a rare type of fine worsted and it is possible that they were discarded at the very beginning of the 15th century when Thomas Dyster, a rich mercer, lived in the tenement (Schofield *et al.* forthcoming).

The textiles dumped along the waterfront for the twin purposes of rubbish disposal and land reclamation generally cannot be traced to a particular source, especially as there was public access to much of the riverside via the narrow lanes that ran between private tenements (Dyson 1989, 17–19). Indeed, few differences can be pinpointed among the waterfront assemblages, apart from those relating to chronology, mainly because the groups were so small. Fragments of silk linings and braids occur alongside plain and striped wool fabrics of varying quality and coarse goathair cloths which may have been used for wrapping goods. By contrast, the accumulation of rubbish at the East Watergate (BC72) gives a very different impression because there is so much of it, both from a deposit dating to the second quarter of the 14th century and from the dock infill which is dated to a few decades later. The latter assemblage constitutes the greatest quantity of finds ever excavated from one deposit in the City and is marked by certain items of good quality and high fashion. They include piked shoes with engraved and openwork patterns (Grew & Neergaard 1988, 29, 32), part of a walrus-ivory diptych (Dyson 1989, fig 22), a wide variety of spurs and spur leathers (Clark *et al.* forthcoming), and the only horseshoes known from England with stamped marks (Clark 1988, 19, 21, nos 8, 9).

It has been suggested that at least part of this late 14th-century assemblage could have come from the Great (royal) Wardrobe. This institution emerged in the middle years of the 13th century as a sub-department of the Wardrobe, a store-house for the increasing quantities of bulky non-perishable goods acquired for the use of the royal household (Tout 1920, I, 269, 273–5). That it was a warehouse is indisputable, but what remains uncertain is what other provisioning activities may have taken place under the same roof. Edward III had his own personal armourers and tailors, and each member of his family also had their own tailors. So far as is known, none of these people carried out their work on the premises of the Great Wardrobe. Instead they worked in houses specially rented elsewhere in the City, visiting the Great Wardrobe to collect the main components for their allotted tasks. They seem to have delivered the completed goods directly to the offices of their master or mistress. What happened in the royal household to clothing once worn and discarded is not clear, but a large part was almost certainly distributed as gifts or favours. The officers of the time, however, do not appear to have indulged in the meticulous list-making frequent a century or two later (Arnold 1980, 9, 22–83).

In 1360 the Great Wardrobe moved out of premises in Lombard Street and by 1361 it had become established in a group of buildings situated west of Knightrider Street and bounded by St Andrew's Hill, Carter Lane and Addle Hill which were acquired by Edward III from the executors of Sir John Beauchamp (Tout 1928, III, 178–9; Dyson 1989, 12, fig 17). This meant that the wardrobe and the dock at the East Watergate were directly connected by a lane which ran down Addle Hill (Dyson 1989, 12), and in view of this it is not impossible that some of the rubbish in the dock came from the Great Wardrobe itself. If one category of artefact could be expected above all others to have come from this source it would be clothing and textiles. These, however, do not appear to have done so. Admittedly, some of the

offcuts of clothing and textiles were, or once had been, fashionable. Chief among these are the edge of a sleeve, finished with at least 46 small buttons and made from a cloth dyed crimson (Fig 144), and snippets of Italian fabrics with bizarre and exotic patterns (Figs 86, 88, 90). However, edgings with similar small buttons that are typical of the close-fitting clothes of the epoch also occur in the earlier Watergate deposit dating to the second quarter of the 14th century, before the Great Wardrobe moved its headquarters to the western edge of the City. Moreover, a site at Nieuwendijk, Amsterdam, yielded similar buttoned edgings dating to the first quarter of the 14th century (Vons-Comis 1982, 152, 155); not only do these predate the London examples, but nowhere has it been suggested that part of this latter group came from a household of the highest status.

An alternative explanation for at least some of the discarded textiles may be sought in the activities of the fripperers. The surviving fragments of clothing, which include neck edgings, armholes, sleeve fastenings, hems and the foot sections of hose, are all parts of dress that would have been subjected to considerable wear and tear, leaving larger areas of cloth available for recycling. These cut-off sections of clothing are characteristic of both 14th-century groups of textiles at BC72. In addition, some offcuts could be waste from the workshops of tailors since a number of these craftsmen are known to have lived in the parish of St Andrews during the late 13th and early 14th centuries. Any hypothesis has to be treated warily, however, especially as different types of artefacts in the two assemblages may suggest different lines of interpretation. The study of one artefact group may give a different impression from the study of another; whereas the *later* 14th-century shoes show little evidence of wear and an abnormally high proportion of decorated uppers or excessive pikes, in some respects it is the *earlier* 14th-century textiles that are of better quality than the later. Silk facings on garment edges with buttonholes are, for example, more common in the earlier group. The sources of the textiles from BC72 and any connection with the Great Wardrobe therefore remains uncertain.

Further information about the deposits from which textiles were recovered and their dating is given in the next chapter.

Chapter content

Little understanding of the significance of the textiles or clothing from London can emerge without a thorough examination of each piece. By this means similarities and differences can be established, enabling certain types to be grouped together. This is a skilled and time-consuming exercise and the information gathered so far cannot be considered exhaustive. Various aspects of the material deserve further attention. For instance only a small sample of the wool fibres has been examined under high magnification in order to establish fleece types (Ryder 1981, 26). Additional analyses could provide evidence as to the way the fleece was sorted to produce cloths of different grades. A study of creasing and wear patterns could also contribute to a fuller understanding of the way that clothes were worn, and how often they were worn, before they were recycled (see Cooke 1990, 8–10); as a result further items of clothing would undoubtedly be identified. Historians might also be able to recognise among the cloths many encountered before only as names in sales and import and export records, legal proceedings, inventories or tailoring accounts.

The concern of this volume is chiefly with the finished product but the raw materials and processes of manufacture are crucial to an understanding of any piece of cloth. A chapter on *techniques used in textile production*, therefore, outlines the equipment and manufacturing methods in use at the time, although it must be borne in mind that many gaps exist in our knowledge. The ensuing chapters describe the excavated textiles in terms of the fibre or fibres from which they were made. The picture provided by the material does not claim to be comprehensive and there are gaps in the chronological sequence. Textiles from the late 12th and early 13th centuries are poorly represented as are those dating to the first half of the 15th century. Despite this, general trends in the types of wool cloths available do emerge, and, to a lesser extent, the types of silk cloths and braids.

Wool textiles are considered first since they are the most numerous. They are classified, as are all the textiles here, according to their basic weave and, within this division, by the way that the yarn was prepared and twisted. The absence, as well as the presence, of certain cloths is significant. Within the period surveyed here there are no examples from the City of four-shed twills with broken-lozenge or chevron patterns. These are cloths that are closely associated with the warp-weighted loom, and their absence offers proof that by the 12th century this form of loom was no longer serving the needs of the urban populace even on a domestic scale. Three-shed lozenge twills were still available in the 12th century but by the following century there is no cloth of this type from London. Plain three-shed twills form a sizeable proportion of the wool cloths until the second half of the 14th century when they gradually disappear, with the result that there are none from London in 15th-century deposits. Three-shed twills from the 14th century include many which show signs of having gone through a series of finishing processes, but when in the 12th or 13th century it became common to full and shear such fabrics cannot be established, nor is it possible at present to distinguish cloths that were fulled by hand or foot from those that were fulled mechanically in a fulling mill. Throughout the 14th century shorn, tabby-woven cloths, which are generally known as broadcloth, increase in proportion to other fabrics. Heavy finishing processes were also accorded to certain four-shed twills in the late 14th and 15th centuries. This emphasis on cloth finishing had an important effect on the way cloth was cut, draped and stitched. Indeed, it minimised fraying so that wide seams and double-folded hems were generally unnecessary, and it also encouraged decorative edgings, such as dagges. Such cloth was extremely hard-wearing and could withstand being returned to a clothworker or tailor to have a fresh nap raised — a process to which Shakespeare was to allude in *King Henry VI, Part II*, written four centuries after the practice first became common, 'Jack Cade the clothier means to dress the commonwealth and turn it, and set a new nap on it' (IV, ii, 6–8).

The wool textiles also provide new information about the range of cloths being woven from combed wool ('worsteds'). Indeed the archaeological evidence shows that, rather than a new yarn being introduced as is asserted sometimes, a new range of fabrics was developed which used worsted yarn. By contrast, changes in spinning 'woollen' yarn emerged during the latter part of the 14th century and can be explained by the diffu-

6

Textiles and Clothing

sion of the spinning wheel (p 45).

New forms of striped patterning, including on occasion the use of silk thread, characterise certain wool fabrics from 14th-century deposits in London. Textiles from other towns in northern Europe, such as Dordrecht in North Brabant, indicate that such innovations had already begun before the end of the 13th century. The stimulus seems to have come, in part at least, from a desire to imitate silk fabrics, combined with changes in weaving technology and the increased use of the counterbalance treadle-loom. These cloths played an important role in clothing since they were often adopted for the livery of retainers. So striking is their appearance that they can easily be identified in many paintings and manuscript illuminations of the period (see Frontispiece and Fig 159). The surviving cloths, however, enable the complexity of the patterns to be understood in a way that was not possible before.

Tapestries and knitting are included in the chapter on wool textiles, as the examples described are made wholly from wool; none are from deposits earlier than the second half of the 14th century. Tapestries point to the importance of furnishings in town houses at this period, while knitted items of wool, particularly caps, appear to have been worn at first for warmth by working men and women before being adopted by those of higher social status. Felt, a non-woven fabric, is also included and encompasses a piece made from a mixture of wool and animal hair, in addition to all-wool felts.

Cloths made from *goathair* form the subject of a separate chapter. These are all of similar construction and are examples of a product in widespread use in medieval Europe which is not well known from written sources.

Linen is the subject of the next chapter. Like cloths woven from wool or silk, the range of linen changed and developed during the middle ages, although any detailed assessment is precluded here by the small size of the sample. It is not known how diverse or extensive the linen industry was in medieval England: linen from Wilton, Wiltshire and Aylsham, Norfolk was supplied to the court in the 13th and 14th centuries (CLR, 1226–1240, 34; Nicolas 1846, 40–55; Safford 1928, 115: Sutton 1989, 202), but the best quality linen continued to be imported from abroad as it had been in the Roman and Anglo-Saxon periods. Not

until around the 14th century did a linen industry flourish in London, when a separate guild of linen weavers was established (Consitt 1933, 60). During the 15th century these weavers produced an ambitious range of napery but of this archaeology has yielded no trace as yet.

Silk textiles from London are second only to those of wool in quantity. This chapter is prefaced with an introduction which places the range of cloths in the more general context of silk imports into England in the medieval period. It has become apparent through the work of archaeologists in the past two decades that silk was not an unusual commodity even in 10th-century towns such as London. While some pieces were hoarded and recycled, such was their value and prestige, a significant feature of the two main 14th-century assemblages of textiles from London is the lack of similarity between the patterned silk cloths. Two of those in the group dating to the second quarter of the 14th century, both weft-faced compound twills, had evidently undergone recycling of some kind before they were discarded, but a third cloth, a twill damask, which was the product of a more distant weaving centre in the Far East, appears to have had a much shorter period of use. Italian silks — *camocas*, *baudekins*, and satins — from the late 14th century all appear to have been discarded fairly rapidly. As the cloths were not any less hardwearing it seems to reflect a slightly more wasteful, consumer-orientated society. The pieces, however, are small and the rest of these cloths was presumably put to further use. This might signify greater affluence among inhabitants in the wake of the Black Death, but it would be rash to speculate on the basis of such slim evidence.

Mixed cloths, or textiles woven from more than one fibre, such as wool and linen or linen and silk, are considered next. They include half-silk velvets. No all-silk velvet has so far been recorded from a deposit in London dating to before 1450, although pieces dyed a beautiful deep red with the costly and highly prized dye, kermes, are familiar as the ground fabric of 14th-century English embroideries, many of which were made in workshops in the City (King 1963, 5; Fitch 1976, 288–95; King 1987, 159–60).

Narrow wares — braids, garters and hairnets — formed an important branch of the textile industry and added a significant dimension to a person's appearance. It was by the quality of an individual's trimmings and accessories, as well as by the colour and richness of fabric, that his status was proclaimed, a fact acknowledged in 14th- and 15th-century sumptuary legislation. The braids from London reveal that many of the simpler varieties were produced continuously throughout the period. Silk fingerloop braids, for example, are present in a late 12th-century pit fill and differ not at all from those of the late 14th century. They clearly served essential needs, including lacing garments and serving as purse drawstrings, and could not be improved upon. More conspicuous braids, especially those worn as girdles or garment trimmings were more influenced by fashion. Workers skilled in tablet weaving adapted their output to imitate samite, and later satin and velvet. Tablet-woven braids from London reflect these changes in a small way, although none are first-rate items. All the braids described in this chapter were probably made locally in the City using imported silk thread, and the thrifty use of this is indicated by tiny knots along the length of the threads where they were joined together (Fig 100B).

Sewing techniques and tailoring are examined in the final chapter. These are aspects of medieval clothing that have been little explored until now and a wealth of information vital in establishing the technical skills of the period is forthcoming. Seams, hems, bindings, facings and fastenings, such as lacing and buttoning, are described and so are the sewing threads used. While this evidence may appear prosaic and less appealing on an aesthetic level than the superb examples of *opus anglicanum* which have rightly attracted considerable attention, much of the stitching was being carried out on workbenches in the same metropolis and at a similar date. Many subtleties are revealed which would not otherwise have been thought of as components of everyday wear in the 14th century; the skilled, regular and firm stitching of the buttonholes, for example, or their carefully applied silk facings. Even more striking is the use of silk tablet-woven braid worked directly on to raw sleeve edges. This is an unexpected touch, although it has often been noted as a finishing method on pouches, and it seems likely that it may also have been used on other edges, perhaps necklines and sleeveless armholes. This refinement, which only the wearer and his or her

most immediate companions would have seen and appreciated, can be traced back through many centuries, and by the second half of the 14th century was close to disappearing from the sewing repertoire in urban centres.

The latter part of the chapter deals with the cutting and shaping of garments. The cloth itself, its draping qualities and colour, appears to have been a central preoccupation of the 13th century, and probably earlier centuries too, producing an elegance of style which has been universally admired in succeeding centuries (Goddard 1927, 20; Evans 1952, 10, 20). The changes which become apparent in the 14th century centre upon a new preoccupation with cut, believed to have been triggered off by developments in plate armour which demanded more closely-fitting padded garments underneath. It was natural for martial fashion to be rapidly transferred to civilian fashion, and to be reflected in turn in female fashions. Increasingly as the 14th century advanced it was the problem of manipulating flat sections of cloth to fit closely to the body form which became the preoccupation of the fashionable. Time after time contemporary chroniclers and commentators decried this 'new' sartorial madness, the inevitable wasting of precious handwoven cloth as a result of cutting it into smaller shaped pieces to fit the human torso. Unlike the earlier practice (still, of course, followed by the less affluent) of using up every piece of cloth by fitting squares or rectangles with triangular sections to create a more shapely garment, the new fashion beguiling European society demanded this wastefulness as part of its creed of conspicuous consumption. Despite this, among the items excavated from London there are no complete clothes, though examples of tunics, hose and hoods can be reconstructed from the remnants. Another aspect of the new wastefulness of resources is to be found in the cutting up of cloth to create decorative effects. This is best exemplified by the dagges found in both 14th-century levels at BC72 which were used to ornament clothing or horse harness, a destructive element of contemporary sartorial style that is echoed in the pierced footwear — 'Gothic window' shoes — of the same years (Grew & Neergaard 1988, 80–82).

Every source of information has its own inherent dangers and limitations and any interpretation is open to question. The large body of textiles

from London serves to challenge many past assumptions about cloth and clothing in medieval
England and provides a new source of material of
extraordinary richness. London has been a major
centre for the creation, display and diffusion of
clothing fashions for more than a thousand years;
here at last is an opportunity to explore the textiles and clothing of the town, rather than of the
nobility, during a period which has often been
considered too remote to merit more than a passing appraisal.

The excavations

Alan Vince

The textiles described in this volume were found during archaeological excavations conducted between 1972 and 1983, and generally come from contexts to which a date and circumstances of deposition can be assigned. In most instances the date was reached by using a combination of methods — the stratigraphic sequence, associated datable objects, especially coins and pottery, tree-ring dating (dendrochronology), and, occasionally historical or documentary references. The main arguments are summarised below, but further information is available in Schofield 1986 or in separate publications as listed. The codes given to each excavation by the Museum of London are used in the Selected Catalogues and Concordance in preference to the full name and address of the site. Here these codes are appended in brackets after the name of the site, while the No/s refer to the numbered items in the Concordance.

Baynard's House, Queen Victoria Street, EC4, 1972 (BC72)
Map 1 (site 1)
The excavation commonly known as Baynard's Castle took place in 1972 (Webster & Cherry 1973, 162–3). It covered an area over 100m wide situated to the south of the original Baynard's Castle built by William I and to the west of a later property of the same name. Two large deposits of medieval date were excavated and these can be related to a stone-walled dock identified by Tony Dyson and Colin Taylor as part of the East Watergate, one of numerous public access ways from Thames Street to the river (Dyson 1989, 10).

(i) The construction of the dock
The northern wall of the dock made use of an earlier timber waterfront, the eastern wall was a pre-existing stone wall, and the west wall was formed by reclaiming an area of foreshore within a new stone wall. The dump behind this latter stone wall included 'sterling' jettons, so-called be-cause they copied the style of the sterling coinage of Edward I and Edward II. These jettons could be of late 13th- or early 14th-century date but are thought to have been still current in the 1330s or later (Rigold 1982, 99). A date in the 1330s or 1340s is considered to be the most likely for the dump which included several hundred textiles of varying quality and character. A Chinese twill damask woven from silk (No 138) is the most exotic piece. Other items include a number of buttoned edges cut from garments (Nos 32–34, 37, 38, 64, 67, 68), dagges (Nos 51 and 70), a false plait of hair trimmed with a tablet-woven braid (No 142), two silk mesh hairnets (Nos 145, 153), and fragments of felt (No 133).

(ii) The use and filling of the dock
A layer of silt within the dock contained a moderate-sized assemblage of pottery and a post-sterling jetton, which suggest that the dock was in use during the third quarter of the 14th century. A vast assemblage was recovered from the backfill of the dock, behind a stone wall which blocked the dock. Coins, pilgrim souvenirs and jettons point to a deposition date in the last quarter of the 14th century. Many hundreds of textiles were packed into this dump and it has proved to be the richest source of organic artefacts excavated in the City. Items include three woollen hoods (Nos 174, 246, 247), buttoned edges of garments (Nos 159, 173, 216–224, 272, 273), fragments of hose (Nos 235–241), dagges (Nos 248–253), silk veils (Nos 332–334), offcuts of Lucchese-type silk cloths (Nos 337–344), pieces of tapestry (Nos 312–315), knitting (Nos 316, 317), half-silk velvets (Nos 349–352), and purpose-made garters (Nos 388–390).

Baynard's House, Queen Victoria Street, EC4, 1975 (BC75)
Map 1 (site 2)
During excavation of a section across Upper Thames Street in 1974 and subsequent observa-

tion a collapsed portion of a Roman riverside wall was recorded (Hill *et al.* 1980, 2). Dumping took place on both sides of this wall in the medieval period and among the rubbish deposited to the south of it to reclaim land were two wool textiles. One is a patterned three-shed twill woven from worsted yard (Fig 10; Crowfoot 1980, 113–15, no 145), the other a reinforced selvedge from a four-shed twill patterned with three different colours in the weft (Crowfoot 1980, 112–14, no 144). This dump was initially described as dating to the 13th century on the basis of pottery analysis but a reassessment of the pottery, which includes only a few sherds of London-type ware, suggests that it dates between the end of the 11th and the middle of the 12th century.

Another revetment deposit situated to the south of the wall, which appears to date to the 14th century, yielded a silk fingerloop braid and a tabby-woven woollen cloth of medium grade (Crowfoot 1980, 113, nos 146, 147).

Baynard's Castle/City of London Boys' School, Upper Thames Street, EC4, 1981 (BYD81)
Map 1 (site 3)
Excavations in 1981 exposed the south-east angle tower of the 15th-century property known as Baynard's Castle. It was found that this octagonal tower and its adjoining walls were part of an extension to the castle, which historical sources indicate was constructed by 1430, after a fire in 1428. The area between the old and new walls was backfilled with rubbish, including pottery of types which first appeared in the early 15th century. Fragments of six wool textiles were found in this dump; two cloths in 2.2 twill — one coarse and woven from S-spun yarn, and the other a fulled woollen with Z-spun warp yarn and S-spun weft yard dyed with madder — and four cloths in tabby weave.

2–3 Trig Lane, Upper Thames Street, EC4, 1974 (TL74)
Map 1 (site 4)
The medieval waterfront sequence excavated at Trig Lane dates from *c.*1250 to *c.*1440 (Milne & Milne 1982). Large assemblages of artefacts of the late 13th century, late 14th century and mid-15th century were recovered but the number of tex-

tiles was relatively small. These came from groups designated G2, G10 and G15.

(i)   G2
The earliest large groups of finds came from dumping behind the G2 revetment. Only the base-plate of this waterfront remained, the superstructure (G3) having been rebuilt about 20 years later, *c.*1290–1335. The date of the construction of G2 is based on a pewter 'Winetavern' token, a type represented elsewhere in London in groups of *c.*1250 to 1280, a worn ampulla of a type made *c.*1250 at Bromholm Priory, Norfolk, and a tentative dendrochronological date obtained from the base-plate. The pottery points to a date later than *c.*1250 for the rubbish in this deposit, so that a deposition date in the second half of the 13th century seems certain. Textiles were recovered from two contexts in the revetment dump. They comprise two wool textiles, namely a fine worsted tabby (No 397) and a 2.2 twill both woven from Z-spun yarn, silk braids (Nos 398–401), a silk mesh hairnet (No 399), and a silk cloth, probably of Spanish origin, woven in 1.3 weft-faced compound twill (No 398).

(ii)   G10
Further reclamation of the Thames waterfront was represented by the G10 revetment, which is dated by dendrochronology between 1336 and 1380. It was repaired over part of its length in *c.*1430 but the finds associated with this repair have been separated from the rest of the artefacts. One textile, a piece of tabby-woven silk cloth, was recovered.

(iii)   G15
The foreshore in front of the G11 revetment dated by dendrochronology to 1351–1383 was examined over a wide area. Jettons and pilgrim souvenirs date the foreshore between *c.*1380 and *c.*1430. The dump above this foreshore was associated with a stone river wall, G15. Textiles were recovered from several deposits within dumps behind the stone wall. These include a number of woollen cloths in tabby weave, a wool cloth patterned with a weft-faced band in extended tabby (No 402), fragments of a plain linen (No 403), a silk tablet-woven braid (No 404), and a tabby-woven silk braid (No 406).

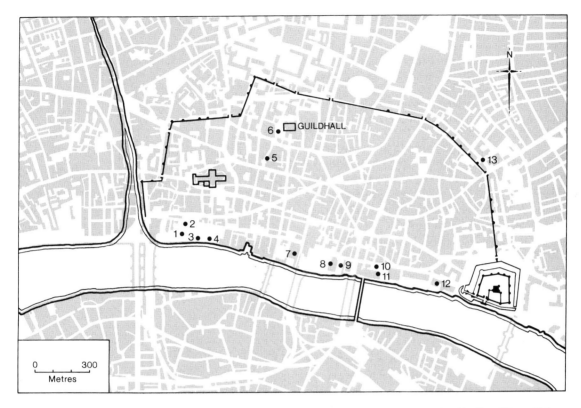

Map 1 Map of the city of London showing the location of sites from which textiles mentioned in the text have been recovered

1–6 Milk Street, EC2, 1976 (MLK76)
Map 1 (site 5)

A series of Saxo-Norman buildings was uncovered, together with a large number of associated pits ranging in date from the 10th to the late 12th centuries; above these was a sequence of later stone buildings fronting Milk Street itself (Roskams & Schofield 1978, 231–4; Schofield *et al.* forthcoming). Two silk fingerloop braids (Nos 407, 408) were recovered from a pit dated by pottery to the late 12th century, and pieces of plain linen (No 409) from a fill of a garderobe dated by pottery and a seal matrix to the second half of the 13th century or a little later. Another piece of plain linen (No 413) and nine cut-up scraps of wool cloth, one woven from worsted yarn in a six-shed twill (No 410) and eight in tabby weave including two with selvedges (Nos 411, 412), were found in a fill of a stone-lined garderobe dated to the late 14th

or early 15th century by a lead bulla of Pope Urban VI (1378–1389).

Guildhall Car Park site, Aldermanbury, EC2, 1965
Map 1 (site 6)

Excavations in the cellar of a demolished building between Aldermanbury and the Guildhall uncovered traces of the robbed out east wall of the Roman fort. Debris, which is dated by pottery to the first half of the 12th century, was recovered from the fill of the wall's robber trench together with charred fragments of a type of huckaback cloth (No 414) which is almost certainly linen.

Public Cleansing Depot, Upper Thames Street, EC3 (Dowgate), 1959
Map 1 (site 7)

During observation of a site on the east side of the mouth of the Walbrook, near the medieval Steelyard and public wharf of Dowgate, a clay river bank, probably of the late 11th or early 12th century, and one or more subsequent timber revetments were recorded. Textiles were recovered from two different deposits. The earlier was a foreshore deposit characterised by a high proportion of imported 12th-century pottery (Dunning 1959), but English pottery showed that the foreshore had remained open into the early 13th century. This foreshore yielded fragments of a coarse tabby-woven cloth woven from plied yarn, which is probably goathair (No 415). The second deposit was a rubbish dump within a timber revetment dated by its pottery assemblage to the middle of the 14th century. A piece of a lozenge-patterned silk cloth was recovered but unfortunately it has not been possible to examine this textile.

Swan Lane/Upper Thames Street, EC4, 1981 (SWA81)
Map 1 (site 8)
A small controlled excavation exposed a clay river bank, from which a small collection of pottery dating somewhere between the late 9th and early 11th centuries was recovered, a series of late 12th-century hearths associated with cloth-working (probably fulling), and a sequence of 12th- and 13th-century revetment dumps. Further revetments and rubbish dumps dating up to the 15th century were identified during a watching brief.

(i)   The late 13th-century waterfronts
The most productive dumps at Swan Lane lay in front of revetments dated by pottery to the middle of the 13th century. A large series of coins and tokens was recovered from these dumps showing that the waterfront across the middle part of the site was reclaimed at a single period, if not as a single operation. The coins suggest a deposition date between *c*.1260 and 1279 since only later issues of the long cross coinage of Henry III were found. Pilgrim souvenirs include a number thought to have been produced to commemorate the centenary of the martyrdom of St Thomas in 1270 and a hat badge dating to 1264 or later from a priory at Toulouse (Brian Spencer pers comm). Textiles recovered from within this dump comprise four tabby-woven silks with twist in the warp yarn only, two silk braids, one plaited (No 421) and one in a silver-brocaded tablet weave (No 420), four wool cloths, two in four-shed twill woven from Z-spun yarn and two in three-shed twill with mixed spinning, and a coarse goathair cloth (No

416). A silk woven in satin damask (No 424) was also supposedly recovered from one of these dumps, but such an early date for this piece must be doubted and it is possible that the context, which was isolated at the top of the sequence and produced no other datable finds, was contaminated by later material.

(ii)   The early 15th-century waterfronts
In the extreme south-east corner of the site large groups of finds were recovered from either side of a timber revetment. Those behind the revetment appear to have been discarded at the very end of the 14th century or beginning of the 15th century and are associated with timbers dated by dendrochronology to 1394 or later. Those in front, which can be divided into those from the foreshore and those from the revetment dump above, are broadly dated by coins to *c*.1422 or later. Two textiles were recovered from the revetment dump, a wool cloth patterned with a series of broad weft-faced bands (No 422) and a silk tablet-woven braid (No 423).

Seal House, 106–8 Upper Thames Street, EC4, 1974 (SH74)
Map 1 (site 9)
The excavation of a long narrow trench, never more than 3m wide, revealed a sequence of 12th- and 13th-century timber revetments. The two earliest revetments, which were dated by dendrochronology to 1133–1170 and 1163–1192 had been robbed before being replaced, but a third dump revetment remained intact (Waterfront III). A date of 1202–1215 was obtained for the felling of the latest timber used in its construction, and the revetment dump behind was cut through by a timber-lined drain from which a date of 1203 or later was obtained. At the time of the discovery the pottery assemblage was considered to be much too late for this dating since it contained sherds from a large number of decorated jugs for which a production date of 1240 was favoured, but as there is no evidence for the reuse of any of the timbers sampled for tree-ring dating, it is now considered that the dating of the pottery should be earlier. A piece of silken cloth (No 426) and part of a fingerloop silk braid (No 427) were recovered from this revetment dump.

New Fresh Wharf, Lower Thames Street, EC3, 1978 (FRE78–watching brief)
Map 1 (site 10)

Traces of a number of medieval revetments were recorded when pile holes were being inserted into the site during redevelopment. Two textiles, a fragment of woollen cloth in tabby weave (No 428) and a piece of knitting (No 429), were recovered from rubbish dumped in one of these revetments. Here the process of reclamation took place no later than the 14th century.

Billingsgate Lorry Park, Lower Thames Street, EC3, 1982–3 (BIG82–excavation, BWB83–watching brief)
Map 1 (site 11)

The Billingsgate Lorry Park excavation examined a large area of medieval waterfront (Youngs *et al.* 1983, 191–2). Finds-recovery methods on site included fine-sieving of up to a quarter of the soil in the reclamation dumps. Despite this, datable artefacts were few until the late 12th century. The medieval sequence will eventually be dated accurately by a combination of dendrochronology, coin-dating, estimates based on the structural sequences and pilgrim souvenirs, but at the time of writing only the earlier tree-ring analyses are available. Textiles were recovered from four different phases of waterfront development. The earliest, a coarse 2.1 twill woven from S-spun wool yarn, came from a revetment dump (Period VIII.1) dating to the late 12th century. Rubbish deposits which infilled the next revetment (Period IX.2, IX.3 and XI.2) dating to the early 13th century yielded four coarse goathair cloths woven from plied yarn (Nos 431–434) and a wool tabby patterned with narrow red bands (No 430). The next revetment dump in the sequence (Period XII.2), which appears to date to the 1250s, yielded two more coarse goathair cloths (Nos 435, 436) and a wool three-shed twill with mixed spinning; a fourth revetment dump was dated later than *c.*1280 and produced a further example of coarse goathair cloth (No 437).

During subsequent work by building contractors, after the formal excavation had been completed and when only limited access to the site was possible, several late medieval revetments were observed and artefacts were salvaged *in situ* or from dumps tipped on and off site. The only textiles recovered were a woollen tabby woven from S-spun yarn, a 2.2 twill woven from Z-spun yarn, a piece of wool knitting (No 438), a coarse cloth of goathair (No 439), a silk tabby (No 440) and a silk and worsted tablet-woven braid (No 441) which came from two separate contexts within a revetment dump dating to the late 14th century.

Custom House, Wool Quay, Lower Thames Street, EC3, 1973 (CUS73)
Map 1 (site 12)

The Custom House excavations took place at the extreme eastern end of the City waterfront, just to the west of the Tower of London (Tatton-Brown, 1974; Tatton-Brown 1975). A foreshore deposit overlying the remains of Roman timber quays contained pottery of the early to mid-14th century in its upper levels (group D1). Textiles from this group consist of two wool cloths in three-shed twill and a tabby-woven silk cloth dyed with kermes.

A dump behind a subsequent timber revetment (C2) is dated by pottery to the early 14th century or later. A tentative dendrochronological date for the revetment gives a *terminus post quem* of 1328 and there is documentary evidence for waterfront activity in the late 1330s, associated with defensive works at the start of the Hundred Years War. This dump yielded a greater quantity and variety of textiles than any of the other sites with the exception of Baynard's Castle. They comprise a group of silk braids of which three are tablet woven (Nos 449–451), three are made by the fingerloop method (Nos 452–454), and three are plaited (Nos 455–457), two pieces of tabby-woven silk cloth with traces of stitching, a coarse four-shed twill with a pattern of open checks woven from wool of different natural colours (No 444), two other four-shed twills both woven from combed yarn, one Z-spun throughout and the other with a Z-spun warp and a S-spun weft (No 443), two types of three-shed twill, namely two fulled and dyed woollens and a coarser cloth woven from natural brown wool (No 442), and two pieces of coarse goathair cloth (Nos 445, 446).

2–7 Dukes Place, EC3, 1977 (DUK77)
Map 1 (site 13)

Excavations at Dukes Place disclosed a wood-lined cesspit (Webster & Cherry 1978, 176). In the medieval period this would have been within the precinct of Holy Trinity Priory, Aldgate. The fills of the pit have been dated by pottery to the second half of the 14th century. One fill produced fragments of two patterned silk cloths (Nos 458, 459), both probably woven in Islamic Spain.

Techniques used in textile production

The appearance of a textile depends upon the raw materials used in its production and the way that it was made. The most common fibres represented in this volume will be discussed individually since the technology applied to them generally developed separately. Processes and tools were, however, sometimes transferred from one type of fibre to another; in the medieval period this adaptability is particularly noticeable in the development of woollen cloths which borrowed various processes from the cotton industry, including the spinning wheel (Mazzaoui 1981, 78–9; Chorley 1987, 376). From the 12th century, statutes and guild regulations governed many aspects of the industry and as a result much can be learned about production methods. These sources, however, are not comprehensive — some documents have been destroyed and many details of this kind were never written down. Where information on textile production is available from London this will be used to illustrate points in preference to that recorded for other towns, though it is not intended to imply that all the excavated textiles were locally made.

Wool

Wool was the chief raw fibre used for textiles in medieval England. Like all natural fibres its quality was fundamental to the finished fabric and the fleece was usually the most expensive item in the making of a cloth. Sheep were smaller and breeds not so highly evolved as they became in the 18th century. There were, nevertheless, regional variations in English wool resulting from differences in climate, pasture and husbandry and this is reflected in a series of wool-price schedules dating from c.1270 to 1499 (Munro 1978; Munro 1979). Each fleece yields a variety of grades of wool according to the part of the sheep from which it comes: that from the shoulders is the top grade, whereas wool from the britch and belly is generally unusable. Written sources imply that in certain monasteries, which were major suppliers

of wool, fleece was sorted into three grades, good, medium and 'locks' or clippings (Munro 1978, 123). Fifty-one wool samples measured by Michael Ryder showed that a wide range of fleece types is present among the cloths from medieval London (Ryder 1981, 25–26, tables 3, 4). Fine wools include two within the merino range (Nos 6 and 48) and a relatively high percentage (30%) of shortwools were identified from the late 14th-century deposit at BC72. Other fibre analyses by Harry M Appleyard indicate that a few cloths and a piece of felt were made from the wool of double-coated sheep (pp 39, 75; Harry M Appleyard pers comm). These were a more primitive type similar to some of the Scottish highland and island breeds, which, like wild sheep, had a hairy outercoat and an undercoat of fine wool (Ryder 1981, 18). Natural brown and grey wools were also used to pattern cloths, sometimes teamed with dyed wool and sometimes wholly undyed (see Pl 4), and the practice of keeping a few coloured sheep in a flock, mentioned by Henry Best in 1641, was perhaps already pursued (Ryder 1983, 480–81). A larger wool sampling programme is needed, however, to gain more detailed information about the types of fleece used for particular cloths.

A lengthy series of processes has to be carried out before fleece is turned into a finished length of cloth; among them are willowing, washing, dyeing, blending, combing, carding, bowing, spinning, winding, warping, sizing, weaving, fulling, stretching, teasling, shearing, and calendering. These varied according to the type of wool and from one region to another leading to divisions within the industry.

Much argument has centred around the length of staple of medieval wool and whether there was any longwool suitable for making worsteds (e.g. Bowden 1956; Ryder 1981, 22, 27). Whatever its precise technical character there is no doubt that worsted yarn, meaning wool prepared by combing, was produced throughout the medieval period. The process was carried out with a pair of woolcombs. These were warmed and dipped into a pot of grease consisting of butter, olive oil or animal fat, which helped to lubricate the wool and prevent the fibres from becoming damaged. The two combs could be held in the hands (Hoffmann 1964, 284–7), but in England it was more usual for one heated comb to be fitted to an upright post, called a combingstock. An appropriate amount of wool was arranged (thrown) on this comb and the second comb was then passed through the wool until it had drawn off all the long fibres leaving the short noils to be cycled separately. The wool was subsequently worked back on to the rigid comb and the process repeated until a sufficient quantity was ready for spinning (Roth 1909, 7). Woolcombing had been practised for centuries in many parts of England and flat iron combs are known from Roman Britain (Wild 1970, 25; Manning 1972, 333–5). By the late 6th century, their form had been modified, and combs found on rural settlements and in graves have rows of teeth bound with iron and set at an angle into a handle of wood or horn. Fragments of similar woolcombs have been found in 10th- and 11th-century deposits in Thetford, York and London, indicating that the task was not at this date confined to rural districts where the wool clip originated.

Combed wool was usually placed (dressed) on a distaff and spun with a spindle fitted with a whorl that helped to weight the implement and to rotate it. In the period 1150–1450, many spindles were lathe-turned from wood and had a swollen shank to hold the whorl in place (Øye 1988, 32, 35–6); a spindle of this type from a late 14th-century deposit in London is a little longer than 254mm (its tip is broken) and is made from coniferous wood (TL74, acc no 2741). If the yarn was to be very fine a spinner might work seated supporting the spindle in a container such as a pot or wooden bowl. However, medieval portrayals indicate that it was more common for a woman to spin standing, drawing out the wool and twisting it until the spindle touched the ground. The direction in which the yarn was twisted depended upon whether the spindle was rotated with the right or left hand. Combed wool was usually Z-twisted in the medieval period (Fig 1), but that used for the weft could be S-twisted and softer spun (Fig 2).

Generally, combed wool was dyed before weaving. This enabled small amounts of wool to be dyed in a batch, thereby requiring less capital outlay on equipment than piece-dyeing. It also meant that the wool used for a length of cloth was

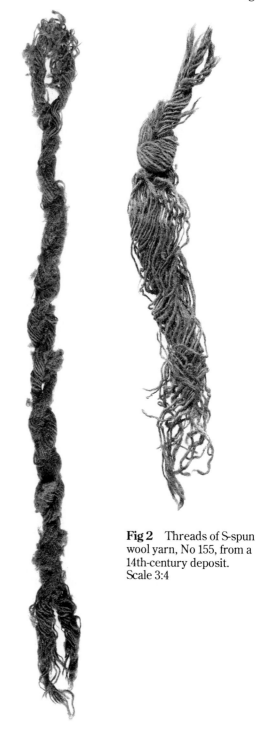

Fig 2 Threads of S-spun wool yarn, No 155, from a 14th-century deposit. Scale 3:4

Fig 1 Part of a hank of combed, Z-spun wool yarn, No 154, from a 14th-century deposit. Scale 1:1

not always exactly the same tint. This enlivened the cloth's appearance but the effect was not favoured in the later middle ages when uniformity of colour was preferred. Worsted yarn was also used for braids and for tapestries where small quantities of coloured yarns were needed for patterning. Another reason why worsteds were cheaper in the later medieval period was that they did not require a complicated series of finishing processes to enhance their texture. Calendering (hot pressing) or polishing, which increased the surface sheen of worsteds, was an exception. Written sources suggest that this process grew in importance from the 15th century (Salzman 1923, 238), but the traditional method of rubbing the surface with a slickstone or heated glass hemisphere, which is also associated with linen, had been practised for centuries.

Cloths woven from worsted yarn were among the most prestigious in the Anglo-Saxon and Viking kingdoms and the finest pieces are found in the graves of persons of high rank in England, Norway, Sweden and Denmark (Carus-Wilson 1969, 159–60; Crowfoot 1983, 457, 460, 468; Ingstad 1982, 88, 94; Ingstad 1988, 136–44; Geijer 1938, 22–29; Hald 1980, 102; Bender Jørgensen 1986, 357–60). The position did not change until around the late 11th or 12th century when heavily finished coloured cloths known as scarlets were introduced (see p 44).

Woollens used short staple wool and the preparation, method of spinning, and finishing differed from that of worsteds. Before the late 13th century, wool that was too short to be combed was sometimes beaten with a bow, an arched strip of wood with a gut string (Mazzaoui 1981, 76–7); the vibration of this tool caused the fibres to separate into a fluffy mass suitable for spinning and for making felt. However, this process, which was also used for goathair and cotton, only appears to have been introduced into western Europe a little before carding, and it was carding rather than bowing that became popular in England. Cards, like woolcombs, were used in pairs. They were wooden boards covered on one side with leather into which rows of small iron hooks were set. Locks of wool were spread across one card, which was held against the thigh and the other card was drawn through the fibres with a stroking motion (Baines 1977, 37). This was repeated several times before the wool was ready for spinning.

Combing and carding sometimes seem to have been carried out in the same workshop — in 1418, Agnes Stubbard of Bury St Edmunds bequeathed to Sibill Chekyneye, a pair of woolcombs, a combingstock, a wheel (*rot*), and a pair of cards (Tymms 1850, 2–3) — and this may have been because many cloths were woven from a combed warp and carded weft. The wheel mentioned in the will was possibly for winding yarn into hanks, balls or bobbins but it could have been a spinning wheel. The latter, the great wheel which the spinster turned standing up, was another implement introduced into England at about the same time as wool cards and was, at first, especially associated with the production of woollen yarn for the weft (see p 45). It speeded up spinning but the yarn was not as fine or as even as that spun with a drop spindle (Lemon 1968, 87–8).

Wool has a tendency to felt and, rather than spoiling the texture of the cloth, this property was exploited to advantage by fulling woollen fabrics after weaving to give a firm texture and soft drape. The process differed slightly from one place to another but it involved soaking the cloth in an alkaline cleansing agent such as fuller's earth or stale human urine to remove grease and dirt (Patterson 1956, 215). After rinsing, the cloth was pounded by hand, underfoot or with wooden hammers rotated by water power. Fulling had been common in the Roman period, when it was often carried out by trampling cloth in large tubs (Wild 1970, 82), but it was unusual in northern Europe in the following centuries when patterned cloths woven from lustrous, combed wool were considered to be more desirable. The subsequent change appears to have spread northwards from Italy where the process may never have died out. Fulling mills are recorded in central and northern Italy during the second half of the 10th century (Malanima 1986, 117–18), around Rouen in Normandy by 1087 (Lennard 1947, 150) and in England by the late 12th century (Carus-Wilson 1954, 189–90). Fulling mills were established close to London at Old Ford, Stratford, Wandsworth, Enfield and the manor of Stepney (Sharpe 1907, Letterbook H, f.xlv, 37; McDonnell 1978, 83–4), but fulling by hand or foot was preferred for certain commodities, such as hats, and in certain cloth-producing regions, particularly Flanders (Gutmann 1938, 486).

Fulling caused cloths to shrink up to about a

third of their original size and to counteract this it became usual to stretch a cloth while it was drying on a wooden tenterframe. The cloth was attached to the parallel bars of the frame by iron hooks spaced along the selvedges at measured intervals to ensure the correct amount of shrinkage, since the width of a cloth, and later its length, was regulated by statute. In 13th-century London, tenterframes were frequently in private ownership. Sir Robert Aguylun, for example, owned a tenterground in the parish of St Swithun's, Candlewickstreet in the 1280s (Cal Wills I, 75) but, in order to maintain quality control and to prevent malpractices, such as the inadequate wetting of cloth, the Drapers and Tailors guilds were granted a petition in 1482 forbidding any freeman to have or keep a tenter (Sharpe 1912, Letterbook L, f.180, 197).

To give the cloth a soft finish it was hung on a beam (perch) and worked over (rowed) with teasles (*Dipsacus fullonum*) set in a wooden frame in order to raise a nap (Carus-Wilson 1957, 110). The nap could be left uncropped, a practice for which there is evidence among early medieval textiles, for example from the early 7th-century ship burial at Sutton Hoo (Crowfoot 1983, 427–8), and from 11th-century deposits at Haithabu, north Germany (Hägg 1984, 121–4, figs 73, 84–87). However, in the later medieval period, it was usual to crop a nap with a pair of large shears after securing the cloth to a curved, padded bench (horse) with double ended metal clips (havettes) (Egan 1979, 190). The process of raising a nap and cropping it could be repeated many times but only if the wool was of sufficiently high quality to withstand such treatment (Munro 1983, 33).

By the 13th century a distinction was made between high quality 'coloured' cloths that were dyed in the piece (e.g. Pl 2B) and cheaper cloths woven from yarn dyed in the hank such as medleys and rays (e.g. Pls 1, 3A, 6; Chorley 1987, 350). However, some wool dyed before weaving was dyed again in the piece (Munro 1983, 53–4).

Hair

Textiles were also produced from the hairs of other animals. Those identified from medieval deposits in London are goat and a species of mustelid, possibly weasel or stoat. The scale patterns affect how hairs can be spun, or felted, and techniques were devised to cope with this. Goathair lacks crimp and, therefore, to produce a thread sufficiently strong for weaving, the yarn was plied (see p 78). The mustelid hairs were used in felt-making where they were combined with wool to give a shiny surface (see p 75). The mixing of animal hair with wool was, however, forbidden in some other branches of the cloth industry, especially in the production of chalons in London where weavers complained that French and other foreign weavers were counterfeiting chalons by mixing the hair of cattle and pigs with that of wool (Consitt 1933, 70).

Linen

The earliest textiles known were produced from plant fibres. Many plants yield suitable fibres but flax (*Linum usitatissimum*) was the principal bast fibre used in the textile industry of medieval Europe. The fibre is obtained from the stem which has to be pulled before the seeds are fully ripe. Processing included soaking (retting) to rot the woody core of the stems — a practice which polluted rivers and caused an unpleasant stench — drying the stems to embrittle them, beating (breaking) the dried stems with wooden mallets, striking (scutching) with a wooden knife against a vertical board to free the fibres from the bark, and combing (heckling) to remove any remaining woody particles and to align the raw fibres for spinning (Baines 1977, 19–24). Although the natural direction of twist of flax fibre is S, throughout northern Europe flax was generally spun with a Z-twist and all the fragments of linen from excavations in London have this characteristic (Figs 54, 56, Table 9). The natural colour of linen is brown and, therefore, it was often bleached to whiten it either before or after weaving. This was a slow process taking several months to complete and added considerably to the cost of the cloth. Little is known about the starching of linen before the 16th century; wheat starch was available in the 14th century (Thirsk 1978, 84) but most recipes probably depended upon particular local plants. It was also common to glaze the surface of linen by rubbing the cloth with a heated, hemispherical glass ball (Cutby 1952, 3275; see also p 81).

Silk

The different stages of silk manufacture likewise demanded skilled labour (Staley 1906, 213–21). As a first step the silk filament had to be freed from the cocoon of the silkworm. The cocoons were heated in a large basin of water to soften the sericin (natural gum); the loosened ends which floated on the surface could then be grasped and the raw silk unravelled (reeled) (Gaddum 1979, 13–16). Two types of reel were in use in Italy in the 18th century, the low reel (*caldara bassa*) on which two threads could be produced simultaneously, and the high reel (*caldara alta*) which more than doubled the output by enabling at least four threads to be reeled side by side, and it is considered that similar machines were used in the medieval period (Roover 1950, 2915–16). The thread was given a very slight twist by crossing the filaments and passing them through an eyelet before winding the thread on to the reel. The fineness of the thread depended upon how many

Fig 3 Splinter of wood wound with undyed raw silk, No 141, from a 14th-century deposit. Scale 1:1

filaments were reeled together, since the silk from a single cocoon was too fine to be used on its own. The aim was to produce a long smooth thread free from fluff, dross and knots but slubs sometimes formed and this thread was used for the weft in less costly fabrics (see Figs 65, 67, 68, 70, 129). It was as raw silk that the fibre was traded (Fig 3) since cocoons are too delicate to be transported safely. Some raw silk was twisted (thrown) to form a stronger warp thread, although this process was strictly unnecessary, and for certain types of heavy fabrics and for braids, hairnets and fringes thrown silk was doubled and redoubled (Roover 1966, 241–2; Dale 1928, 78). Water-powered throwing mills were introduced to speed up the process in Italy during the 13th century (Born 1939, 995; see p 124) but these did not spread into northern Europe until later. After the silk had been reeled or thrown, any remaining gum was usually boiled off, although this was not always done in the Far East or in the early medieval period (see pp 82, 85, 141), and the silk was washed in clear water and dried (Roover 1950, 2919; Roover 1966, 242–3). At this stage the silk was usually dyed, or bleached with sulphur if it was to be pure white.

Dyes

Dyeing, as already mentioned, played a vital part in textile production. Natural dyes were obtained from plants, lichens, insects and molluscs but only a few were used on a commercial scale and most of these had to be imported into England. Merchants, as well as craftsmen, specialised in particular dyes. Woad (*Isatis tinctoria* L.), which gave a blue dye and was used as a base for other colours, was imported in casks into London in the form of dried balls of pulped leaves (Carus-Wilson 1944, 36). These balls had to be pulverised, moistened and left to ferment at temperatures not exceeding 50°C before the dye was ready for use (Salzman 1923, 209; Hurry 1930, 25–7). If properly prepared, woad balls can be stored for several years without deteriorating, and it is not unusual to find bequests of casks of woad — Adam de la Pole, a London stockfishmonger, bequeathed four casks of it to his granddaughter Katherine in 1358 (Cal Wills II, 3). Supplies mainly came from Picardy during the 12th and 13th centuries, supplemented in the late 13th and 14th centuries by imports from Brabant, the Low Countries, Germany, Lombardy and Languedoc (Carus-Wilson 1953; Childs 1978, 107–8). During the 14th and 15th centuries many woadmongers in London were associated with the parish of St Andrew's Baynard's Castle, the parish in which most of the excavated textiles were found (Cal Wills II, 73, 423, 494). This was close to the Thames where most dyehouses were established because of the river's constant supply of running water.

Madder (*Rubia tinctorum* L.) was another important vegetable dye and its popularity is shown by the dye results from the London textiles (see Appendix) and by the fact that three madder bags were chosen to form the arms of the London Dyers' Company. Unlike woad, the roots, not the leaves, yield the dye and a mordant, such as alum or iron, has to be applied to the fibre before the dye can be fixed. Sherds of cooking pots of different shapes and sizes stained with a residue which matches the chemical composition of madder have been recorded from deposits in London dating from the 10th to the 12th centuries (Pritchard 1991, 168–9). These are not common in later deposits, which seems to confirm that dyeing changed from being a domestic handicraft to a more commercial enterprise.

A more expensive red dye was obtained from the insect popularly referred to as kermes or grain, on account of its small round shape. This insect is found in Mediterranean countries where it lives on the kermes oak (*Quercus coccifera*). The dye was obtained by collecting the bodies of mature females during May or June when their eggs were ready to be hatched, and by making a *pastel* from sieving the eggs with vinegar (Verhecken & Wouters 1988/9, 212, 215–16). It was then packed in leather bags for shipment. This dye does not appear to have been imported into England before the 12th century for, although it has been identified on wool fabrics of the Roman period, its use was probably restricted to the Mediterranean provinces of the empire. No wool cloths dyed with kermes are known from northern Europe between the 5th and 11th centuries though it is not unusual on silk textiles. Records refer to its use in 13th-century England (Carus-Wilson 1944, 38); in 1248, for example, a payment of £7 10s. was authorised to Bernard Curuzan for dyeing cloth in grain for the king's use (CLR, 1241–1288, 216). Perhaps

the introduction of kermes into England can be linked to Jewish traders and dyers who are reported to have had a monopoly on its collection in some places (Serjeant 1972, 66, 71). The main sources for the importation of the dye appear to have been Spain and Portugal (Childs 1978, 104–6), although some may have also come from north Africa and southern France.

It is becoming evident from dye analyses of archaeological textiles that kermes supplanted lichen purple dyes on wool fabrics in northern Europe around the 12th century. Lichen purple dyes are not light fast but they have been identified on many patterned cloths of good quality woven in northern Europe between the 1st and 11th centuries (Taylor & Walton 1983, 15; Walton 1986, 39–40; Walton 1989B, 17–18), including three chevron twills from 10th-century London (Pritchard 1984, 58, nos 18, 20, 21, fig 6). By contrast, orcein, the active dye element in purple-producing lichens, has not been detected from the much larger quantity of wool textiles sampled from 14th-century deposits in London and it seems reasonable to conclude it was no longer as popular as it had been. Written sources, nevertheless, indicate that lichens were imported into England for dyeing in the 13th to 15th centuries from Norway and the Canary Islands (Carus-Wilson 1944, 38; Childs 1978, 107; and Appendix, p 200). While lichen purple dyes declined in importance for wool textiles outside rural areas after the 11th century, their use on silk increased, at least in Italy and, as will be described, the dyestuff was detected on threads removed from a patterned silk cloth and a half-silk velvet (pp 115, 128), both of which were recovered from a late 14th-century deposit.

The chief commercial yellow dye was weld (*Reseda luteola* L.) which could be used on its own or top-dyed over woad to give green, or brightened with madder to produce shades of orange and gold (see Appendix). Written references to it are few (Carus-Wilson 1944, 38; Childs 1978, 107). However, its cultivation in England was probably sufficient to meet home demand, for analyses of seeds sampled from archaeological deposits indicate that it was very common (Hall *et al.* 1984, 59; Tomlinson 1985, 280–81).

Looms

Changes in cloth production in the medieval period were not confined to spinning and finishing. New looms were introduced, which were used as well as older, traditional looms, but exactly when and how they came to be accepted remains uncertain. The earliest type of loom known from England is the warp-weighted loom which, by the 10th century, had been in use for over a millennium (Wild 1970, 61). The warp was prepared by weaving a starting border on a small band loom and extending the weft loops round

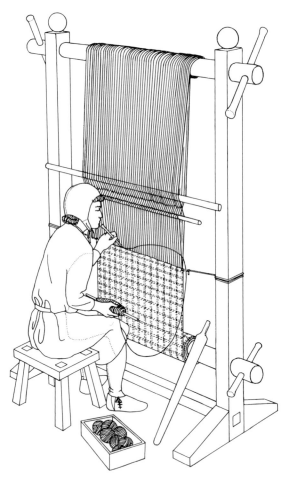

Fig 4 Upright two-beam loom as it might have looked in the 13th century. A heddle-bracket would probably have been used although this is not depicted

pegs (Hoffmann 1964, 63–70, 154–6). The weft became the warp once the border was sewn on to the cloth beam of the larger loom. Tensioning was achieved by tying clay or stone weights to groups of ends, which were carefully spaced apart by chaining a cord across the lower edge of the warp. The loom was placed at an angle against a wall for weaving so that a natural shed was formed between the warp and the wooden uprights of the loom. The weaver stood to do her work beating the weft upwards with a pin-beater of polished bone and a sword-beater of whalebone, wood or iron. Different types of cloth could be woven on this loom but four-shed twills with broken lozenge patterns were closely linked with it. Around the late 9th century, the heddle-bracket on the loom appears to have been modified and a second notch was added to it which, experiments have shown, enabled three-shed twills and lozenge patterns with a point repeat to be produced more easily (Haynes 1975, 160–63; Lise Dokkedal pers comm). This change is indicated by the appearance of three-shed lozenge twills in high status graves at Birka, Sweden (Geijer 1938, 26), and also by the identification of double-notched heddle-brackets from excavations in Trondheim, Norway.

Also apparently in use in England during the Anglo-Saxon period was the upright two-beam loom which was probably introduced into Britain by the Romans although there is no direct evidence for it (Wild 1970, 70; see p 27). On this the warp was tensioned vertically between two wooden beams, the warp beam at the top and the cloth beam below, and the cloth was woven from the bottom upwards, in contrast to the warp-weighted loom, so that the weaver worked seated (Fig 4). In prehistoric times and in certain countries, including Syria, it was common to weave a circular or tubular cloth on this type of loom by looping the warp round an extra rod; the cloth could then be opened flat once it was removed from the loom (Hald 1980, 167–75). This resulted in a shorter piece than if a revolving cloth beam was used, for which evidence is lacking (Hoffmann 1964, 333). Short loom lengths may have been typical, and if so cloths with the length of 23.75m (26 yards) first mentioned in royal proclamations of the 13th century (Bridbury 1982, 107) could not easily have been woven on it. It is difficult to judge how widely this loom was used in

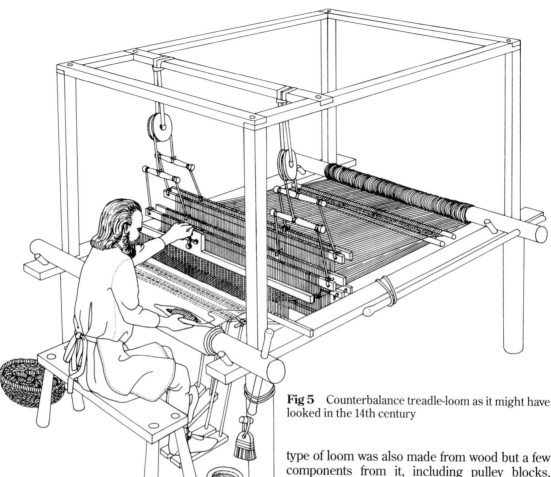

Fig 5 Counterbalance treadle-loom as it might have looked in the 14th century

medieval Europe since tangible evidence is absent. It has been suggested, however, that certain asymmetrical, double-ended bone tools, which have been found on many English sites, were characteristic of it (Brown 1990, 227).

A warp could also be tensioned horizontally on a loom. There are many ways of doing this but written evidence suggests that it was a foot-operated counterbalance treadle-loom that became more widely diffused in western Europe during the 11th century (Hoffmann 1964, 258–60; Carus-Wilson 1969, 164–5). The treadles were linked by pulleys to shafts which could be raised and depressed to open sheds in the warp (Fig 5). This

type of loom was also made from wood but a few components from it, including pulley blocks, treadles and heddle-horses, have been identified from urban sites in northern and eastern Europe (Kaminska & Nahlik 1960, 93–7; Thompson 1968, 146–7; Nyberg 1984, 145–7; Øye 1988, 73–5). The earliest of these come from 11th-century deposits in Haithabu, north Germany, and Gdansk, Poland. The method of beating in the weft differed from that used on upright looms. Instead of a weaving sword, pin-beater or comb, a reed was fitted to the loom between the harness and the cloth beam which the weaver pulled towards himself. By varying the degree to which the weft was beaten, texture could be added to a cloth, and this method of patterning was used in the weaving of rays in the late 13th and 14th centuries (see p 52). The reed had a further function, for the warp ends were threaded between metal teeth (dents) to ensure that they were correctly spaced.

Other types of horizontal loom were also

known in medieval Europe, including the draw-loom, damask loom, velvet loom and low warp tapestry loom. The drawloom was an extremely complex machine and its historical development remains obscure. Indeed, only through analyses of ancient textiles has a clearer understanding of the loom emerged. Its key component was a system of cords or figure harness which controlled the lifting of individual warp ends spaced at regular intervals across the warp (Fig 6). With one person (the drawboy) pulling selected cords and another (the weaver) changing the shed and

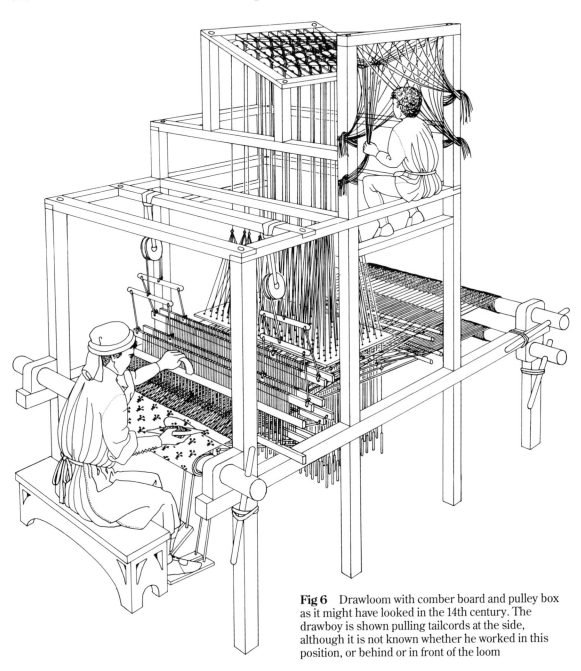

Fig 6 Drawloom with comber board and pulley box as it might have looked in the 14th century. The drawboy is shown pulling tailcords at the side, although it is not known whether he worked in this position, or behind or in front of the loom

Fig 7 Band loom set up for tablet weaving, as it
might have looked in the 14th century

throwing the weft, an elaborate pattern could be
repeated across the cloth (King 1981, 95–6). The
irregular size of the pattern repeat on many early
textiles shows that the figure harness was not
perfected for many centuries. Modifications included the addition of a comber board and pulley
box to help control the pattern mechanism
(Becker 1987, 267–70) but there is little information about them in medieval records (Monnas
1986, 76, fn 11).

The looms described so far were chiefly used
for weaving broad widths of cloth and a fair
amount of workspace was essential for them.
Braid-making, by contrast, took up less space; the
equipment for it was extremely simple and could
easily be improvised. A shedding device was the
main requirement, coupled with a small blunt-
edged beater or sword which could be made from
wood or bone and, for brocading, probably a pin
or needle.

A pack of tablets made from wood, antler or
hide was one type of shedding device, for by rotat-
ing the tablets forward or backwards an opening
was created in the warp (Fig 7). Each tablet was
usually about 25–40mm square and pierced with
four holes, although hexagonal tablets with six
holes were sometimes used. The warp was
threaded through the holes and tensioned either
by running it from a fixed point and tying it to the
weaver's waist, or by stretching it between two
posts (Fig 7; Collingwood 1982, 32). Manuscript
illuminations indicate that the latter method was
favoured at least by the 14th century. This led to
the use of a warp spreader which helped to keep
the threads evenly spaced while the tablets were
turned and the braid woven (Collingwood 1982,
33).

For making tabby-woven ribbons a rigid heddle or heddle-frame was suitable (see p 141). The frame consisted of a series of pierced slats through which alternate ends were threaded enabling a shed and countershed to be created when the frame was raised or depressed; it could either be used on its own with the warp tensioned as for tablet weaving, or fitted into a small box loom supported on the lap (Fig 8). An elk antler heddle-frame from a 13th- or early 14th-century deposit in Bergen, Norway, shows that extra rows of holes for the warp were sometimes pierced through the edge of the frame at the top and bottom to assist with patterning (Øye 1988, 79–80).

Fig 8   Box loom with a rigid heddle as it might have looked in the 14th century

Wool textiles

State of preservation

In examining wool textiles from waterlogged sites two types of damage caused by the damp conditions of preservation have to be borne in mind — damage to texture and damage to colour. Overall matting as fibres disintegrate, particularly with the pressure of packed layers of cloth in the enclosed conditions of a large deposit, makes it difficult in many cases to determine the original degree of fulling and finishing. Discarded material often contained a mixture of old and new fabrics. Small strips and corners, perhaps thrown away new during tailoring, may give some idea of a cloth's original appearance, but in larger pieces cut from garments too worn to be reused and where a raised surface is present only in patches, it is hard to judge if this is the remains of actual cloth finishing processes, or later matting while subjected to wear or to pressure during burial. This particularly applies to woollens, though the shine on the long-staple combed wool of a good worsted sometimes shows even when the fibres have deteriorated.

Damage to colour is even more noticeable. All wool textiles are inclined to darken with age, but preservation in damp, sealed conditions produces severe staining in most cases completely obscuring the original colour. Dye analysis has not been possible on every fragment studied, but in 1978 a random test by M C Whiting on material from BC72 produced very similar results, sometimes unexpected, to those found before on pieces selected by eye for dye-testing (see Appendix). Many undyed cloths now appearing to be light brown were probably the white or off-white of much sheep's wool, but among the darker shades, from near black to pale pinkish-brown, many, though also of natural white wool, also gave no dye reaction. Some strong reddish-browns dyed with madder were visibly no different from others giving a negative result; and after a striking red-purple (No 50; Pl 2B) was identified as kermes (grain), the most expensive medieval dyestuff, pieces selected for their similar appearance in all cases but one proved again to be madder-dyed. The fugitive nature of many vegetable dyes, leakage of dye from one piece to another during burial in the soil, and the practice of using several different dyebaths for one piece of cloth have also complicated the results. The universally brown appearance of so many of these fragments gives no idea of the variety of the colours which from written descriptions must have been vividly present — sanguin, vermilion, crimson, violet, red, yellow, green, azure, murrey, russet, grey, perse (dark blue) — or the 'exotic dyeing' and 'subtle blending of colour' which recent study suggests was so important a feature of English cloth exports of the 13th and 14th centuries (Bridbury 1982, 103).

The weaves of the cloths

From Table 1 it will be seen that a very high proportion of the textiles is tabby woven; twills, apart from a small group of six-shed weaves, include only the simplest three-shed and four-shed constructions. Variety is provided by the use of different spinning, yarn thicknesses, and colour effects using both dyed and natural grey or brown wool among which are checks and mottled patterns, and an impressive range of transverse stripes with special weave effects sometimes incorporating silk thread.

The date of the ultimate disposal of the textiles is fortunately very precise, and the significance of this accurate dating in charting the rise and fall in the use of different bindings can be seen clearly in Table 1, together with another highly important dating factor, the variation in spinning directions, and their association at different periods with different weaves. Similar spinning in warp and weft — Z/Z, S/S — throws up the pattern of a weave, for example the diagonals and reverses of a twill, particularly when combined with a hard-spun, worsted thread. Mixed spinning — Z-spun warp, S-spun weft — where the fibres all lie in the same direction when woven, gives a firmer cloth, par-

Table 1 The weaves of wool textiles present in London deposits of *c.*1150 to 1450

	1151-1200	1201-1250	1251-1300	1301-1350	1351-1400	1401-1450
2.1 Twill						
z-spun	–	–	–	20	9	–
z/s-spun	–	–	3	136	5	–
s-spun	1	–	–	4	4	–
2.2 Twill						
z-spun	–	–	3	27	37	–
z/s-spun	–	–	–	7	3	1
s-spun	–	–	–	1	-	1
3.3 Twill						
z-spun	–	–	–	4	2	1
Tabby						
z-spun	–	–	1	4	33	1
z/s-spun	–	1	–	144	328	9
s-spun	–	–	–	2	102	6
Tabby with weft-faced bands	–	–	–	54	35	2
Date	1151-1200	1201-1250	1251-1300	1301-1350	1351-1400	1401-1450

ticularly suitable for raising a nap and for other forms of finishing. The rise of S/S spinning in the late 14th century was, however, probably due more to changes in spinning practices, particularly the increased use of the spinning wheel, than to any connection with weaving or finishing.

The striking differences between the textiles preserved from the first half of the 14th century and the late 14th century provide invaluable evidence of the changes in production at a crucial stage in the standardisation of the cloth industry. These differences particularly concern the twill weaves which are, therefore, considered first.

Three-shed twills

The three-shed twill made an early appearance in the Roman-occupied territories of Europe and the Near East. The unevenly balanced construction of this weave has often been described as unsuited to the warp-weighted loom of the Mediterranean and Celtic world, with which the early production of four-shed twills was closely associated in the north (Hald 1980; Hoffmann 1964, 183–5, 200–4). But the Romans were also familiar with the vertical two-beam loom, known in Egypt since the New Kingdom *c.*1570–1070 BC. (Forbes 1956, 195–8), and the distribution of three-shed twill in areas once under their occupation, for example in England in Anglo-Saxon cemeteries, may be due to a Roman legacy (Wild 1970, 69–72; Crowfoot 1983, 440–42). The continued life of the two-beam loom in medieval England is suggested by recent finds at Winchester (Keene 1990, 204–8), and it is indeed used to the present day for specialised weaves such as tapestry.

The production of three-shed twills increased throughout northern Europe from the 10th century onwards, until by the 13th century this had become perhaps the most prevalent weave for wool fabrics. The rise in its output in north-west Europe has been attributed to the spread of the treadle-operated horizontal loom (Kaminska & Nahlik 1960, 107), which evidence indicates was becoming more widely employed from the 11th century onwards (Hoffmann 1964, 260; Carus-Wilson 1969, 165), and three-shed twills were woven for domestic consumption on treadle-looms in Scandinavia in recent centuries (Hoffmann 1964, 201). But just as the three-shed binding was ill-matched to the warp-weighted loom, it was also poorly suited to the counter-balanced treadle-loom which operated more effectively where an even number of shafts was used. From the 14th century the weave began to lose its popularity. This is clear from a document dating to 1369 which sets out the guild regulations of Chalons in north-east France. This stipulated what cloths were to be produced locally, namely 'fabrics for which two treadles are used, as is the practice in other cities ...', and, in addition, 'fabrics requiring three treadles, which were usual according to old practice' (Hoffmann 1964, 263–4), wording indicating that the three-shed twill was becoming outdated.

This picture is strikingly confirmed in the two 14th-century deposits at BC72. In the earlier deposit (*c*.1330–1340) the proportion of pieces of 2.1 twill discarded is 38% of all textiles present, while in the main dock filling dated to a few decades later, the quantity is under 4%. Elsewhere in London, cloths with this weave have also only been recorded from deposits dating up to the middle of the 14th century, although it appears to have undergone a limited revival in the 16th century when it is associated with some lightweight union cloths with wool being combined with another fibre such as silk. A similar picture of decline emerges from other towns and countries in north-west Europe, notably The Netherlands, where the comparative scarcity of the binding after *c*.1325 contrasts with its frequency in 13th- and early 14th-century deposits (Vons-Comis 1982, 162), though in less commercialised areas such as Oslo three-shed twills were still *c*.31% of the textiles in a group dated towards the end of the 15th century (Kjellberg 1979, 84–6).

No complete loomwidths have survived from London, and it is not possible to estimate the width of the looms on which three-shed twills were made. The use of reinforced selvedges is, however, a characteristic of many of the London cloths (Figs 11, 12, Table 2), which suggests that they must have been sufficiently wide to require strengthened edges. In southern Sweden the clothing worn by the Bocksten man, who was probably murdered in the 14th century, includes a mantle made from a 2.1 twill which is 600mm (23 ⁵/₈ins) wide (Nockert 1985, 47; Nockert & Possnert 1989, 74), and in Assisi, Tuscany, a mantle woven in 2.1 twill worn by St Clare (died 1253) has a loomwidth of 550mm (21 ⁵/₈ins) (Flury-Lemberg 1988, 314, 485, no 57). Both are, therefore, relatively narrow and capable of being woven by one person.

Cloths with this twill binding are not all alike. The majority fall into two types — cloths woven from combed wool, which is usually Z-spun, with little or no finishing, and cloths with mixed spinning, where the Z-spun warp is smooth and even and the S-spun weft is coarse and often uneven. Many of the latter show signs that may indicate fulling and they also include cloths patterned with colour or texture. A small number of other twills

are not so clearly placed; they include cloths with S-spun yarn in both systems and a miscellaneous group of coarse cloths, mainly from the late 14th-century deposit at BC72. On all the 2.1 twills from London the warp face appears to have been regarded as the right side. This is clear from the way that seams are turned on clothing and from buttoned garments, many of which were made from this type of twill (see Figs 137, 151, 163).

Worsteds

This group of cloths is easily recognisable with its hard combed yarn, slightly higher thread density in the warp, and rather shiny surface (Fig 9).

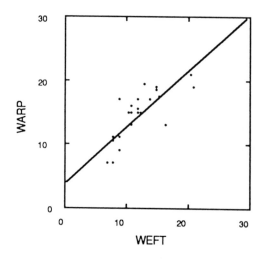

Fig 9   Scatter diagram showing the thread density of three-shed twills woven from Z-spun wool yarn based on 28 examples

They are good quality fabrics and, although now stained brown, were probably usually coloured; of the five samples analysed for dyes four gave positive results, one kermes, the three others madder. All these worsteds are simple diagonal twills, without the lozenge patterns found on three cloths from London deposits of the 11th and 12th centuries (Fig 10; Crowfoot 1980, 113–15, no 145; Pritchard 1984, 56–7, nos 28, 29). A few worsted three-shed twills have mixed spinning, a feature that is also evident in a small number of the earlier three-shed lozenge twills, including one from late 11th-century London (Pritchard 1984, 56–7, no 29), but in other respects they are indistinguish-

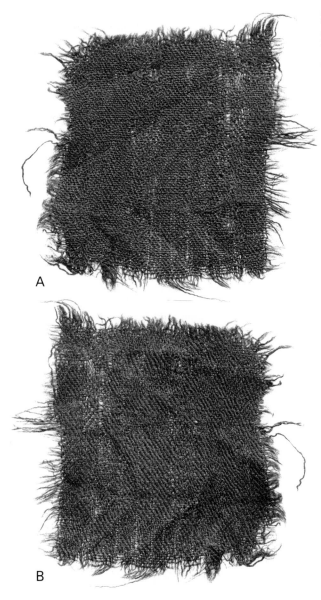

A

B

Fig 10 Three-shed lozenge twill woven from combed, Z-spun wool yarn from a deposit dating to the middle of the 12th century: (A) warp face, (B) weft face. Scale 1:1

Table 2   Selvedges on three-shed twills woven from Z-spun wool yarn

Cat. No	No of threads per cm warp/weft	Description of selvedge
Second quarter 14th century		
1	19/15	2 edge cords of paired ends
2	17/14	unreinforced, the 5th and 8th ends are a darker colour; 2 shuttles used pick-and-pick (Fig 11A)
3	16/11	2 edge cords of paired ends; 2 shuttles used pick-and-pick (Fig 11B)
4	14–15/12–13	edge cord of 3 ends, 2 pairs of ends; 3 shuttles (Fig 11C)
5	14–16/12	edge cord of 3 ends; 3 shuttles (Fig 12)

Selvedges on five pieces woven from Z-spun yard (Table 2) throw valuable light on weaving practices. Four of the five reveal the use of more than one shuttle; two of these have pick-and-pick selvedges (Nos 2–3, Fig 11A and B), while for two others at least three shuttles were used (Nos 4–5, Figs 11C and 12). Unfortunately, in no example are both selvedges preserved and the exact passage of the weft cannot be determined. Indeed, these and many other selvedges survive only as offcuts with the weft loops often damaged so that the character of the main weave is uncertain. Patterned worsted three-shed twills from Novgorod were apparently manufactured by throwing the weft with three shuttles (Nahlik 1963, 262), a method which was also used on three-shed textiles preserved from excavations at Gdansk (Kaminska & Nahlik 1960, 104), and mentioned in written sources (Nahlik 1963, 36). If a greater number of selvedges from three-shed twills were preserved in good condition, this practice might be found to be more general, but at present the evidence from London confirms the findings from Novgorod that this is typical only of worsted three-shed twills. One cloth has a coloured selvedge consisting of two darker coloured ends (No 2, Fig 11A), which is otherwise rare on cloths woven from worsted yarn.

The small proportion of worsted 2.1 twills re-covered from 14th-century deposits in London in-

able from those made from Z-spun yarn. One piece is woven from an undyed merino-type fleece with a visibly red colour, an unusual kind of wool which perhaps came from the famous Spanish red sheep (No 6, Harry M Appleyard pers comm).

A

B

C

Fig 11 Selvedges on three-shed twills woven from Z-spun yarn: (A) No 2, (B) No 3, (C) No 4

dicates that they were no longer common at this period, and a similar picture of decline emerges for the output of tabbies woven from worsted yarn (see p 43). At the same time experiments with new bindings for cloths woven from this type of yarn appear to have occurred, indicating that a shift took place in this branch of the industry which was able to develop new fabrics to meet changing demand and competition with growing imports of silk cloths.

Fig 12 Selvedge strip, No 5, folded and stitched to form a trimming. Scale 1:1

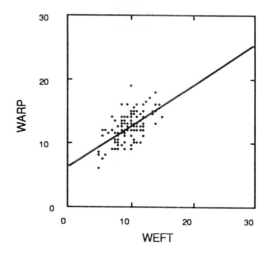

Fig 13 Scatter diagram showing the thread density of three-shed twills woven from Z-spun warp yarn and S-spun weft yarn based on 144 examples

Cloths with mixed spinning

Most three-shed twills from 14th-century deposits in London are woven from Z-spun warp yarn and S-spun weft yarn (Fig 13). The warp yarn is smooth and fine and was probably combed before spinning. The weft yarn usually has less twist and because of its longer float on the reverse of the cloth has often become woolly and matted, obscuring the back of the weave. Where the front surface is also matted it may be assumed that the cloth was fulled, but the degree of finishing that these cloths were given is very difficult to estimate. This difficulty is compounded by documentary evidence indicating that cloths were often reshorn (*retonsura*) during cleaning.

Some of these cloths from deposits dating to the first half of the 14th century are patterned with checks and stripes. These can be coloured (Nos 7–9, Fig 14), or textured by using threads of different weight, or ply, and by varying the spin direction, particularly in the weft (Nos 10–11, Fig 15). Twills with similar patterning have been found in earlier town deposits, for example from a late 10th-century deposit in Winchester and an 11th-century deposit in Durham (Crowfoot 1990, 475, no 1033, pl xxxixa, fig 119; Crowfoot 1979, 37–9). The colour in these early pieces was at least partly carried out by using different shades of natural brown wool, whereas in these later examples from London the use of dyed fleece appears to have been more usual. Three-shed twills

Fig 14 Three-shed twills with colour effects: (A) No 7 warp and weft face, (B) No 8 warp face, (C) No 9 warp face

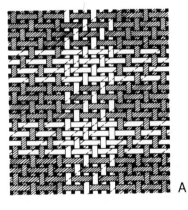

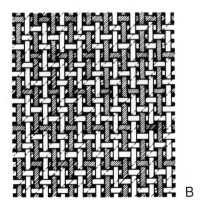

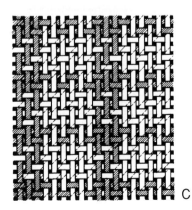

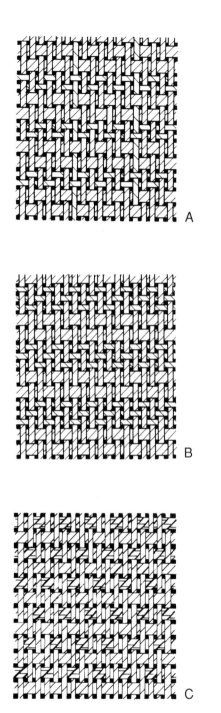

Fig 15 Three-shed twills with colour and spin effects: (A) No 10, (B) No 11, (C) No 12 which has a S-diagonal on the face of the twill rather than the usual Z-diagonal

Fig 16 Three-shed twill woven with a thick weft yarn, No 442: (A) warp face, (B) weft face. Scale 1:1

with coloured stripes in warp or weft were also present at Novgorod (Nahlik 1963, 264).

The thick yarns used for pattern effects are different from those woven into other three-shed twills which often have a knobbly weft that has been unevenly spun (Fig 16), and which was deliberately used to produce a warm, matted inner surface. Some of these cloths are woven from natural grey-brown wool and none appear to have been fulled, suggesting that they were a cheap type of cloth.

A number of three-shed twills, which appear to have been fulled, have coloured selvedges. This feature is more generally associated with tabby weaves (p 48), but it was clearly not restricted to one type of weave and the fact that the cloths were fulled may be more pertinent. Two selvedges are similar with a pair of red edge cords on brown cloths (Nos 17–18, Table 3 and Fig 17A). The third is a light brown cloth which has three cords of paired ends followed by a narrow stripe of ends that are partly in a darker coloured yarn (No 19, Table 3, Figs 17B and 18). Single shuttle working is found on these cloths with coloured selvedges and they were presumably monochrome apart from the selvedge. A coloured selvedge was similarly noted on a fulled three-shed twill from Novgorod, where it was argued that the cloth was a foreign import (Nahlik 1963, 264). Other 2.1 twills with mixed spinning from London have two weft yarns with pick-and-pick selvedges (Nos 13–15, 20, 23, 24, Table 3, Figs 17C and D) which also occur on twills woven from Z-spun yarn (p 29). In one example with a reinforced edge, the second shuttle seems only to have been used occasionally, perhaps carrying a different-coloured yarn, returning after two or three shots of the other weft to pull the heavy, four-warp outer cords on to each other to make a sort of false tubular edge (No 27, Table 3 and Fig 17E). A similar effect was sometimes produced in more regular selvedges by tightening the longer weft loops to pull them level with the shorter return of the third throw of the twill (e.g. No 30, Table 3 and Fig 17F).

No trace of a starting edge is preserved on any of these cloths, but part of a decorative fringe which was used to finish an edge is present on one piece (No 31). This fringe was made by plying groups of three ends together and then tying ten of these groups in a finger knot.

Table 3   Selvedges on three-shed twills with mixed spinning

Cat. No	No of threads per cm warp/weft	Description of selvedge
Second quarter 14th century		
13	9/8	unreinforced; 2 shuttles used pick-and-pick (Fig 17C)
14	15/12	unreinforced; 2 shuttles used pick-and-pick
15	12/11	unreinforced; 2 shuttles used pick-and-pick
16	10/8	edge cord of paired ends
17	11/8	2 edge cords of paired red ends (Fig 17A)
18	9/7–8	2 edge cords of paired red ends
19	10/7–8	3 edge cords of paired ends (brown), 1 end (brownish-black), 1 pair of ends (1 brown, 1 brownish-black), 1 end (brownish black) (Figs 17B, 18)
20	9/7	4 or 5 edge cords of paired ends; 2 shuttles used pick-and-pick
21	14/11	5 edge cords of paired ends
22	13/12	5 edge cords of paired ends
23	13–14/11–12	edge cord of 3 ends, 2 pairs of ends; 2 shuttles used pick-and-pick
24	14/9	edge cord of 4 ends, 2 pairs of ends; 2 shuttles used pick-and-pick (Fig 17D)
25	?7–8	4 edge cords of 3 ends, 2 pairs of ends; probably 3 shuttles
26	12–13/9–10	edge cord of 4 ends, probably 3 shuttles
27	12–13/9	2 edge cords of 4 ends, 5 pairs of ends; 3 or shuttles (Fig 17E)
28	?/11	3 edge cords of 4 ends, 3 pairs of ends (incomplete)
29	?/?	4 edge cords of paired ends
30	?/?	2 edge cords (S/Z-ply), 7 pairs of ends (incomplete) (Fig 17F)
Last quarter 14th century		
157	10–11/10–11	2 edge cords of 3 ends
158	6/5	4 edge cords of paired ends

Fig 17   Selvedges on
three-shed twills with
mixed spinning: (A) No
17, (B) No 19, (C) No 13,
(D) No 24, (E) No 27,
(F) No 30

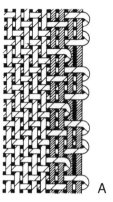

A

B

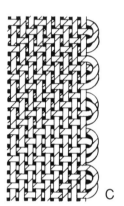

C

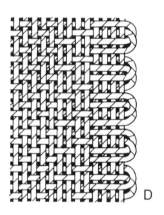

D

E

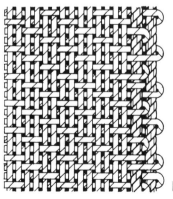

F

Fig 18 Three-shed twill with coloured selvedge, No 19, from a deposit dating to the second quarter of the 14th century. Scale 1:1

Fig 19 Three-shed twill woven from S-spun yarn, No 160, from a late 14th-century deposit. Scale 1:1

Cloths woven from S-spun yarn and coarse cloths

The remaining 2.1 twills do not form a coherent group. Six examples, all recovered from 14th-century deposits, can be described as medium-grade fabrics woven from S-spun yarns (No 160, Fig 19). None have been heavily fulled and shorn and no selvedges are preserved.

Twenty other examples are all coarse cloths with less than ten threads per cm in both warp and weft. The earliest piece, from a deposit of the late 12th century at BIG82, is woven from S-spun yarn of a similar quality in both warp and weft. The 14th-century twills include 11 with mixed spinning, six Z-spun, and two S-spun. At least four are woven from wool that has a natural brown fleck and another proved to be dyed from madder. One Z-spun example has paired threads in the ?weft, possibly from a band running across the cloth. Another, also Z-spun throughout, is rolled and stitched, as if used for a belt, with wool thread (No 156, see p 153). The coarse grade, and in many the lack of any fulling or finishing, suggest that these cloths were domestically produced. Appropriately, the patched cowl of St Francis and mantle of St Clare, which have been preserved as relics,

were made from twills of this coarse grade, the natural grey and brown wool Z-spun throughout (Flury-Lemberg 1988, 314–17, 485, nos 56 and 57).

Fulling and finishing

It has been suggested that by the 13th century practically all professionally-woven wool fabrics were fulled, the only exceptions being fine worsteds mainly produced in four-shed bindings (Carus-Wilson 1969, 183–209; Hoffmann 1964, 264). Three-shed twills, as survivals of an earlier technique, perhaps represent an intermediate stage. Some certainly have been fulled and probably teasled and shorn, but on many it is difficult to tell from the surviving fragments what the original surface appearance would have been. In the case of those with coloured stripes and checks, while the thick weft face is matted, it seems unlikely that the front was subjected to any fulling. The threads on the front are smooth, and even allowing for stronger contrast in the original colours, raising a nap would have blurred the narrow lines or concealed the different qualities of the yarns used in other stripes.

Apart from its decorative value, the long lie of the threads in the diagonal of a twill gives extra warmth and thickness, but with the spread of fulling, and the demand that cloth should have a finished surface, the extra bulk of the twills ceased to be an advantage; the thickening resulting from the fulling process could add warmth and solidity to the simplest weaves, and the production of twill became unnecessarily time consuming if the pattern of the weave was not to be seen. The simplification of technology and appeal to widening markets have been pointed out as factors leading to the decrease of the 2.1 twill in the 13th to 15th centuries in eastern Europe (Nahlik 1963, 99–100). The London material is consistent with this verdict, while providing an even closer dating for the professional rejection of the three-shed twill.

Four-shed twills

The history of four-shed twills is clearer. The basic 2.2 diagonal twill, a balanced weave easily adapted to any hand loom, was continuously produced in northern Europe from the late Iron Age onwards. Coarse twills with S-spun thread, probably woven on a tubular loom during the Late and pre-Roman Iron Ages in Denmark, *c.*500 BC– AD 200. (Hald 1980, 181–4), were contemporary with fabrics woven from Z-spun yarn in other areas of Scandinavia, where the evidence of loomweights and starting-borders on textiles indicate that the upright warp-weighted loom was already in use. On this loom, with a simple arrangement using the natural shed and three-rod heddles, coarse to medium weight diagonal twills produced from Z-spun yarn were followed in the Halstatt-La Tène cultures and the northern Roman provinces by finer twills with mixed (Z/S) spinning and a variety of dog's tooth, herringbone and broken lozenge patterns (Bender Jørgensen 1984, 126; Wild 1970, 96–100, 112–6; Wild 1977, 12–26). This preference for mixed spinning in patterned twills persisted in England throughout the post-Roman period (Crowfoot 1983, 418–28) and was still to be found among four-shed twills of the 10th century in English towns including Gloucester and London (Hedges 1982, 112–13; Pritchard 1984, 53–5). But from the 7th century onwards the combination of Z-spinning and combed wool seems to predominate (Crowfoot 1978, 103–5; Crowfoot 1981, 96; Crowfoot 1987, 171–2). However, the very high proportion of mineralised fibres in the excavated English material, mainly from Anglo-Saxon cemeteries, means that it is not always possible to distinguish how many of these twills with Z-spun yarn are of wool and how many of flax.

Four-shed twills from 13th-and 14th-century London are all simple 2.2 diagonal weaves. There are no starting-borders among them, and there is little doubt that these twills were being woven on the horizontal loom, where the four shafts, hung in two pairs of pulleys, were set in motion by four treadles. Unlike 2.1 twills, there is little difference between 2.2 twills from the 13th and 14th centuries, and in all deposits they form a small but fairly consistent proportion of the total number of textiles (Table 1). Textiles from other European towns show the same picture, with the small proportion of four-shed twills continuing, while 2.1 twills gradually disappear and give first place to tabby weaves (Kjellberg 1979, 86–7; Tidow 1982, 177). The east European material suggests a higher proportion of 2.2 twills in the 14th and 15th centuries, perhaps reflecting a later urbanisation and continued use of the warp-weighted loom (Nahlik 1963, 294), but the record is incomplete, as some sites which have produced important evidence have no material published from later than the 13th century.

Worsteds
Of the eighty 2.2 twills from deposits in London dating from the late 13th to the early 15th centuries all but 13 are woven from Z-spun yarn (Fig

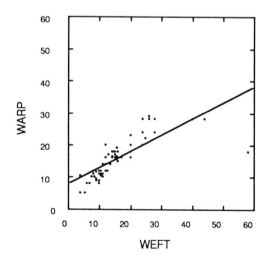

Fig 20   Scatter diagram showing the thread density of four-shed twills woven from Z-spun wool yarn based on 68 examples

Fig 21 2.2 twill with colour effects, Nos 38, 159

Fig 22 Worsted four-shed twill with simple unreinforced selvedge, No 39, from a deposit dating to the second quarter of the 14th century. Scale 1:1

Fig 23 Worsted weft-faced four-shed twill, No 162, from a late 14th-century deposit. Scale 1:1

20). Most of these are cloths that can be classified as worsteds. The wool is mainly fine to medium, including one within the merino range. The fleece was combed before spinning and the yarns evenly spun showing up the diagonal wale (line) of the weave; this was emphasised by using a balanced number of warp and weft threads and occasionally warp and weft yarns of contrasting tints. In two examples from London where this type of colour effect was employed the yarn used for one system was dyed red with madder while the other was white or perhaps yellow (Nos 38, 159, Fig 21). Both are good quality cloths which were used to line fashionable buttoned garments made from coarser 2.1 twills (Figs 143A, 163). They were perhaps different pieces of the same garment, for although they were recovered from deposits of different dates at BC72 the better preserved piece comes from the earlier deposit. A worsted 2.2 twill of similar quality (No 392) was used for another

stylish buttoned garment (Fig 162), and for this item the twill formed the main fabric as well as the lining. The two twills used for this garment are so similar that they may have been cut from the same length of cloth.

While most worsted 2.2 twills are balanced weaves, two cloths (Nos 161, 162) from late 14th-century deposits are weft-faced, with the weft threads concealing the ends of the warp in the ratio of 1.5:1 to 3:1 (Figs 20, 23), a trend foreshadowed by a cloth from a deposit of the second quarter of the 14th century (No 39, Fig 22). This type of cloth is not otherwise found until the 16th century in London, perhaps owing to the lack of 15th-century material preserved from the City. Written records indicate a growth in output of weft-faced worsteds at the end of the 14th century, since they refer to the making of worsteds 'with double or half again as many weft threads' as warp threads (Kerridge 1985, 9). It is probable that this

Table 4   Selvedges on four-shed twills

Cat. No	Spin direction warp/weft	No of threads per cm	Description of selvedge
Second quarter 14th century			
39	Z/Z	28/40	unreinforced (Fig 22)
40	Z/Z	8/7	unreinforced
41	Z/Z	24/24	edge cord of paired ends
42	Z/Z	16–17/14	edge cord of paired ends
43	Z/Z	12/12–13	edge cord of 4 ends
433	Z/S	18/9	edge cord Z/S-ply, 2 pairs of ends (Fig 24A)
Last quarter 14th century			
164	Z/Z	15/16	unreinforced
163	Z/Z	16/20	edge cord of paired ends, 14 ends in 5mm (Fig 25)
165	Z/Z	10/11	2-edge cords of 4 ends
166	Z/Z	9–10/9	edge cord Z/S-ply, 8 pairs of ends (Fig 24B)
167	Z/Z	8/10	edge cord of 3 ends
168	Z/S	10–11/10	4 edge cords of paired ends
Unstratified			
392	Z/Z	17/13	unreinforced (Fig 162)

was the type of cloth that John Paston was referring to when, in September 1465, he wrote to his wife Margaret requesting her to inquire 'where William Paston bought his tepet of fyne worsted whech is almost like silke' (Davis 1971, 140).

Visual examination and dye tests established little about the range of colours used for these cloths. Twelve samples gave positive results when tested and the dye identified was madder with three exceptions. In these a yellow or brown dye, which could not be identified, was used and in one piece this dye appears to have been top-dyed over woad (indigotin), presumably resulting in a shade of green (see Appendix).

Selvedges on worsted 2.2 twills from London in the 14th century are all of simple construction and they are not strengthened apart from sometimes having an edge cord of paired or multiple ends (Table 4). An exception is a coarse cloth from a late 14th-century deposit which has a plied edge cord and at least eight pairs of ends (No 166, Fig 24B), but as the rest of this cloth is not preserved its overall character cannot be determined. The absence of a series of strong cords which takes the strain on the edge of a stretched cloth, reflects both the general lack of finishing on cloths of this nature and the likelihood that they were woven to narrower widths. Also, by contrast to three-shed twills and to a number of tabby-woven cloths, no differently coloured ends are apparent among these selvedges.

As well as preserving a selvedge, one of these twills has a fringe of loosely twisted ends (No 163, Fig 25). It also has a cord consisting of a throw of four S-ply weft threads, 17mm above the end of the web, with the end of the cord run back into the weave. This cord, rather than forming part of a pattern, probably marks the end of the piece of cloth and was therefore cut off and discarded (*cf.* six-shed twills No 170, p 43).

Worsted yarn was also used in combination

Fig 24 Reinforced selvedges on four-shed twills: (A) No 443, (B) No 166

A

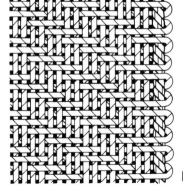

B

Fig 25 Worsted four-shed twill with selvedge, fringe and cord marking cloth length, No 163, from a late 14th-century deposit. Scale 1:1

cushion covers — for the hard surface had the virtue of not gathering dust, while the decorative effect of the diagonal lines would have shown to advantage. These items were made as piece goods (Sutton 1989, 203). Clothing was cut from longer bolts and the elastic texture of the cloth was particularly useful for hose before knitted stockings became commonly available, although no worsted hose has been identified from 14th-century deposits in the City, and for lightweight clothing, especially for summer wear or for hotter climates. At the end of the 13th century worsted was taken abroad for the clothing of the knightly orders, to Cyprus for the Templars, and to Jerusalem for the Hospitallers (CCR, 51; Sutton, 203), while in England it was bought by monks at Durham and Norwich for summer clothing, in spite of an attempted prohibition on the grounds that it was too fine.

Non-worsteds woven wholly from Z-spun or S-spun yarn

Of the four-shed twills woven from Z-spun yarn which do not come into the category of worsteds, four from BC72 appear to have been fulled. There are also six examples of coarser cloths with less than 10 threads per cm in both systems. Four-shed twills woven wholly from S-spun yarn are rare, especially by contrast to later centuries when wheel-spun yarn became common. One cloth from an early 15th-century deposit is heavily fulled, while another, a coarse cloth, is dyed with madder.

Twills with mixed spinning

Four-shed twills with mixed spinning total only 11 from deposits of the 14th and early 15th centuries. None has more than 20 ends or 15 picks per cm.

Five pieces woven from hairy, natural brown or grey wool are relatively coarse (Fig 26). The wool, which usually includes both fine and coarse fibres, appears to have come from a type of double-coated sheep. The Z-spun yarn has a harder twist, and a selvedge preserved on one cloth (No 168, Table 4) indicates that this yarn is the warp. Different shades of natural-coloured wool were sometimes used to pattern the cloths; on one piece the warp appears to have lighter coloured stripes of differing widths (No 45, Fig 27A). Colour effects were also combined with yarns of different thicknesses and there is a cloth

with four-shed twill in patterned bands on cloths woven with a tabby main weave. These are discussed later (see p 55).

Worsted fabrics woven from combed wool have always been an English speciality. The derivation of the name from the north Norfolk village of Worstead (Anglo-Saxon Worthstede) is generally accepted; the earliest reference so far found of weavers there is in 1290. By the early 14th century the name had already been transferred to the cloth; 'draps qe homme appelle Worthstedes and Aylehams', are recorded in the Rolls of Parliament for 1314–15. The town of Aylsham, situated a little further west, in its turn gave its name to a type of linen (Salzman 1923, 229; Sutton 1989, 202). Throughout the 14th and 15th centuries the production of worsteds was concentrated in east Norfolk, the worsteds being bought to Norwich for inspection and sealing, and exported to the Continent through the port of Yarmouth (Carus-Wilson & Coleman 1963, 15).

English worsteds were invariably cheaper than fulled cloths, because the wool and labour costs were lower. They were valued at home and abroad for special uses; in medieval records they are particularly linked with household furnishings — bedhangings, wallhangings, coverlets and

Fig 26 Coarse cloth with mixed spinning woven in 2.2 twill, No 169, from a late 14th-century deposit. Scale 1:1

Fig 27 Coarse four-shed twills with colour effects and mixed spinning: (A) No 45, (B) No 444

A

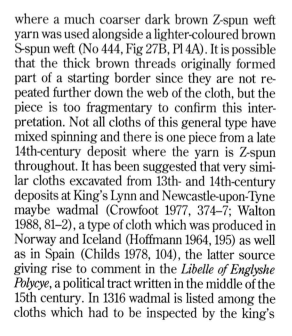

B

where a much coarser dark brown Z-spun weft yarn was used alongside a lighter-coloured brown S-spun weft (No 444, Fig 27B, Pl 4A). It is possible that the thick brown threads originally formed part of a starting border since they are not repeated further down the web of the cloth, but the piece is too fragmentary to confirm this interpretation. Not all cloths of this general type have mixed spinning and there is one piece from a late 14th-century deposit where the yarn is Z-spun throughout. It has been suggested that very similar cloths excavated from 13th- and 14th-century deposits at King's Lynn and Newcastle-upon-Tyne maybe wadmal (Crowfoot 1977, 374–7; Walton 1988, 81–2), a type of cloth which was produced in Norway and Iceland (Hoffmann 1964, 195) as well as in Spain (Childs 1978, 104), the latter source giving rise to comment in the *Libelle of Englyshe Polycye*, a political tract written in the middle of the 15th century. In 1316 wadmal is listed among the cloths which had to be inspected by the king's

aulnager to check that it conformed with statutory regulations as to length and width (Salzman 1923, 202; Hoffmann 1964, 223).

The other four-shed twills with mixed spinning include one from a mid-14th century deposit woven from combed wool with a much softer spun weft (No 443, Table 4, Fig 24A). This was a type of cloth more common in earlier centuries (see p 36). Three others are medium to coarse fabrics, which were probably fulled, while a long strip of a heavily-fulled woollen dyed with madder from an early 15th-century deposit can be seen as a forerunner of the woollen twills that were to become popular in the later 15th and 16th centuries.

It has been suggested that the cloths say and sayette, distinguished in medieval regulations as unfulled and woven of long-staple wool, were 2.2 twills. Marta Hoffmann quotes descriptions of the cloth from documents dating to the 13th to 15th centuries from the Flemish towns of Bruges and Hondschoote that suggest a balanced four-shed twill: it is described as a weave with a warp and a weft face made on a loom with four treadles (Hoffmann 1964, 264–5). It is a possibility that some of the 2.2 twills from London may have been sayes, and this argument is strengthened by a find from a 16th-century Thames riverside deposit of a leaden aulnage seal for a 'Colchester Dutch' say which is affixed to a small piece of its original cloth (Geoff Egan pers comm). This is a 2.2 twill woven from long-staple wool with a Z-spun warp, S-spun weft, and 26 threads per cm in both systems; it also has a reinforced selvedge, 4mm wide, woven in tabby weave. Whether this say was typical of those made in other towns and in earlier centuries is uncertain but the use of mixed spinning could provide an important guide to its identification.

Six-shed twills

A small but very interesting group of 14th-century worsteds are in a six-shed binding (Table 5). They include fragments of up to four cloths from the deposit at BC72 dating to the second quarter of the 14th century, and three later examples, two from the late 14th-century deposit at BC72 and one from a late 14th- or early 15th-century fill of a stone garderobe at MLK76. All were woven from fine, Z-spun worsted yarn, and are clearly skilled

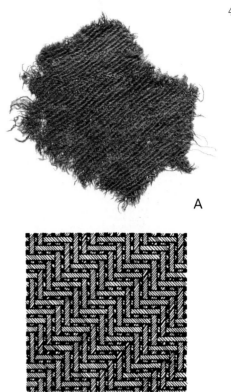

A

B

Fig 28 Six-shed twill, No 48, from a deposit dating to the second quarter of the 14th century: (A) photograph, scale 1:1, (B) weave diagram

Table 5 Six-shed twills

Cat. No	Spin direction warp/weft	No of threads per cm warp/weft	Dyestuff/s
Second quarter 14th century			
46	Z/Z	21/33	madder
47	Z/Z	25/26	madder
48	Z/Z	25/36	madder (Fig 28A)
49	(i) Z (ii) Z (iii) Z	27/27 & 30	madder for red and purple yarns (Fig 29, Pl 2A)
Last quarter 14th century			
170	Z/Z	17/36 & 75–86	negative (Fig 30)
171	Z/Z	18/100	not tested (Fig 150)
410	Z/Z	18/80	not tested

professional products. A small piece from a castle at Voorst, Overijssel, in the Low Countries, dating to 1362 or a little earlier, is the only contemporary example of such a fabric so far noted from the Continent (Vons-Comis 1983, 85–6).

The type of wool used for the four earliest examples varies. In one cloth (No 48) it is a very fine fleece-type within the merino range, in two others (Nos 46 and 49) it is in the fine to medium range, while in the fourth (No 47) the wool has been identified as coming from a double-coated sheep since kemp hairs as well as fine fibres are present (Harry M Appleyard pers comm). But all the yarns shine and the diagonal wale of the weave is very evident. Three of the fragments are unpatterned (Nos 46–48, Fig 28), although their size is too small for the overall design of the cloth to be determined with certainty, and despite now being different shades of pink and reddish-brown,

all were apparently madder-dyed. No selvedges are preserved, but from the evidence of the fourth cloth, which is patterned, the system with slightly closer-spaced threads must be the weft.

Fortunately two rather larger pieces have survived of the beautiful patterned fabric (No 49, Fig 29, Pl 2A). Both show areas of the same weft-chevron pattern, the warp yarn dyed reddish-pink and the weft possibly undyed. Across the centre is a band of similar chevrons but woven from a reddish-pink weft yarn similar to the warp. The band is edged in extended tabby with the weft passing under and over three ends, half woven in a light purple yarn and half in a white yarn; the band was beaten harder on the loom than the twill-woven part of the web. Both the red and purple yarns were dyed with madder. The maximum height preserved of the cloth is only 45mm, and it is possible that the two fragments came from a wide decorative band on a monochrome main weave of diagonal twill rather than that the whole fabric was patterned with waved chevrons.

The appearance of six-shed twills from deposits of the late 14th century is very different. The weave is the same diagonal 3.3 twill, but the closely beaten weft (only slightly anticipated in those fabrics produced earlier in the century) hides the diagonal wale, giving the fabrics the

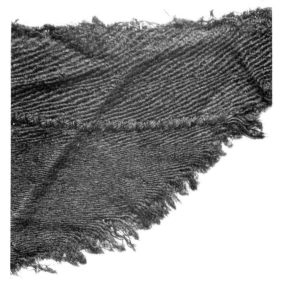

Fig 29   Patterned six-shed twill, No 49

Fig 30   Weft-faced six-shed twill, No 170, from a late 14th-century deposit. Scale 1:1

look of sateen rather than twill, except that, unlike sateen, the twills are reversible. One piece appears at first to be two fragments of cloth, one fine and one coarser, joined across the middle (No 170, Fig 30). The weave is, however, continuous, the 'join' being a single throw of *c*.22 threads in one shed, with the remains of a similar cord run in several throws further along the loom length. On one side the weft was densely beaten up covering the warp by a ratio of 5:1; on the other the weave is looser with a weft to warp ratio of only 2:1. It seems probable that this weft cord was thrown, with its tail run roughly back into the binding to hold it firm, to mark the end of a length of cloth, and, therefore, the unevenly woven area was the beginning of the loompiece (see above, p 38). Other fragments of a weft-faced six-shed twill from the 1380s deposit at BC72 are covered with rows of silk stitching and probably formed part of a garment (No 171, Fig 150). The piece from MLK76 is of a similar fine quality with a weft to warp thread density of 4.5:1. These weft-preponderant fabrics are very similar in appearance to two weft-faced 2.2 twills from a contemporary late 14th-century deposit in London (see p 37). Weft-faced 2.2 twills continued to be produced into the 16th century whereas six-shed twills apparently disappeared during the early 15th century. The realisation, therefore, that the same effect could be obtained with less effort in a four-shed construction may perhaps account for the limited life and distribution of these six-shed worsteds.

The unusual character of the binding, and the brief period of their appearance, point to these high quality worsteds being produced in a specialised centre, perhaps in Norfolk where the worsted industry was concentrated (Sutton 1989, 201). The weft-chevron pattern has been compared to similar bands on 13th-century Hispano-Moresque silk fabrics (Pritchard 1985, 30), and the weft-faced character of the later six-shed twills seems likely to have been designed to imitate the newly-introduced silk satins.

Tabby weaves

Tabby weave, as its old name 'linen weave' (*Leinenbindung*) implies, has always been closely associated with flax. The binding was popular for textiles produced from either animal or vegetable

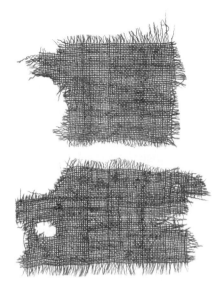

Fig 31 Worsted tabby, No 397, from a late 13th-century deposit. Scale 1:1

fibres in the Roman period, and its apparent decline in post-Roman Europe can be partly explained by the damp conditions in which many textiles have been preserved. Study of mineralised textile remains from Anglo-Saxon cemeteries of the 6th and 7th centuries shows a regular and, in some areas, such as Kent, an increasing proportion of tabby weaves, some certainly of wool. It is apparent, however, from other material of the 7th to 10th centuries, and even later in the north, that the emphasis was still on twills for outer garments.

A few tabby-woven cloths from London exhibit the worsted yarn and slightly open-textured, balanced weave which characterise many of the earlier fabrics, particularly a fine worsted from TL74 dating to *c*.1270 (No 397, Fig 31). These worsted fabrics, however, ceased to be produced in any quantity. The very different appearance of most tabby-woven cloths from 14th-century deposits — generally woollens with traces of a nap — should be connected with the establishment of fulling mills, and the production of cloth with a finished surface.

The shift in output from twills to tabbies is reflected very clearly in 14th- and 15th-century textiles from London. Tabby predominates in the textiles recovered from a late 14th- or early 15th-century fill of a garderobe at MLK76 and in an early 15th-century revetment dump at TL74. The percentage of tabby weaves in the BC72 group of textiles rises from 49% in the deposit of the 1340s to 90% in the late 14th-century dock filling. A similar trend is present throughout north-west Europe; for example, tabby dominates the textile finds dating from the 13th to 16th centuries in The Netherlands (Vons-Comis 1982, 162, fig 3), the 15th-century material from the north German towns of Lübeck and Hameln (Tidow 1982, 177), and those from late medieval deposits in Oslo (Kjellberg 1979, 95–101). It has been pointed out that among late medieval cloth regulations for Flemish and French towns all aspects of production seem to be dealt with: the wool, tools, dimensions and dressing of the cloth, indeed everything except the actual weaving (Hoffmann 1964, 264, fn 26). The binding was apparently not considered to be of such importance when the weave itself was to be obscured. Tabby weave, the simplest construction, was the quickest and easiest for warpers and weavers to produce, and the even surface which resulted was ideal for later finishing treatments.

Broadcloth

Broadcloth woven, dyed, fulled, teasled and sheared in England was by the 14th century one of the country's most important exports, its dimensions regulated by statute and its standards jealously guarded (Bridbury 1982, 44). A fortunate find among documents in Toulouse shows what one quality of broadcloth was like in the 15th century (Wolff 1983, 120–25). This document records the sale in 1458 of four pieces of English cloth, and still sewn to the parchment are samples of three of them. They are woven in a tabby binding with mixed (Z/S) spinning, described as teasled, on both sides. The finishing, however, appears not to have been very heavy, and on one sample where the raised nap has disappeared the weave structure can be seen to have approximately 12–13/10 threads per cm. One example, described as red, was dyed with madder; the two others 'rosatz' (a rich bordeaux colour to the eye) were dyed with madder and slight indigo (woad), the darker one intensified by the addition of brazilwood. The changed appearance of late medieval cloth due to finishing processes is seen here as a fact, and the description of these cloths as 'good middle quality' corresponds to many of the pieces from

14th-century deposits in London which were manufactured at least a century earlier.

Mixed spinning, as mentioned before, gives a very firm cloth, particularly suitable for fulling and finishing. Of the BC72 tabbies, 144 (all but six) in the group dating to the second quarter of the 14th century, and 327 in the group of the late 14th century, are Z/S spun. Damage caused by deterioration after the cloths were discarded makes the thread density in most pieces variable. Nevertheless, the cloths can be divided roughly into three grades: fine (18/18 threads per 10mm and over), coarse (under 10/10 threads per 10mm) and medium, between fine and coarse. Twenty-two cloths with mixed spinning, all from the late 14th-century deposit at BC72, are of a fine grade, 440 are medium grade and only twenty are of a coarse grade (Fig 32). A large number of these can be seen to have received some degree of fulling or finishing, though many of the others, too worn to show it clearly, may have undergone similar treatment. If the Toulouse samples are taken as a guide, most of the London pieces would have come from what can be accepted as English broadcloths. The dyes present on the London cloths also correspond with the samples at Toulouse, with madder used very frequently, indigotin less often, and brazilwood possibly surviving in one example (No 51, see p 200).

The 'good middle quality' of the Toulouse samples is certainly the grade most commonly represented among the textiles from 14th-century deposits in London. Whether any of the best grade cloths from the assemblage could come into the category of 'scarlet' is uncertain. Probably of similar construction to the lower grades of broadcloth, the quality of scarlet — a word which in early medieval usage had nothing to do with colour — apparently depended upon its finishing, including the number of times a nap was raised with teasles and sheared, four times being the expected degree for these luxury fabrics (Hoffmann 1964, 265–9). This process left the cloth soft and flexible and enhanced its draping quality. The expense of the fabric was due not to only the skilled labour involved, but to the immense quantity of wool needed, and the superior grade required to withstand the rigours of the treatment (Endrei 1983, 111). It has also been suggested that the use of costly grain for dyeing was another important ingredient in the production of

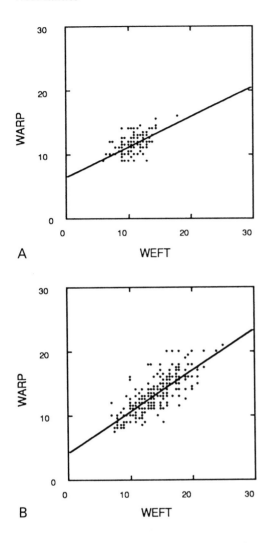

Fig 32 Scatter diagrams showing the thread densities of tabby-woven cloths with mixed spinning: (A) early to mid-14th century based on 139 examples, (B) late 14th to early 15th century based on 322 examples

true scarlet (Munro 1983, 39–63). References to scarlet appear from the 11th century onwards (Hoffmann 1964, 265–8; Munro 1983, 19 and 27–8), but it seems that at first the English cloth industry had no workers skilled enough to carry out the shearing, and the cloth was sent abroad, often as far as Italy, to be finished. By the 12th century, however, all stages of the work could be completed satisfactorily in England. It is, perhaps,

too much to expect scarlets to be recognisable here among the excavated fragments. There are, nevertheless, at least nine medium to fine grade pieces of tabby-woven cloth dyed with kermes which now range from dark purple and red to bright pink (e.g. No 50, Pl 2B). The six examples of kermes-dyed cloth from the late 14th-century deposit are finer than those from the earlier part of the century. The coarsest is a mottled cloth with kermes-dyed threads in the weft only (No 66) and, therefore, it would not have been fulled to the same degree as the unpatterned cloths.

A gradual change in the production of medium grade tabby-woven cloths is evident from the London material. In both 14th-century deposits at BC72 there is a small number of tabby-woven pieces with yarn of a similar spin and count in the warp and weft (Table 1). Examples from the second quarter of the 14th century comprise just three Z-spun and two S-spun woollens. By the late 14th century, the percentage of cloths woven from Z-spun yarn had risen slightly (8%), and there is a more noticeable rise in those cloths with S-spinning (20.8%), a trend which was to increase significantly in succeeding centuries.

This trend coincides with a technological development, namely an increased use of the spinning wheel, and adds to our knowledge of the way in which the wheel came to be accepted. Guild regulations laid down in the second half of the 13th century in a number of widely dispersed European towns, including Bologna (Italy) and Speyer (Germany), permitted the use of the wheel only for spinning weft yarn (Mazzaoui 1981, 194, fn 13), and it can be inferred from other sources, including a Flemish schoolmaster's rhyme composed *c.*1369, which refers to the unevenness of yarn which was produced on spinning wheels by inexperienced spinsters (Baines 1977, 94), that this was also the general rule in northern Europe. It has already been pointed out that there was a long tradition of using S-spun yarn for the weft, and consequently the spinning wheel, which had no built-in design tendency to twist yarn in a particular direction, was used to produce yarn with a S-twist to conform with the requirements of the cloth industry. S-spun yarn thus became established as the normal product of the spinning wheel and once the resistance to wheel-spun yarn had been overcome similar yarn was also used for the warp. The growth in S-spun yarn at this

Table 6   Selvedges on wool tabbies with mixed spinning

Cat. No	No of threads per cm warp/weft	Description of selvedge	Cat. No	No of threads per cm warp/weft	Description of selvedge
Second quarter 14th century			*Last quarter 14th century*		
52	14/9	2 edge cords of paired ends	187	13/13	3 edge cords of paired ends
53	13/14	3 edge cords of paired ends	428	13/11	edge cord decayed (weft loops only)
54	13/12	3 edge cords of paired ends (golden-brown) (Fig 34A, Pl 6A)	188	12–13/10	2 edge cords of thick single ends
55	12/10	2 edge cords of paired Z-spun ends, 2 cords Z/S-ply	189	12/14	2 edge cords Z/S-ply (both 1 black and 1 brown end, 3 pairs of ends (black), 1 pair of ends (1 black, 1 brown)
56	10–12/10–12	2 edge cords of 3 ends			
57	10/10	2 edge cords Z/S-ply, 2 pairs of ends	190	12/13–14	3 edge cords Z/S-ply
58	?/10	4 edge cords of Z/S-ply ends	191	12/12	1 edge cord Z/S-ply, 2 pairs of ends
59	?/9–10	2 edge cords of thick ends, 1 pair of ends, 3 singles, 2 pairs of ends	192	12/11–12	10 pairs of ends (incomplete)
			193	12/11	3 edge cords Z/S-ply (light brown)
60	?/9–10	8 edge cords Z/S-ply	194	12/10	5 edge cords of paired ends (light brown), 3 pairs of ends (same colour as cloth)
61	?/8	3 edge cords of 3 ends, 2 pairs of ends, 1 single end, 1 pair of ends; 2 shuttles used pick-and-pick			
			195	*c.* 12/10	7 edge cords Z/S-ply (black), 1 pair of ends (red), width 7mm; main weave red (Pl 5A)
Last quarter 14th century			196	10/12	1 edge cord Z/S-ply, 1 pair of ends
176	20/20	9 edge cords of paired ends (Fig 34B)	197	10–12/11–12	2 edge cords of paired Z/S-ply ends
177	20/16	6 edge cords Z/S-ply, 2 pairs of ends	198	10–12/10–11	edge cord of 6 pink ends
178	18/18	edge cord of paired ends, 2 cords of 3 ends, 1 pair of ends	199	10/9–10	3 edge cords Z/S-ply (light brown)
179	18/13–14	7 edge cords of paired ends	200	10–11/8–9	5 edge cords Z/S-ply (brown, black, brown, black, black), width 7mm
180	18/13	8 edge cords of paired ends			
181	17–18/18	5 edge cords Z/S-ply	201	9/15–16	5 edge cords Z/S-ply, 5 pairs of ends (Fig 37C)
411	17/18	edge cord of paired Z/S-ply ends, 4 cords Z/S-ply, 2 pairs of ends (Figs 34C, 35)	202	7–9/7–8	2 edge cords of 3 ends
			203	?/14	3 edge cords Z/S-ply, 6–7 pairs of ends
182	16/16	7 or 8 edge cords of paired ends	204	?/12	9 edge cords of paired ends, width 10mm
183	16/14	6 edge cords of paired ends or Z/S-ply	205	?/11	3 edge cords Z/S-ply
412	15/13	10 edge cords of thick single ends	206	?/10	6 edge cords Z/S-ply (yellowish)
184	14–15/20	6 edge cords Z/S-ply, 2 pairs of ends (brown); main weave red	207	?/9	8 edge cords Z/S-ply
			208	?/9	4 edge cords Z/S-ply (pale brown)
185	14/15	3 edge cords Z/S-ply (with dark fibres), 2 pairs of ends (reddish-purple), 1 pair of ends (with dark fibres)	209	?/8	6–7 edge cords of paired ends (mid brown), 1 pair of ends (dark red), width 8–9mm
			First quarter 15th century		
186	14/12	4 edge cords Z/S-ply	396	12/11	unreinforced

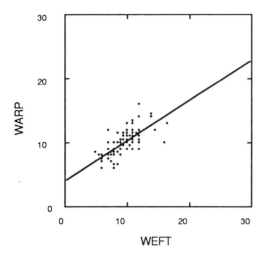

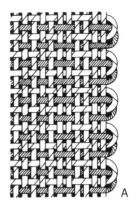

Fig 33 Scatter diagram showing the thread density of tabby cloths woven from S-spun wool yarn based on 104 examples. All but two are from deposits of the late 14th or early 15th centuries

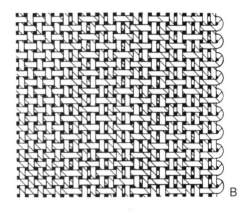

period, therefore, reflects another step towards greater mechanisation in the industry. The chief advantage of the spinning wheel was to increase the speed by which yarn was produced, thereby helping to meet the demands of weavers of treadle-operated looms who quickly used up large amounts of yarn.

Wheel-spun yarn was not as fine as that which could be spun with a drop spindle and it is not surprising, therefore, that no woollen cloth woven from S-spun yarn included here is of a fine grade. The maximum number of warp and weft threads per cm is 16 and 14 respectively but most range from nine to 11 threads per cm (Fig 33). Furthermore, the dyestuff kermes has not been identified on any of the pieces of S-spun woollen cloth tested for dyes in contrast to tabby-woven cloths with mixed spinning. Out of 19 S-spun tabby-woven cloths sampled 11 proved to be dyed with madder, one with a yellow dye and the remaining seven gave negative results.

Selvedges

Selvedges on cloths woven in tabby are, with few exceptions, reinforced (Tables 6, 7, Figs 34, 35). They have an edge cord of plied or thick ends and often a series of pairs of ends before the single

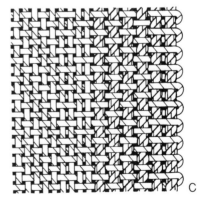

Fig 34 Reinforced selvedges on wool tabbies with mixed spinning: (A) No 54, (B) No 176, (C) No 411

Table 7   Selvedges on wool tabbies woven from S-spun yarn

Cat. No	No of threads per cm warp/weft	Description of selvedge
Last quarter 14th century		
255	?/12	2 edge cords Z-ply, 5 pairs of ends, width 10mm
256	13–14/11	5 or 6 edge cords S/Z-ply, 6 pairs of ends
257	12/14–15	3 edge cords of paired ends (mid-brown), 3 pairs of ends (dark brown)
258	12/11	2 cords Z-ply (incomplete)
259	?/10–11	7 edge cords of paired ends, width 9mm
260	?/10	5 or 6 edge cords S/Z-ply (light brown)
261	?/10	4 thick ends (dark brown), 4 pairs of ends
262	?/10	6 edge cords Z-ply (dark brown)
263	?/9	6 edge cords of paired ends
264	?/8	4 edge cords S/Z-ply (black), 2 pairs of ends (brown)
265	12/6–8	4 edge cords S/Z-ply, 3 pairs of ends
266	11–12/8–9	2 purplish-pink ends
267	10/16	4 edge cords of paired ends
268	10/9	edge cords of 3 S/Z-ply ends
269	8/7	5 edge cords of paired ends
270	8/6	6 edge cords of paired ends
271	7/6	edge cord decayed (weft loops only)

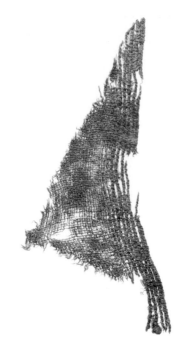

Fig 35   Reinforced selvedge on wool tabby with mixed spinning, No 411, from a deposit dating to the late 14th or early 15th century. Scale 1:1

ends of the main web begin. This arrangement resulted in an edge strong enough to hold tenterhooks when the cloth was stretched during finishing. Some selvedges include ends of a different colour from the rest of the cloth. When found on textiles from sites in eastern Europe, coloured selvedges have been considered as a sign of cloths imported from weaving centres in the west. Adam Nahlik suggested that the different colours and the numbers of coloured threads might indicate the producer and the quality of the cloth (Nahlik 1963, 249). The num-ber of coloured selvedges preserved on cloths from London raised hopes that some clarification of this argument could be attempted but, unfortunately, many of the selvedges have been cut off so closely that the number of coloured ends and the character of the cloth is uncertain. Furthermore, the difficulties of ascertaining the original colours and the poor condition of the edges have made conclusions tentative.

Most coloured selvedges come from tabbies with Z-spun warp and S-spun weft and many of these have been heavily fulled (e.g. No 195, Pl 5A). The commonest colour for selvedges is light brown (possibly originally white, or in some cases yellow) on pink, red or dark brown (probably also red) cloths. These cloths are of medium grade but the shades of colour and the number of ends are variable. Three fine grade cloths from a late 14th-century deposit at BC72 are tints of red or red-purple with darker coloured selvedge cords, now black and brown, but possibly originally dark purple. Two of these have six dark cords (Nos 177, 184) and the other only three (No 185). These

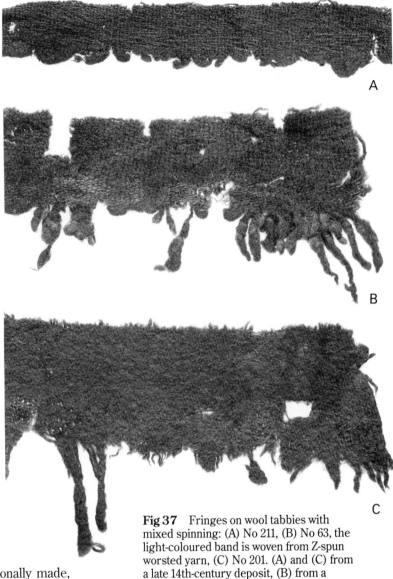

A

B

C

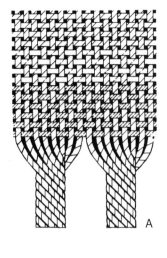

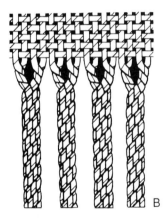

Fig 36 Diagrams of fringes on wool tabbies with mixed spinning: (A) No 210, (B) No 62

Fig 37 Fringes on wool tabbies with mixed spinning: (A) No 211, (B) No 63, the light-coloured band is woven from Z-spun worsted yarn, (C) No 201. (A) and (C) from a late 14th-century deposit, (B) from a deposit dating to the second quarter of the 14th century. Scale 1:1

cloths would all have been professionally made, and with such a bewildering variety of numbers of cords and colours it is perhaps more reasonable to assume that they indicate a producer rather than the quality of the cloth.

Fringes

Fringes are preserved on seven tabby-woven cloths, six with mixed spinning and one S-spun throughout. Usually groups of ends were simply plied together in groups of four, six or eight (e.g. No 210, Fig 36A, and No 211, Fig 37A), but one cloth has ends which were plied in pairs and then paired again and twisted in the opposite direction to form more prominent tassels (No. 62, Fig 36B). Two cloths are patterned with bands of contrasting colours woven just above the fringe (No 210, Fig 36A, and No 63, Fig 37B) and this decoration was sometimes exploited in making up garments; hoods, for example, are depicted in many manuscript illuminations with shoulder capes edged with coloured bands and fringes.

The fringes are preserved as narrow strips; none appear to have been discarded unused. A blob of red pigment identified by XRF analysis as vermilion (Helen Ganiaris pers comm) is also present in the corner of one cloth with a fringe (No 201, Fig 37C) but it does not appear to have formed part of a painted design.

Colour and weave effects

Patterning on wool tabbies is confined to checks and stripes of two distinct types, simple colour effects in warp and/or weft, and a wider variety of weft-faced bands incorporating both colour and weave effects. Of the first type, three from 14th-century deposits are simple checks. This form of pattern has a long history in northern Europe. Most earlier examples are woven in twill, a tradition that continues with Scottish plaids, but in England by the 6th and 7th centuries such patterns are also found on tabby-woven cloths.

One checked cloth from a deposit of the second quarter of the 14th century is part of a buttoned sleeve. In this weave, the warp and weft are arranged in groups of red (madder) and white (apparently undyed) threads, with two darker coloured threads outlining the checks (No 64, Fig 38A, Pl 1). The cloth is worn threadbare on the outside, and has become rubbed and matted inside; it was probably only lightly fulled in order to prevent the pattern from becoming blurred. It was, however, originally a firm fabric that did not fray when cut.

The other cloths with checked patterns come from a deposit of the late 14th century. They are in two colours, pink and near black. One with a regular sized check is a coarse woollen woven from S-spun yarn (No 275, Fig 38B, Pl 3A). The other, patterned with lines and checks, is a medium grade Z-spun worsted (No 172, Fig 38C, Pl 3B). Madder was the only dyestuff detected on either of these two cloths; it was used in different concentrations for the two colours of No 275, but apparently only for the black of No 172, where the pink appearance may be due to leakage during burial in waterlogged conditions. The black could have been produced by the use of a mordant such as iron.

Cloths patterned with coloured bands were also produced in simple tabby weave. The earliest

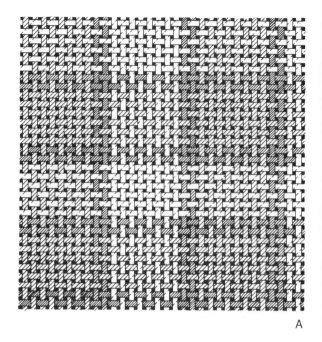

A

Fig 38 Checked patterns on wool tabbies:
(A) No 64,
(B) No 275,
(C) No 172

B

represented here, a cloth with narrow alternating bands of red and orangish-brown yarns (No 430, Fig 39), comes from an early 13th-century deposit; it is coarse and includes many weaving errors, particularly in the shuttling of the weft. From 14th-century deposits, there are cloths with contrasting bands close to fringes (see p 49, No 210, Fig 36A, and No 63, Fig 37B), and in possible all-over patterns (Nos 202, 212–214). In No 202, madder was again identified on both light and dark brown

C

threads, the darker hue produced from over-dyeing natural brown wool. This practice was forbidden in some English towns, for example Leicester (Carus-Wilson 1944, 36, 47), but this does not appear to have prevented it taking place.

A cloth with a narrow yellow band shows another type of simple colour effect, the use of warp and weft yarns of different colours, giving the main weave a mottled appearance, in this case two shades of brown (No 65). Other cloths have contrasting light brown and pink yarns; in one of these kermes was used to dye the weft yarn pink (No 66), while in another two alternating weft yarns of pink and light brown are combined with a light brown warp (No 54, Fig 34A, Pl 6A). These cloths are perhaps examples of the fabrics described as of mixed colours, known as 'medleys' (see also Selected Catalogue I, Nos 125–127, 293).

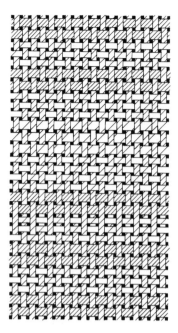

Fig 39 Coloured bands on a wool tabby including weaving error, No 430

Tabby weaves with weft-faced bands

The commonest form of patterning on tabby cloths from 14th-century deposits in London is the weft-faced band woven in extended tabby with the weft yarn passing under and over two ends. This gives a ribbed appearance forming a contrast with the texture of the main weave. Mixed spinning with the warp yarn Z-spun and the weft S-spun prevails, except for three examples from the late 14th century which are Z-spun throughout the main weave (Nos 280, 303, 306). In general the pattern wefts have the same spin as the main weft but in some, where at least two pattern wefts were employed, one, or more rarely two, may be Z-spun and is usually finer (Nos 106, 120, 124, 132, 289–291, 297, 299–305, 307, 309, 310, 422). None of these cloths is of a fine grade with more than 15 threads per cm in the warp or main weft. Generally there are between nine and 11 ends and eight and 12 picks per cm. Two cloths with a lower number of picks have a main weft of a different colour to the warp (Nos 125 and 126), and the greater

thickness of the weft yarn, which is the reason here for the low number of picks, would have emphasised the mottled effect. The bands were beaten more closely during weaving than the main web and conceal the warp, which resulted in as many as 52 picks per cm, that is four times the density of the weft threads in the ground (No 296), but a density ratio of between 2:1 and 3:1 is more usual. There can be little doubt that these are the cloths called 'rays' which were woven at centres in Flanders, Brabant and northern France as well as in England during the late middle ages (e.g. Bridbury 1982, 68–9; Chorley 1987; Harding 1987, 211), and which have been recovered from excavations in Amsterdam and Dordrecht in The Netherlands (Vons-Comis 1982, 156), Lübeck in Germany (Tidow 1990, 168–9, fig 19.3), and Novgorod in Russia (Nahlik 1963, 252–4), as well as in London and York (Walton 1989A, 383).

Altogether there are 93 examples of these cloths from London. Most preserve only part of one band, but a few have two or even three bands remaining and there is no doubt that they come from cloths that were striped throughout. The range of variations shows an increasing virtuosity on the part of weavers, who introduced twill-woven patterns into the bands alongside extended tabby. Where selvedges are preserved they are always reinforced (e.g. No 79, Fig 40A, No 125, Fig 41, Pl 6B, and No 112, Fig 42) and they often include threads of another colour (e.g. No 277, Pl 5B).

Some cloths appear to show signs of fulling but this may reflect the natural woolliness of the yarn. If the pieces were fulled it is probable that this was always lighter than the treatment given to plain-coloured broadcloths since heavy fulling would have obscured the delicate lines in the bands, where up to five colours were sometimes used. The lower price charged for shearing rayed scarlets, which was a third that of shearing unstriped scarlets (Munro 1983, 37), together with the evidence of an account for shearing a ray-cloth 'in which all rays vary' with 'small shears' (Eleanora Carus-Wilson letter dated 29 August 1975), suggests that teasling and shearing were confined to the tabby-woven surface between the weft-faced bands so that the pattern was not harmed.

Most bands are woven from wool or from wool and silk but there are two cloths from the earlier

A

B

Fig 40 Tabby-woven wool cloths patterned with bands in silk thread: (A) No 79, including detail of reinforced selvedge, (B) No 80, both from a deposit dating to the second quarter of the 14th century. Scale 1:1

deposit at BC72 where the pattern weft is a two-ply thread of silk (No 78, Fig 131, and No 79, Fig 40A), and a cloth of similar appearance has a silk stripe running in what appears to be the direction of the

warp (No 80, Fig 40B). On this cloth and No 79, however, the silk thread is bound in tabby rather than passing over and under two threads at a time. Six to 12 throws were used in these silk bands, presumably reflecting the greater expense of the yarn, but the result was nevertheless effective and marked a new departure in cloth design in northern Europe. The silk bands appear to have been evenly spaced to produce a regular all-over pattern. A variation identified on a cloth recovered from a deposit dating to the first quarter of the 14th century in Amsterdam alternates bands of silk with bands of wool spaced at intervals of 28–30mm (Vons-Comis 1982, 156). Other cloths which combine silk and wool in the same band are discussed below.

Cloths patterned with monochrome bands of wool comprise 23 examples from the deposit dating to the second quarter of the 14th century (Nos 81–100, 125–127) and one from that of the late 14th century at BC72 (No 277, Pl 5B). These bands range in width from 4mm to 35mm. A wider band of 40mm on a cloth stained a uniform dark blackish-brown, which was recovered from a deposit of the first half of the 15th century at TL74, may not have been monochrome originally (No 402). Some of the narrower bands are arranged in pairs (e.g. No 82), and a cloth of this type with pairs of pink bands on a light brown ground was recovered from a 13th-century deposit in Dordrecht (PUT III 1978, no 1072, Sandra Vons-Comis pers comm). A variation was to weave monochrome bands either singly or in pairs on a two-toned ground so that sometimes three colours of yarn were used in these cloths, one for the warp, another for the main weft and a third for the pattern weft (e.g. No 125, Fig 41, Pl 6B). Another cloth has a mottled ground woven from two alternating weft yarns, one now a light brown matching the colour of the warp and the other a pinkish-red, across which run narrow bands of yellow (No 127).

Cloths with bands of two colours offered greater scope for patterning. Most of the 20 all-wool examples have a band edged with a few throws of a contrasting hue (e.g. No 107, Pl 7B), but a few have an approximately even width of each colour (e.g. No 112, Fig 42, and No 115, Pl 4B). Two fabrics are patterned with pairs of monochrome bands, each of a different colour (Nos 103, 113). A similar diversity of colouring is mentioned

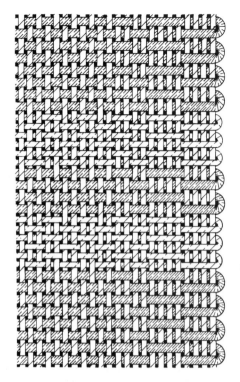

Fig 41 Wool cloth woven in tabby with warp and weft yarns of contrasting colour and thickness patterned with two bands in extended tabby, No 125

Fig 42 Tabby-woven wool cloth patterned with a band woven in extended tabby in two colours, No 112, from a deposit dating to the second quarter of the 14th century. Weft loops at the edge of the cloth show that the selvedge cords have decayed. Scale 1:1

in written sources; among three rayed cloths of Dendermond (Flanders), forfeited to the king's aulnager at Boston fair in 1329–30 for not complying with statutory regulations on width, was a cloth coloured *'fleur de vesce'* patterned with twin bands of black and white and green and red, and another piece with a ground dyed partly in grain and patterned with twin bands of red and white, and a yellow band (Buyse 1956, 184).

Occasionally, instead of being dyed, one of the wefts is naturally-coloured wool. Two examples have been identified here. One is a cloth with a mottled ground where the main weft is brown wool (No 125, Pl 6B). The other, a cloth with two pattern wefts, one natural brown wool and the other dyed red, has narrow bands spaced at intervals of 35mm (No 115, Pl 4B). Among other coloured yarns used for these cloths, a dark purplish-black is distinctive. The yarn dyed this tint is often thicker than the other pattern wefts (e.g. Nos 299, 304, 305, 310, 311) and sometimes has decayed more than the other threads, possibly because an iron mordant was used when the wool was dyed (e.g. No 123, Pl 9A, and No 309, Pl 11A). When dye tested two of these purple yarns proved to be dyed with both madder and indigotin (Nos 286, 305, Pl 9B), although others gave negative results (e.g. No 299), and from this it may be suggested that a yarn dyed with the same two dyestuffs on a cloth which is now stained a uniform dark brown originally was a similar shade of purple (No 422). Pale buff yarns also appear to have been especially susceptible to decay (e.g. No 112, Fig 42).

In deposits of the late 14th century, cloths with bands of three colours are more common than those with just one or two colours. Bands woven solely in extended tabby range in width from 22mm to 39mm, whereas those which include 2.2 twill as well as extended tabby tend to be broader, 29–53mm. The colours are generally arranged in contrasting light and dark zones of differing widths with narrow lines marking the edges (e.g. Nos 287, 394, Pl 8A and B). The spacing of the bands differs. One cloth has two similar bands, each 28mm wide, separated by 112mm of main weave (No 117), another has two bands separated by 90mm of main weave (No 292), and a third has two bands each differently patterned separated by 4mm of main weave (No 284). The latter piece also indicates that bands were not always identical on a single length of cloth.

The patterning is enhanced with bands of 2.2 twill on 17 cloths (Nos 296–311, 422). Sometimes the twill was woven as a block in the centre of a band where, by the simple expedient of reversing the direction of the diagonals, a weft-chevron twill was produced (e.g. No 298, Pl 10A). On a few cloths, where the twill areas are separated by zones of extended tabby, the diagonals are reversed in each section (e.g. No 308, Pl 12B). In addition, a weaver might introduce alternating threads of two different colours for the twill which accentuated the diagonals (e.g. No 299, Pl 10B). The fineness of the thread also often differed for the twill; Z-spun worsted yarn was frequently used (e.g. Nos 305, 309, Pls 9B, 11A) and more rarely silk (e.g. No 308, Pl 12B, No 311). One cloth has spin patterning in the warp (No 300) and perhaps the two yarns were originally different colours.

Silk thread is combined with wool in bands in 12 cloths. Five of these are from the deposit of the second quarter of the 14th century at BC72 and seven from that of the late 14th century. The former have fewer pattern wefts and the patterning is less complex. Thus, from the earlier deposit, two cloths have narrow bands with silk lines flanking the wool in the centre which is of a different colour to the main web (Nos 128, 129). A wider band has a centre of silk flanked by rows of wool which in turn are edged with silk (No 130), and another has four bands of silk alternating with three of wool (No 131). The fifth cloth has narrow lines of silk edging a brown band with a pinkish-brown centre, all these yarns contrasting with the colour of the ground (No 132).

Cloths with silk and wool bands from the later deposit have three to five pattern wefts and usually include areas of 2.2 twill. An exception is a dark red cloth which has a band woven wholly in extended tabby (No 294, Pl 12A). The others include a cloth where the silk thread is woven in four blocks of 2.2 twill, divided by bands of extended tabby, with the diagonals of the twill reversing in each silk block (No 308, Pl 12B). Another piece has a narrow silk line flanked by wider zones of 2.2 twill woven with a pattern weft of fine Z-spun worsted (No 309, Pl 11A). A third cloth, with a band 43mm wide, also has a narrow line of silk running through the centre with areas of 2.2 twill on either side, but here the twill is accentuated by the use of alternate threads of two colours and a coarser pattern weft edges the twill (No 310, Pl 11B). Another cloth with five pattern wefts has lines of silk thread restricted to the very edge of the band where it is bound in extended tabby, and to each side of the centre throw where it is bound in 2.2 twill (No 311). It is not surprising that because of the number of spools needed for the different colours there are occasional mistakes in the reverses of the bands.

While it can probably be safely assumed that most bands went from selvedge to selvedge, there are two cloths where they run only a short distance into the cloth, the rest being unpatterned (Nos 118, 295). Number 295 has a series of narrow silk bands with the silk thread floating on the back in between. As the piece is now so small and deteriorated it is difficult to determine whether the bands were woven, or darned in afterwards, or how they were used as decoration.

An indication of the cost of different qualities of rayed cloths can be gained from the rolls of purchase of the Great Wardrobe. For example, in 1332–3 William la Zouche bought 12 rayed cloths from Simon de Swanlande, a London draper who was a former alderman and mayor of the City, and a further 23½ cloths from a Genoese merchant, Antonio Bache. The cheapest cloths with a red ground cost 36s. each, three green and red cloths patterned with white silk cost 70s. each, and the most expensive were those with a red ground dyed in grain which cost 106s. 8d. per cloth (PRO E101/386/5 membrane 3); this difference in price can be explained since the amount of silk woven into the cloths was very small. No examples of rayed cloths dyed in grain have been identified among the London textiles but there are many with grounds dyed various shades of red with madder (e.g. Nos 92, 101, 112, 128, 279, 286, 290, 308, 402, 422).

Selected catalogue I

Tabby-woven cloths patterned with bands or stripes in silk thread

Second quarter 14th century

78　Dimensions: h 140mm, w 90mm
　　Warp: brown (negative), Z-spun, 9 ends per cm
　　Weft: brown (negative), S-spun, 10 picks per cm
　　Pattern weft: silk, golden brown, Z/S-ply
　　Width of bands: two bands 2mm wide (6 throws) in extended tabby separated by 90mm of main weave
　　Fig 131

79　Dimensions: h 152mm, w 29mm
　　Warp: dark brown, Z-spun, 10–11 ends per cm
　　Weft: dark brown, S-spun, 12–14 picks per cm
　　Pattern weft: silk, golden brown
　　Selvedge: 3 edge cords mid-brown Z/S-ply, 2 pairs of ends, w 6mm
　　Width of bands: three bands 1.5mm wide (7 throws) in tabby separated by 48mm and 46mm of main weave
　　Fig 40A

80　Dimensions: h 46mm, w 12mm
　　Warp: dark brown, Z-spun, 11 ends per cm
　　Weft: dark brown, S-spun, 10 picks per cm
　　Pattern warp: silk, golden-brown, Z/S-ply
　　Width of stripe: 3mm (12 throws)
　　Fig 40B

Tabby-woven cloths patterned with weft-faced bands in extended tabby

Cloths with one pattern weft

Second quarter 14th century

81　Dimensions: h 93mm, w 20mm
　　Warp: light brown, Z-spun, 10 ends per cm
　　Weft: light brown, S-spun, 11 picks per cm
　　Pattern weft: reddish-purple, S-spun
　　Width of band: 3mm (13 throws)

82　Dimensions: h 65mm, w 110mm
　　Warp: pinkish-mauve, Z-spun, 9–10 ends per cm
　　Weft: pinkish-mauve, S-spun, 9 picks per cm
　　Pattern weft: yellowish-brown, coarse yarn, S-spun
　　Width of bands: two bands 4–5mm wide (6 throws) separated by 30mm of main weave

83　Dimensions: h 50mm, w 50mm
　　Warp: pale brown (negative), Z-spun, 11 ends per cm

　　Weft: pale brown (negative), S-spun, 9 picks per cm
　　Pattern weft: purplish-brown, S-spun, 20 picks per cm
　　Width of band: incomplete, greater than 20mm (38+ throws)

84　Dimensions: h 34mm, w 75mm
　　Warp: dark brown, Z-spun, 10–11 ends per cm
　　Weft: dark brown, S-spun, 9–11 picks per cm
　　Pattern weft: reddish-purple, S-spun, 20 picks per cm
　　Width of band: incomplete, greater than 22mm (44+ throws)

85　Dimensions: h 22m, w 110mm
　　Warp: reddish-purple, Z-spun, 13 ends per cm
　　Weft: reddish-purple, S-spun (hard twist), 14–15 picks per cm
　　Pattern weft: reddish-purple, S-spun
　　Width of band: incomplete, greater than 3mm (14+ throws)

86　Dimensions: h 95mm, w 12mm
　　Warp: greyish-brown, Z-spun, 10 ends per cm
　　Weft: greyish-brown, S-spun, 10 picks per cm
　　Pattern weft: brown, S-spun, 24 picks per cm
　　Width of band: 22mm

87　Dimensions: h 62mm, w 100mm
　　Warp: light brown, Z-spun, 9 ends per cm
　　Weft: light brown, S-spun, 11 picks per cm
　　Pattern weft: light brown, S-spun, *c.*36 picks per cm
　　Width of band: incomplete, greater than 5mm

88　Dimensions: (i) h 100mm, w 15mm; (ii) h 170mm, w 17mm
　　Warp: dark brown, Z-spun, 9–10 ends per cm
　　Weft: dark brown, S-spun, 10 picks per cm
　　Pattern weft: dark brown (madder), S-spun, 24 picks per cm
　　Width of bands: two bands, one 30mm wide, other incomplete, separated by 83mm of main weave

89　Dimensions: h 120mm, w 20mm
　　Warp: dark brown (negative), Z-spun, 9 ends per cm
　　Weft: dark brown (negative), S-spun, 9 picks per cm
　　Pattern weft: dark brown (madder), S-spun, 20 picks per cm
　　Width of band: incomplete, greater than 15mm

90　Dimensions: h 70mm, w 35mm
　　Warp: medium brown, Z-spun, 10 ends per cm

Weft: medium brown, S-spun, 10 picks per cm
Pattern weft: reddish-purple, S-spun
Width of band: incomplete, greater than 10mm

91 Dimensions: h 90mm, w 80mm
Warp: reddish-brown, Z-spun, 11 ends per cm
Weft: reddish-brown, S-spun, 10–11 picks per cm
Pattern weft: reddish-brown, S-spun, 20 picks per cm
Selvedge: 3 pairs of ends (incomplete)
Width of band: incomplete, greater than 20mm

92 Dimensions: h 57mm, w 95mm
Warp: crimson (madder), Z-spun, 10 ends per cm
Weft: crimson (madder), S-spun, 8 picks per cm
Pattern weft: olive-green (negative), S-spun
Width of band: 8mm wide (11 throws)
Pl 7A

93 Dimensions: h 65mm, w 75mm
Warp: brown (negative), Z-spun, 10 ends per cm
Weft: brown (negative), S-spun, 11 picks per cm
Pattern weft: crimson, S-spun, 22 picks per cm
Width of band: incomplete, greater than 20mm

94 Dimensions: h 60mm, w 130mm
Warp: mid-brown, Z-spun, 11 ends per cm
Weft: mid-brown, S-spun, 9 picks per cm
Pattern weft: pinkish-purple, S-spun
Width of band: 5mm (13 throws)

95 Dimensions: h 50mm, w 15mm
Warp: brown, Z-spun, 8 ends per cm
Weft: brown, S-spun, 9–10 picks per cm
Pattern weft: brown, S-spun, 20 picks per cm
Width of band: 12mm

96 Dimensions: (i) h 25mm, w 40mm; (ii) h 7mm, w 68mm
Warp: medium-brown, Z-spun, 8 ends per cm
Weft: ?
Pattern weft: brown (madder), S-spun, 24 picks per cm
Width of band: incomplete, greater than 20mm

97 Dimensions: h 70mm, w 6mm
Warp: brown, Z-spun, 11 ends per cm
Weft: brown, S-spun, ? picks per cm
Pattern weft: red, S-spun
Width of band: incomplete, greater than 3mm

98 Dimensions: h 43mm, w 90mm
Warp: brown, Z-spun, 9 ends per cm
Weft: brown, S-spun, 8 picks per cm
Pattern weft: brown, S-spun, 20 picks per cm
Width of band: incomplete, greater than 20mm

99 Dimensions: h 10mm, w 40mm
Warp: dark brown (negative), Z-spun, 10 ends per cm
Weft: dark brown (negative), S-spun, 8 picks per cm
Pattern weft: light brown, S-spun, *c.*24 picks per cm
Width of band: incomplete, greater than 9mm

100 Dimensions: (i) h 90mm, w 105mm; (ii) h 60mm, w 45mm
Warp: brown, Z-spun, 8 ends per cm
Weft: brown, S-spun, 12 picks per cm
Pattern weft: yellowish-brown, S-spun, 26 picks per cm
Width of band: incomplete, greater than 23mm

Last quarter 14th century
277 Dimensions: h 135mm, w 50mm
Warp: yellowish-brown, Z-spun, 10 ends per cm
Weft: yellowish-brown, S-spun, 12 picks per cm
Pattern weft: yellow, S-spun, 28 picks per cm
Selvedge: edge cord Z/S-ply (one yellow end, S-spun, and one red end, Z-spun), one cord S/Z-ply (yellow), two cords Z/S-ply (as for edge cord)
Fringe: selvedge cords tied in pairs, other ends S-plied in groups of eight
Width of bands: two bands 12mm wide (one incomplete) separated by 18mm main weave
Pl 5B

First half 15th century
402 Dimensions: h 120mm, w 145mm
Warp: dark blackish-brown (madder), Z-spun, 10–11 ends per cm
Weft: dark blackish-brown (madder), S-spun, 10 picks per cm
Pattern weft: dark blackish-brown, S-spun, 32 picks per cm
Width of band: 40mm (126 throws)

Cloths with two pattern wefts

Second quarter 14th century
101 Dimensions: h 120mm, w 60mm
Warp: mauvish-brown (madder), Z-spun, 8 ends per cm
Weft: mauvish-brown (madder), S-spun, 10 picks per cm
Pattern wefts: (i) reddish-purple, S-spun
(ii) yellowish-brown (negative), S-spun
24 picks per cm
Width of band: 22mm

Pattern: 8 throws reddish-purple
        30 throws yellowish-brown
        8 throws reddish-purple

102 Dimensions: h 80mm, w 20mm
    Warp: pale mauvish-brown, Z-spun, 10–11 ends
      per cm
    Weft: pale mauvish-brown, S-spun, 10–11 picks
      per cm
    Pattern wefts: (i) yellow, finer than (ii), S-spun
               (ii) red, S-spun
             26 picks per cm
    Width of band: 16mm
    Pattern: 4 throws yellow
        *c.*38 throws red
        4 throws yellow

103 Dimensions: h 35mm, w 43mm
    Warp: reddish-purple, Z-spun, 10 ends per cm
    Weft: reddish-purple, S-spun, 10 picks per cm
    Pattern wefts: (i) reddish-purple, S-spun
               (ii) light brown, S-spun
             20 picks per cm
    Selvedge: edge cord of 4 ends (2 reddish-brown
      ends, 2 brown ends), 2nd cord of 3 brown ends,
      w 4mm
    Width of bands: reddish-purple band 15mm (24
      throws), light brown band 14mm, separated by
      6mm (6 throws) of main weave

104 Dimensions: h 10mm, w 32mm
    Warp: dark brown, Z-spun, 12 ends per cm
    Weft: ?
    Pattern wefts: (i) red, Z-spun
               (ii) dark brown, Z-spun
             28–30 picks per cm
    Width of band: incomplete, greater than 10mm
    Pattern: 2+ throws dark brown
        5 throws red
        5 throws dark brown
        5 throws red
        10+ throws dark brown

105 Dimensions: h 165mm, w 35mm
    Warp: brown, Z-spun, 10–11 ends per cm
    Weft: brown, S-spun, 9–11 picks per cm
    Pattern wefts: (i) red, S-spun
               (ii) brown, S-spun
             22 picks per cm
    Selvedge: 4 edge cords Z/S-ply (dark brown),
      1 pair of ends, w 8mm
    Width of band: 20mm
    Pattern: 10 throws red
          10 throws brown
          4 throws red
          10 throws brown
          10 throws red

106 Dimensions: (i) h 100mm, w 185mm; (ii) h 40mm,
    w 23mm
    Warp: brown, Z-spun, 9 ends per cm
    Weft: brown, S-spun, 10–11 picks per cm
    Pattern wefts: (i) pink, Z-spun
               (ii) brown, finer than (i), S-spun
             *c.*30 picks per cm
    Width of band: 21mm
    Pattern: *c.*24 throws brown (7mm)
          *c.*16 throws pink (7mm)
          *c.*24 throws brown (7mm)

107 Dimensions: h 95mm, w 100mm
    Warp: dark brown, Z-spun, 11 ends per cm
    Weft: dark brown, S-spun, 12–13 picks per cm
    Pattern wefts: (i) reddish purple, S-spun
               (ii) orange, S-spun
             *c.*23 picks per cm
    Width of band: 11mm
    Pattern: 5 throws reddish-purple
        *c.*14 throws orange
        6 throws reddish-purple
    Pl 7B

108 Dimensions: h 100mm, w 8mm
    Warp: brown, Z-spun, ? ends per cm
    Weft: brown, S-spun, 12 picks per cm
    Pattern wefts: (i) red, S-spun
               (ii) brown, S-spun
    Selvedge: 3 edge cords of paired ends (one end
      S-spun and the other Z-spun), w 8mm
    Width of band: incomplete, greater than 46mm
    Pattern: too worn

109 Dimensions: h 80mm, w 300mm
    Warp: brown, Z-spun, 10 ends per cm
    Weft: brown, S-spun, 10–11 picks per cm
    Pattern wefts: (i) brown, S-spun
               (ii) red, S-spun
             *c.*24 picks per cm
    Width of band: 8mm
    Pattern: *c.*10 throws brown
          *c.*10 throws red

110 Dimensions: h 18mm, w 140mm
    Warp: brown, Z-spun, 11 ends per cm
    Weft: brown, S-spun, 14 picks per cm
    Pattern wefts: (i) dark brown, S-spun
               (ii) brown, S-spun
    Width of band: incomplete, greater than 5mm
    Pattern: *c.*7 throws brown
        5+ throws dark brown

111 Dimensions: h 14mm, w 120mm
    Warp: dark brown, Z-spun, 9 ends per cm
    Weft: dark brown, S-spun, 9 picks per cm

Pattern wefts: (i) brown, S-spun
                (ii) crimson, S-spun
            25 picks per cm
Width of band: incomplete, greater than 10mm
Pattern: *c*.18 throws brown (7mm)
           7+ throws crimson (3mm)

112 Dimensions: h 65mm, w 72mm
Warp: brown (madder), Z-spun, 10 ends per cm
Weft: brown (madder), S-spun, 10 picks per cm
Pattern wefts: (i) dark purplish-brown (nega-
                tive), coarser yarn, S-spun
            (ii) buff (negative), finer than (i),
                S-spun (partly decayed)
            c.30 picks per cm
Selvedge: 3 edge cords of two-ply ends (light
    brown), 2 pairs of ends, w 8mm
Width of band: 23mm
Pattern: 16 throws purplish-brown (6mm)
        c.24 throws buff (8mm)
        16 throws purplish-brown (9mm)
Fig 42

113 Dimensions: h 135mm, w 50mm
Warp: brown, Z-spun, 10 ends per cm
Weft: brown, S-spun, 10 picks per cm
Pattern wefts: (i) grey brown, S-spun
            (ii) crimson, S-spun
            26 picks per cm
Width of bands: grey-brown band 10mm, crimson
    band 10mm, separated by 8mm (7 throws) of
    main weave

114 Dimensions: h 20mm, w 105mm. Bias cut
Warp: dark brown, Z-spun, 9 ends per cm
Weft: dark brown, S-spun, 10 picks per cm
Pattern wefts: (i) brown, S-spun
            (ii) crimson, S-spun
            17 picks per cm
Width of band: incomplete, greater than 20mm
Pattern: 8+ throws brown
        12 throws crimson
        14+ throws brown

115 Dimensions: h 109mm, w 240mm
Warp: mid-brown, Z-spun, 8–9 ends per cm
Weft: mid-brown, S-spun, 7–8 picks per cm
Pattern wefts: (i) dark brown (natural pigment),
                S-spun
            (ii) red (madder), S-spun
Width of bands: 5–6mm separated by 35mm of
    main weave
Pattern: 3/4 throws brown
           4 throws red
Pl 4B

116 Dimensions: h 28mm w 25mm
Warp: pale brown, Z-spun, 12 ends per cm
Weft: pale brown, S-spun, 10 picks per cm
Pattern wefts: (i) bright brown, S-spun
            (ii) red, S-spun
            16 picks per cm
Selvedge: 3 red edge cords, Z/S-ply
Width of band: 10mm
Pattern: 5 throws brown
      c.18 throws red
      5 throws brown
      c.18 throws red
      5 throws brown

Last quarter 14th century
278 Dimensions: h 128mm, w 8mm
Warp: reddish-brown, Z-spun, *c*.10 ends per cm
Weft: reddish-brown, S-spun, 10 picks per cm
Pattern wefts: (i) brown, S-spun
            (ii) purple, S-spun
            15–23 picks per cm
Selvedge: 5 edge cords S/Z-ply, w 8mm
Width of bands: two bands of 16mm and 18mm,
    both incomplete, separated by 85mm of main
    weave
Pattern: (A) 12+ throws brown
            2 throws purple
          10 throws brown

        (B) 8 throws brown
           3 throws purple
          24 throws brown
          2 throws purple
         6+ throws brown

279 Dimensions: h 90mm, w 45mm
Warp: mid-brown (madder), Z-spun, 9 ends per
    cm
Weft: mid-brown (madder), S-spun, 8–9 picks per
    cm
Pattern wefts: (i) mid brown (madder), S-spun
            (ii) purple (madder), S-spun
            c.23 picks per cm
Width of band: incomplete, greater than 8mm
Pattern: 8 throws mid-brown
      6 throws purple
      5+ throws mid-brown

280 Dimensions: h 140mm, w 27mm
Warp: brown (negative), Z-spun, 11 ends per cm
Weft: brown (negative), Z-spun, 10 picks per cm
Pattern wefts: (i) brown, S-spun
            (ii) purplish-black, S-spun
            c.28 picks per cm
Width of bands: three bands, 5–6mm wide, separ-
    ated by 45–48mm of main weave

Pattern: 2 throws brown
    11 throws purplish-black
    2 throws brown

281 Dimensions: h 7mm, 2 120mm
 Warp: light brown, Z-spun, *c.*10 ends per cm
 Weft: ?
 Pattern wefts: (i) pinkish-red, S-spun
      (ii) light brown, S-spun
 Width of band: incomplete, greater than 7mm
 Pattern: 7+ throws pinkish red
    5+ throws light brown

Cloths with three pattern wefts

Second quarter 14th century

117 Dimensions: h 210mm, w 30mm
 Warp: brown (negative), Z-spun, 11 ends per cm
 Weft: brown (negative), S-spun, 11 picks per cm
 Pattern wefts: (i) chocolate-brown, S-spun
      (ii) reddish-purple, S-spun
      (iii) light brown, S-spun (decayed)
      *c.*20 picks per cm
 Width of bands: two bands 28mm wide separated
  by 112mm of main weave
 Pattern: 4 throws chocolate-brown
    16 throws reddish-purple (8mm)
    ? throws light brown (7mm), partly
     decayed
    16 throws reddish-purple (8mm)
    4 throws chocolate-brown

118 Dimensions: h 45mm, w 30mm
 Warp: yellowish-brown, Z-spun, 11 ends per cm
 Weft: yellowish-brown, S-spun, 9 picks per cm
 Pattern wefts: (i) yellow, fine yarn, Z-spun
      (ii) red, S-spun
      (iii) yellowish brown, S-spun
      *c.*22 picks per cm
 Width of band: incomplete, greater than 8mm
  (NB the band does not extend across the full
  width of the cloth)
 Pattern: 4 throws yellow
    2 throws yellowish-brown, tabby weave
    2 throws red
    3 throws yellowish-brown
    2 throws red
    3 throws yellowish-brown, tabby weave
    2+ throws red

119 Dimensions: (i) h 30mm, w 140mm; (ii) h 30mm,
  w 90mm. Bias cut
 Warp: brown, Z-spun, 10 ends per cm
 Weft: brown, S-spun, 9 picks per cm

Pattern wefts: (i) red, S-spun
      (ii) brown, S-spun
      (iii) ? (decayed)
      36 picks per cm
Width of band: 24mm
Pattern: 6 throws brown
    12 throws red
    6 throws brown
    ? decayed
    8 throws brown
    8 throws red
    8 throws brown
    ? decayed
    6 throws brown
    12 throws red
    6 throws brown

120 Dimensions: h 118, w 85mm
 Warp: dark brown, Z-spun, 10–11 ends per cm
 Weft: dark brown, S-spun, 10–11 picks per cm
 Pattern wefts: (i) light brown, S-spun
      (ii) mid-brown, S-spun
      (iii) pink, Z-spun
      *c.*34 picks per cm
 Width of band: 23mm
 Pattern: 4 throws light brown
    4 throws mid-brown
    7 throws pink
    4 throws mid-brown
    6 throws pink
    4 throws mid-brown
    7 throws light brown
    4 throws mid-brown
    4 throws light brown

121 Dimensions: h 85mm, w 35mm
 Warp: dark reddish-brown, Z-spun, 9 ends per cm
 Weft: dark reddish-brown, S-spun, 9 picks per cm
 Pattern wefts: (i) crimson, S-spun
      (ii) dark brown, S-spun
      (iii) pale brown, S-spun
      22 picks per cm
 Selvedge: 2 edge cords Z/S-ply
 Width of band: 25mm
 Pattern: 8 throws crimson
    4 throws dark brown
    30 throws pale brown
    4 throws dark brown
    8 throws crimson

122 Dimensions: h 90mm, w 35mm
 Warp: light brown (madder), Z-spun, 11 ends per
  cm
 Weft: light brown (madder), S-spun, thicker than
  warp, 6–7 picks per cm

Pattern wefts: (i) dark brown, S-spun
(ii) natural, S-spun
(iii) purple, S-spun
22 picks per cm
Width of band: 22mm
Pattern: 4 throws dark brown
4 throws natural
4 throws dark brown
*c.*26 throws purple (15mm)
4 throws dark brown
4 throws natural
4 throws dark brown

Last quarter 14th century

282 Dimensions: h 10mm, w 65mm
Warp: pinkish-brown, Z-spun, 9 ends per cm
Weft: ?
Pattern wefts: (i) white, S-spun
(ii) dark brown, S-spun
(iii) reddish-purple, S-spun
*c.*33 picks per cm
Width of band: greater than 10mm (incomplete)
Pattern: 2+ throws white
7 throws dark brown
8 throws white
12 throws reddish-purple
4+ throws white

283 Dimensions: h 120mm, w 15mm
Warp: dark brown, Z-spun, 10 ends per cm
Weft: dark brown, S-spun, 10 picks per cm
Pattern wefts: (i) red, S-spun
(ii) light brown, S-spun
(iii) purplish-black, S-spun
32 picks per cm
Width of band: 39mm
Pattern: 16 throws red (5mm)
32 throws light brown (7mm)
12 throws red
10 throws purplish-black
12 throws red
32 throws light brown (7mm)
16 throws red (5mm)

284 Dimensions: h 80mm, w 45mm
Warp: light brown, Z-spun, 10 ends per cm
Weft: light brown, S-spun, 9 picks per cm
Pattern wefts: (i) red, S-spun
(ii) purplish-black, S-spun
(iii) light brown, S-spun
Selvedge: 3 edge cords Z/S-ply (light brown), 3
cords of paired or plied ends (each cord consists of one light brown and one dark brown
end), w 10mm

Width of bands: two bands, 13–16mm and 9mm
wide, with different patterns, separated by
4mm (8 throws) of main weave
Pattern: (A) 3 throws light brown
1 throw red
1 throw purplish-black
8 throws light brown (3mm)
16 throws purplish-black (5mm)
10 throws light brown (3mm)
2 throws purplish-black

(B) 10 throws light brown
14 throws red
10 throws light brown

285 Dimensions: (i) h 48mm, w 17mm; (ii) 35mm,
w 13mm. The two pieces are stitched together
Warp: dark brown, Z-spun, 9 ends per cm
Weft: dark brown, S-spun, 10 picks per cm
Pattern wefts: (i) brown, S-spun
(ii) purplish black, S-spun
(iii) red, S-spun
*c.*22 picks per cm
Width of band: greater than 21mm (incomplete)
Pattern: *c.*4 throws brown
12 throws purplish-black
*c.*26 throws brown
5+ throws red

286 Dimensions: (i) h 100mm, w 203mm; (ii) h
130mm, w 175mm; (iii) h 28mm, w 33mm
Warp: dark brown (madder), Z-spun, 10 ends per
cm
Weft: dark brown (madder), S-spun, 11 picks per
cm
Pattern wefts: (i) purplish-black (madder + indigotin), S-spun
(ii) mauvish-brown (madder), fine
yarn, S-spun
(iii) pink (madder), S-spun
*c.*32 picks per cm
Width of band: 24mm
Pattern: 4 throws purplish-black
*c.*24 throws mauvish-brown (5mm)
6 throws pink
14 throws purplish-black (5mm)
6 throws pink
*c.*20 throws mauvish-brown (5mm)
4 throws purplish-black

287 Dimensions: h 165mm, w 68mm
Warp: light brown, Z-spun, 10 ends per cm
Weft: light brown, S-spun, 10 picks per cm
Pattern wefts: (i) light brown, S-spun
(ii) purple, S-spun
(iii) red, S-spun
32–34 picks per cm
Width of band: 31mm

Pattern: 8 throws light brown
          4 throws purple
          4 throws light brown
          6 throws purple
          4 throws light brown
          2 throws purple
          15 throws light brown
          2 throws purple
          10 throws red
          2 throws purple
          14 throws light brown
          2 throws purple
          5 throws light brown
          6 throws purple
          4 throws light brown
          2 throws purple
          9 throws light brown
Pl 8A

288 Dimensions: h 210mm, w 20mm
     Warp: dark brown, Z-spun, 11 ends per cm
     Weft: dark brown, S-spun, 9 picks per cm
     Pattern wefts: (i) red, S-spun
                     (ii) light brown, S-spun
                     (iii) dark purple, S-spun
                     22 picks per cm
     Selvedge: 6 edge cords Z/S-ply (light brown),
       w 9mm
Width of band: 38mm
Pattern: 6 throws red
             *c.*20 throws light brown
               16 throws dark purple
               10 throws light brown
               16 throws dark purple
             *c.*20 throws light brown
                6 throws red

289 Dimensions: h 100mm, w 11mm
     Warp: dark brown, Z-spun
     Weft: dark brown, S-spun, 9 picks per cm
     Pattern wefts: (i) light brown, S-spun
                     (ii) purplish black, S-spun
                     (iii) mid brown, Z-spun
                     28 picks per cm
     Selvedge: 5 edge cords Z/S-ply, w 7–9mm
     Width of band: incomplete, greater than 28mm
     Pattern: 9   throws light brown
               6   throws purplish-black
               25   throws light brown
               2   throws purplish-black
               8   throws mid-brown
               2   throws purplish-black
               20+ throws light brown

290 Dimensions: h 90mm, w 25mm. Bias cut
     Warp: brown (madder), Z-spun, 10 ends per cm

Weft: brown (madder), S-spun, 12 picks per cm
Pattern wefts: (i) dark purple, S-spun
                (ii) reddish-brown, S-spun
                (iii) brown, Z-spun
                23 picks per cm
Width of band: incomplete, greater than 22mm
Pattern: 6 throws brown
           20 throws dark purple
        *c.*26 throws reddish-brown
          1+ throw dark purple

291 Dimensions: h 40mm, w 148mm. Partly bias cut
     Warp: dark brown, Z-spun, 10 ends per cm
     Weft: dark brown, S-spun, 14 picks per cm
     Pattern wefts: (i) light brown, S-spun
                     (ii) dark brown, S-spun
                     (iii) pale brown, Z-spun
                     32 picks per cm
     Width of band: incomplete, greater than 20mm
     Pattern: 16   throws light brown
               2   throws dark brown
              16   throws light brown
               2   throws dark brown
              16   throws pale brown
               2   throws dark brown
              10+ throws light brown

Unstratified
394 Dimensions: h 140mm, w 210mm
     Warp: mid-brown (unidentified dye), Z-spun, 11
       ends per cm
     Weft: mid-brown (unidentified dye), S-spun, 11
       picks per cm
     Pattern wefts: (i) dark purplish-brown, S-spun
                     (ii) light brown, S-spun
                     (iii) reddish-brown, S-spun
                     36 picks per cm
     Width of band: 26mm
     Pattern: 3 throws dark purplish-brown
               3 throws light brown
              32 throws reddish-brown (9mm)
               6 throws light brown
              30 throws reddish-brown (9mm)
               3 throws light brown
               3 throws dark purplish-brown
Pl 8B

Cloths with four pattern wefts

Second quarter 14th century
123 Dimensions: (i) h 45mm, w 90mm; (ii) h 75mm,
       w 85mm; (iii) h 55mm, w 23mm
     Warp: dark brown (negative), Z-spun, 10–11 ends
       per cm
     Weft: dark brown (negative), S-spun, 9–10 picks
       per cm

Pattern wefts: (i) red (madder), S-spun
(ii) buff, S-spun
(iii) dark brown, S-spun
(iv) purple, S-spun (decayed)
24 picks per cm
Width of band: 25mm
Pattern: 5 throws red
5 throws buff
17 throws dark brown
5 throws purple
16 throws red
5 throws buff
5 throws red
Pl 9A

124 Dimensions: h 50mm, w 35mm
Warp: dark brown, Z-spun, 10 ends per cm
Weft: dark brown, S-spun, 8 picks per cm
Pattern Wefts: (i) brown, S-spun
(ii) black, S-spun
(iii) red, S-spun
(iv) brown, Z-spun, finer than (i)
*c.*16 picks per cm
Width of band: 27mm
Pattern: 4 throws brown (ii)
*c.*14 throws brown (i)
3 throws black
3 throws red
2 throws brown (i)
4 throws brown (ii)
2 throws brown (i)
3 throws red
3 throws black
*c.*14 throws brown (i)
4 throws brown (ii)

Last quarter 14th century
292 Dimensions: h *c.*200mm, w 12mm. Knotted strip
Warp: mid-brown, Z-spun, 12 ends per cm
Weft: mid-brown, S-spun, 9 picks per cm
Pattern wefts: (i) brown, S-spun
(ii) purple, S-spun
(iii) red, S-spun
(iv) brown, Z-spun
Selvedge: *c.*10 edge cords, w 10mm
Width of bands: two bands, (A) 33m wide, (B) incomplete, separated by 90mm of main weave
Pattern: (A) 8 throws brown
4 throws purple
20 throws brown
5 throws red
*c.*22 throws brown (iv)
5 throws red
24 throws brown
4 throws purple
10 throws brown

Tabby-woven cloths with warp and weft of contrasting colours and weft-faced bands in extended tabby

Second quarter 14th century
125 Dimensions: (i) h 95mm, w 84mm; (ii) h 33mm, w 30mm
Warp: light brown (negative), Z-spun, 8–10 ends per cm
Weft: black (natural pigment), S-spun, 4–5 picks per cm
Pattern weft: yellowish-brown (negative), fine yarn, S-spun
Selvedge: 2 edge cords of 4 ends, 2 pairs of ends, w 8mm
Width of bands: pairs of bands each 4mm wide (6 throws) separated by 6mm (4 throws) of main weave, 35mm main weave between the pairs of bands
Fig 41, Pl 6B

126 Dimensions: h 50mm, w 16mm
Warp: reddish-purple (madder), Z-spun, 10 ends per cm
Weft: dark brown, S-spun, 6–7 picks per cm
Pattern weft: light grey-brown, S-spun
Width of band: 6mm (14 throws)

127 Dimensions: (i) h 95mm, w 100mm; (ii) h 45mm, w 40mm
Warp: light brown, Z-spun, 9 ends per cm
Weft: alternate throws (i) light brown, S-spun
(ii) red, S-spun
10 picks per cm
Pattern weft: yellowish-brown, S-spun, 24–26 picks per cm
Width of band: greater than 11mm

Last quarter 14th century
293 Dimensions: (i) h 70mm, w 50mm, and a smaller second fragment
Warp: brownish-black, Z-spun, 12 ends per cm
Weft: pale brown, S-spun, 14 picks per cm
Pattern wefts: (i) pinkish-brown (madder), S-spun
(ii) brown, S-spun
(iii) brownish-black, S-spun
Width of band: 18mm
Pattern: *c.*10 throws brownish-black
12 throws light brown
8 throws pinkish-brown
12 throws light brown
*c.*10 throws brownish-black

Tabby-woven cloths patterned with silk and wool weft-faced bands in extended tabby

Cloths with two pattern wefts

Second quarter 14th century

128   Dimensions: (i) h 90mm, w 80mm; (ii) h 38mm, w 27mm
Warp: pinkish-brown (madder), Z-spun, 9–10 ends per cm
Weft: pinkish-brown (madder), S-spun, 10–11 picks per cm
Pattern wefts: (i) brown, S-spun
(ii) silk, golden-brown, Z/S-ply
Width of band: 2mm
Pattern: 3 throws silk
2 throws brown
3 throws silk

129   Dimensions: (i) h 27, w 35mm; (ii) h 10mm, w 13mm
Warp: light brown, Z-spun, 8–9 ends per cm
Weft: light brown, S-spun, 9–11 picks per cm
Pattern wefts: (i) dark brown, S-spun
(ii) silk, golden-brown, Z/S-ply
Width of band: 3mm
Pattern: 6 throws silk
4 throws brown
6 throws silk

130   Dimensions: (i) h 230mm, w 20mm; (ii) h 110mm, w 23mm
Warp: dark brown, Z-spun, 10–11 ends per cm
Weft: dark brown, S-spun, 10 picks per cm
Pattern wefts: (i) dark brown, S-spun
(ii) silk, golden brown, Z/S-ply
30 picks per cm
Width of band: 14mm
Pattern: 4 throws silk
*c.*16 throws dark brown
4 throws silk
*c.*16 throws dark brown
4 throws silk

131   Dimensions: h 115mm, w 12mm
Warp: dark brown, Z-spun
Weft: dark brown, S-spun, 8 picks per cm
Pattern wefts: (i) dark brown, S-spun
(ii) silk, golden-brown, Z/S-ply
Selvedge: 4 edge cords Z/S-ply (dark brown), 2 pairs of ends, w 9mm
Width of band: 5mm

Pattern: 4 throws silk
3 throws brown
4 throws silk
3 throws brown
4 throws silk
4 throws brown
4 throws silk

Cloths with three pattern wefts

Second quarter 14th century

132   Dimensions: h 85mm, w 65mm
Warp: dark brown, Z-spun, 9–10 ends per cm
Weft: dark brown, S-spun, 9 picks per cm
Pattern wefts: (i) brown, Z-spun
(ii) pinkish-brown (madder), coarser than (i)
(iii) silk, golden brown, Z/S-ply
25 picks per cm
Width of band: 20 mm
Pattern: 2 throws silk
8 throws brown
32 throws pinkish-brown
8 throws brown
2 throws silk

Last quarter 14th century

294   Dimensions: (i) h 55mm, w 80mm; (ii) h 45mm, w 40mm
Warp: dark reddish-purple (madder), Z-spun, 10 ends per cm
Weft: dark reddish-purple (madder), S-spun, 11–12 picks per cm
Pattern wefts: (i) light brown, S-spun
(ii) black, S-spun
(iii) silk, golden-brown, Z/S-ply
*c.*50 picks per cm
Width of band: 14mm
Pattern: 2 throws silk
10 throws light brown
10 throws black
4 throws light brown
2 throws silk
4 throws light brown
10 throws black
4 throws light brown
2 throws silk
4 throws light brown
10 throws black
10 throws light brown
2 throws silk
Pl 12A

295   Dimensions: h 130mm, w 13mm
Warp: dark brown, Z-spun, 10 ends per cm
Weft: dark brown, S-spun, 11 picks per cm

Pattern wefts: (i) dark brown, S-spun
            (ii) mid-brown, Z-spun
            (iii) silk, golden-brown, Z/S-ply
Width of band: 54mm
Pattern: Uncertain, very deteriorated (NB band
    does not extend across full width of cloth)

Tabby-woven cloths patterned with weft-faced bands in extended tabby and 2.2 twill

Cloth with two pattern wefts
Last quarter 14th century
296 Dimensions: h 60mm, w 50mm
Warp: dark red, Z-spun, 15 ends per cm
Weft: dark red, S-spun, 13 picks per cm
Pattern wefts: (i) brown, S-spun
            (ii) black, S-spun
            *c.*52 picks per cm
Width of band: 38mm
Pattern: *c.*30 throws brown (5mm)
        16 throws black (3.5mm)
        *c.*24 throws brown (5mm)
        *c.*19 throws 2.2 twill with point repeat in
          weft
        *c.*32 throws brown (6.5mm)
        14 throws black (3mm)
        *c.*28 throws brown (5mm)

Cloths with three pattern wefts
Last quarter 14th century
297 Dimensions: h 10mm, w 42mm
Warp: mid-brown, Z-spun, 11 ends per cm
Weft: ?
Pattern wefts: (i) dark purplish-brown, S-spun
            (ii) light brown, Z-spun
            (iii) reddish-brown, Z-spun
            *c.*48–50 picks per cm
Width of band: incomplete, greater than 10mm
Pattern: 9+ throws dark purplish-brown
    4 throws light brown, 2.2 twill,
       Z-diagonal
    3 throws reddish-brown, 2.2 twill with
       point repeat in weft
    4 throws light brown, 2.2 twill,
       S-diagonal
    8+ throws reddish-brown, 2.2 twill,
       Z-diagonal

298 Dimensions: (i) h 115mm, w 95mm; (ii) h 85mm,
    w 110mm; (iii) h 60mm, 90mm; (iv) h 70mm, w
    80mm
Warp: light brown, Z-spun, 11–12 ends per cm

Weft: light brown, S-spun, 12 picks per cm
Pattern wefts: (i) light brown, S-spun
            (ii) purple (madder), S-spun
            (iii) red (madder), S-spun
            31 picks per cm
Width of band: 32mm
Pattern: 4 throws light brown
        8 throws purple
     20 throws light brown
       2 throws purple
       5 throws red
       4 throws light brown
       2 throws purple
     31 throws light brown, 2.2 twill with point
       repeat in weft
       2 throws purple
       4 throws light brown
       5 throws red
       2 throws purple
     20 throws light brown
       8 throws purple
       4 throws light brown
Pl 10A

299 Dimensions: (i) h 50mm, w 45mm; (ii) h 38mm,
    w 40mm
Warp: brown, Z-spun, 10 ends per cm
Weft: brown, S-spun, thicker than pattern wefts,
    10 picks per cm
Pattern wefts: (i) buff (negative), S-spun (partly
            decayed)
            (ii) purple (negative), coarse yarn,
            S-spun
            (iii) dark red, Z-spun
Width of band: 29mm
Pattern: *c.*12 throws buff
        6 throws purple
        8 throws buff
        2 throws purple
        *c.*20 throws alternate red and buff 2.2
        twill, Z-diagnonal
        8 throws buff
        *c.*20 throws alternate red and buff, 2.2
        twill, S-diagonal
        2 throws purple
     10 throws buff
        6 throws purple
        ? throws buff
Pl 10B

300 Dimensions: h 13mm, w 23mm
Warp: (i) brown, Z-spun
     (ii) brown, S-spun
     10 ends per cm (Z,Z,S,S,Z,Z,S,S etc)
Weft: ?

Pattern wefts: (i)light brown, S-spun
                 (ii)red, Z-spun
                 (iii)light brown, finer than (i),
                     Z-spun
                 *c.*20 picks per cm
Width of band: incomplete, greater than 12mm
Pattern: 8 throws light brown (i)
        6 throws light brown (ii)
        6 alternate red and light brown (ii), 2.2
            twill, Z-diagonal
        6 throws light brown (ii)
        8 throws light brown (i)

301 Dimensions: h 27mm, w 78mm
      Warp: red, Z-spun, *c.*20 ends per cm
      Weft: ?
      Pattern wefts: (i) purplish-brown, fine yarn,
                          Z-spun
                       (ii) mid-brown, S-spun
                       (iii) red, S-spun
      Width of band: incomplete, greater than 30mm
      Pattern: 4mm purplish-brown, 2.2 twill,
                  Z-diagonal
              5mm mid-brown, 2.2 twill, S-diagonal
              4 throws red
              4 throws mid-brown
              2mm purplish-brown, 2.2 twill,
                  Z-diagonal
              2mm mid-brown, 2.2 twill, Z-diagonal
              2mm purplish-brown, 2.2 twill,
                  Z-diagonal
              4 throws mid-brown
              4 throws red
              5mm mid-brown, 2.2 twill, S-diagonal
              5mm purplish-brown, 2.2 twill, Z-diag-
                  onal

302 Dimensions: h 51mm, w 57mm
      Warp: dark reddish-brown, Z-spun, 9 ends per
          cm
      Weft: dark reddish-brown, S-spun, 9 picks per cm
      Pattern wefts: (i)light brown, S-spun
                       (ii)purplish-black, S-spun
                       (iii)light brown, finer than (i),
                           Z-spun
      Width of band: incomplete, greater than 13mm
      Pattern: 8 throws light brown (i)
              6 throws purplish-black
              4 throws light brown (i)
              6mm   light brown (iii), 2.2 twill,
                       Z-diagonal

303 Dimensions: h 195mm, w 40mm. Bias cut
      Warp: brown, Z-spun, 9 ends per cm
      Weft: brown, Z-spun, 9 picks per cm

Pattern wefts: (i)brown, S-spun
                 (ii)purple, S-spun
                 (iii)reddish-brown, Z-spun
Width of band: 45mm
Pattern: 9 throws brown
            10 throws purple
             6 throws brown (8mm)
             8 throws reddish-brown, 2.2 twill,
                 Z-diagonal
            40 throws brown (8mm)
            *c.*8 throws reddish-brown, 2.2 twill,
                 Z-diagonal
             6 throws brown (8mm)
            10 throws purple
            12 throws brown

First quarter 15th century
422 Dimensions: ten fragments, largest (i) h 265mm,
          w 405mm; (ii) h 70mm, w 140mm
      Warp: dark blackish-brown (madder), Z-spun, 10
          ends per cm
      Weft: dark blackish-brown (madder), S-spun, 9
          picks per cm
      Pattern wefts: (i) Z-spun, fine yarn
                       (ii) S-spun (madder + indigotin)
                       (iii) S-spun
                       *c.*36 picks per cm
      Width of bands: 52mm and 53mm separated by
          54mm of main weave
      Pattern: 6 throws (i)
                  32 throws S-spun yarn
                  12 throws S-spun yarn, 2.2 twill,
                      S-diagonal
                  26 throws S-spun yarn
                  *c.*16 throws S-spun yarn, 2.2 twill with
                      point repeat in weft (S,Z,S diagonals)
                  24 throws S-spun yarn
                  10 throws S-spun yarn, 2/2 twill,
                      S-diagonal
                  34 throws S-spun yarn
                   6 throws (i)

Cloths with four pattern wefts

Last quarter 14th century
304 Dimensions: h 250mm, w 20mm
      Warp: mid-brown, Z-spun, 10 ends per cm
      Weft: mid-brown, S-spun, 10–11 picks per cm
      Pattern wefts: (i) brown, S-spun
                       (ii) purplish-black, coarse yarn,
                           S-spun
                       (iii) red, S-spun
                       (iv) brown, Z-spun
                       29 picks per cm
      Selvedge: 5 edge cords Z/S-ply

Width of bands: 32mm and 38mm separated by
   85mm of main weave
Pattern: 6–8 throws brown (i)
        8 throws purplish-black
        6 throws red
        8 throws brown (i)
        3 throws black
       *c.*10 throws brown (iv), 2.2 twill,
        S-diagonal
        4 throws brown (i)
       10 throws black
        4 throws brown (i)
       *c.*10 throws brown (iv), 2.2 twill,
        Z-diagonal
        3 throws black
        8 throws brown (i)
        6 throws red
        8 throws black
        6–8 throws brown

305 Dimensions: h 95mm, w 122mm
     Warp: grey-brown (negative), Z-spun, 10 ends per
       cm
     Weft: grey-brown (negative), S-spun, 9 picks per
       cm
     Pattern wefts: (i)purplish-black (madder + indi-
             gotin), coarse yarn, S-spun
          (ii)light brown, S-spun
          (iii)mid-brown, fine yarn, Z-spun
          (iv)red, coarse yarn, S-spun
          26 picks per cm
     Width of band: 35mm
     Pattern: 2 throws purplish-black, tabby weave
        10 throws light brown
        8 throws purplish-black
       15 throws light brown
        8 throws mid-brown, 2.2 twill,
         S-diagonal
        3 throws light brown
       10 throws red
        3 throws light brown
        8 throws mid-brown, 2.2 twill,
         Z-diagonal
       14 throws light brown
        8 throws purplish-black
       10 throws light brown
        2 throws purplish-black, tabby weave
     Pl 9B

306 Dimensions: h 110mm, w 25mm
     Warp: dark red, Z-spun, 9 ends per cm
     Weft: dark red, Z-spun, 9 picks per cm
     Pattern wefts: (i)brown, S-spun
             (ii)purplish-black, S-spun
             (iii)buff, S-spun
             (iv)brown, Z-spun

Width of band: two bands 12mm and 2mm wide,
    both incomplete, separated by 82mm of main
    weave
Pattern: (A)   16 throws brown (i)
            9 throws purplish-black
        *c.*6 throws buff

      (B)   ? throws brown (iv), 2.2 twill,
            S-diagonal
          8 throws brown (i), tabby weave
          9 throws purplish-black
       *c.*6 throws buff

Cloths with four pattern wefts including silk

Last quarter 14th century

307 Dimensions: h 85mm, w 12mm. Bias cut
     Warp: brown, Z-spun, 10 ends per cm
     Weft: brown, S-spun, 10 ends per cm
     Pattern wefts: (i)purplish-black, S-spun,
             (ii)red, Z-spun
             (iii)light brown, Z-spun
             (iv)? silk (decayed)
          *c.*32 picks per cm
     Width of band: 50mm
     Pattern: 2 throws purplish-black
        4mm   red, 2.2 twill, Z-diagonal
        4mm   light brown, 2.2 twill, Z-diagonal
        8 throws purplish-black
        9mm   light brown and red (colour
               changes indistinct), 2.2 twill,
               Z-diagonal
        2 throws silk
        11mm   light brown, red, light brown,
               red, light brown (colour
               changes indistinct), 2.2 twill,
               Z-diagonal
        6 throws purplish-black
        11mm   light brown and ? red, 2.2 twill,
               Z-diagonal
        2 throws purplish-black

308 Dimensions: (i) h 65mm, w 124mm; (ii) 60mm, w
          104mm; (iii)h 55mm, w 31mm; (iv)
          h 52mm, w 30mm
     Warp: reddish-purple (madder), Z-spun, 11 ends
       per cm
     Weft: reddish-purple (madder), S-spun, 11 picks
       per cm
     Pattern wefts: (i)purplish-black, S-spun
             (ii)reddish-brown, S-spun
             (iii)brown, S-spun
             (iv)silk, Z/S-ply
          *c.*40 picks per cm
     Width of band: 30mm

Pattern: 2 throws purplish-black, tabby weave
14 throws reddish-purple
2 throws purplish-black
3 throws brown
3 throws silk, 2.2 twill, Z-diagonal
3 throws brown
2 throws purplish-black
14 throws reddish-purple
2 throws purplish-black
3 throws brown
3 throws silk, 2/2 twill, S-diagonal
3 throws brown
2 throws purplish-black
12 throws reddish-purple
2 throws purplish-black
3 throws brown
3 throws silk, 2.2 twill, Z-diagonal
3 throws brown
2 throws purplish-black
12 throws reddish-purple
2 throws purplish-black
3 throws brown
3 throws silk, 2.2 twill, S-diagonal
3 throws brown
2 throws purplish-black
12 throws reddish-purple
2 throws purplish-black, tabby weave
Pl 12B

309 Dimensions: h 105mm, w 85mm
Warp: light brown, Z-spun, 10 ends per cm
Weft: light brown, S-spun, 12 picks per cm
Pattern wefts: (i)red, S-spun
(ii)purple, S-spun (partly decayed)
(iii)light brown, fine yarn, Z-spun
(iv)silk, Z/S-ply
*c.*30 picks per cm
Width of bands: 17mm separated by 65mm of
main weave
Pattern: 2 throws purple
6 throws red
2 throws purple
*c.*12 light brown, 2.2 twill, Z diagonal
2 throws purple
3 throws silk
2 throws purple
*c.*12 light brown, 2.2 twill, Z diagonal
2 throws purple
6 throws red
2 throws purple
Pl 11A

Cloths with five pattern wefts including silk

Last quarter 14th century
310 Dimensions: h 72mm, w 27mm
Warp: dark red, Z-spun, 10 ends per cm
Weft: dark red, S-spun, 12 picks per cm
Pattern wefts: (i)light brown, S-spun
(ii)purplish-black, coarse yarn,
S-spun
(iii)dark red, Z-spun
(iv)light brown, finer than (i),
Z-spun
(v)silk, Z/S-ply
*c.*30 picks per cm
Width of band: 43mm
Pattern: 8   throws light brown (i)
6   throws purplish-black
26 throws light brown (i)
7mm alternate throws red and light
brown (iv), 2.2 twill, Z-diagonal
2   throws silk
7mm alternate throws red and light
brown (iv), 2.2 twill, S-diagonal
26 throws light brown (i)
6   throws purplish-black
8   throws light brown (i)
Pl 11B

311 Dimensions: h 160mm, w 30mm
Warp: dark brown (negative), Z-spun, 14 ends per cm
Weft: dark brown (negative), S-spun, 12 picks per cm
Pattern wefts: (i)light brown, S-spun
(ii)dark brown, S-spun
(iii)purplish-black, coarse yarn,
S-spun
(iv)red, S-spun
(v)silk, Z/S-ply
34 picks per cm
Width of band: 40mm, with at least 80mm of main
weave before the next band
Pattern: 1 throw silk
*c.*12 throws light brown (3mm)
4 throws purplish-black (2mm)
*c.*24 throws dark brown (5mm)
6 throws purplish-black (2mm)
*c.*24 throws light brown (5mm)
3 throws red
3 throws alternate silk, red, silk, 2.2
twill, Z-diagonal
3 throws red
*c.*24 throws light brown (6mm)
6 throws purplish-black (2mm)
*c.*24 throws dark brown (6mm)
4 throws purplish-black (2mm)
*c.*12 throws light brown (2mm)
? 1 throw silk

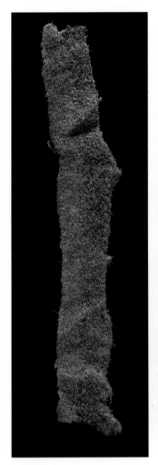

A

Plate 5
(A) Red wool cloth with reinforced selvedge of black threads, No 195. Height 109 mm

(B) Corner of a tabby-woven cloth patterned with yellow weft-faced bands in extended tabby, No 277. The cloth has a fringe and a reinforced selvedge which includes a red stripe. Height 137 mm

Both are from a late 14th-century deposit

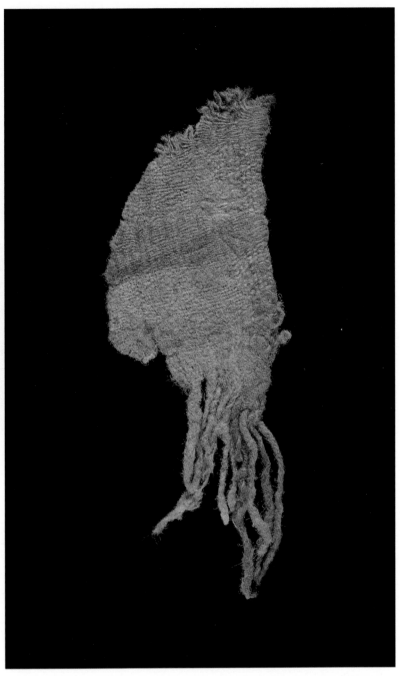

B

A

B

Plate 6

(A) Wool tabby-woven cloth with a mottled pattern produced by using two colours of weft yarn, No 54. It has a reinforced selvedge shown on the right. Height 115 mm

(B) Wool cloth with a mottled patterned main weave and pairs of yellowish-orange weft-faced bands woven in extended tabby, No 125. It has a reinforced selvedge shown on the right. Height 92 mm

Both are from a deposit dating to the second quarter of the 14th century

A

B

Plate 7
(A) Red wool cloth patterned with a green, weft-faced band in extended tabby, No 92. Height 55mm
(B) Wool cloth patterned with an orange weft-faced band outlined in reddish-purple yarn and woven in extended tabby, No 107. Height 91mm
Both are from a deposit dating to the second quarter of the 14th century

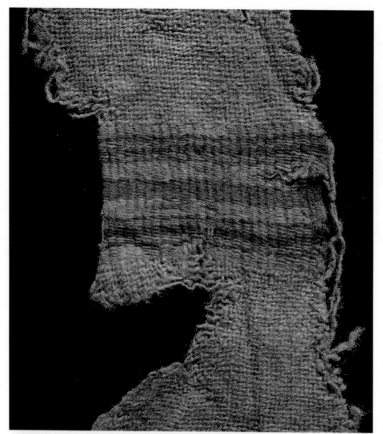

A

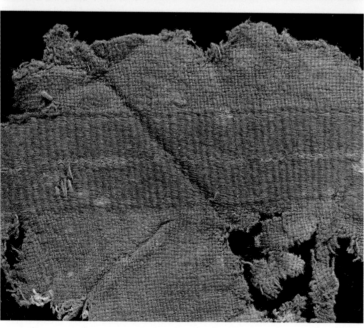

B

Plate 8
Wool cloths patterned with weft-faced bands of three colours woven in extended tabby: (A) No 287, from a late 14th-century deposit. Width of band 31mm. (B) No 394. Width of band 26mm

Tapestry

Tapestry is a technique whereby 'the weft threads are not thrown completely across the loom but are introduced to cover short spaces with various tints and colours as required by the design. The warp is thus completely hidden in the finished fabric' (Kendrick 1924, 1). Four textiles from the late 14th-century deposit at BC72 bear the remains of patterns woven in this way (Nos 312–315). All are woven from wool, the warp being two-ply worsted yarn, and the different coloured weft yarns, either Z-spun or S-spun, used double. Despite the fragmentary state of these tapestries a few additional features can be observed, including the use of four different coloured yarns in the finest of them (No 314), and a consistent use of unlinked slits (Fig 43).

The use of double yarn in the weft on a plied wool warp was not uncommon among tapestries woven in French, Flemish and Burgundian towns during the late 14th century. By doubling the weft yarn, the speed with which a tapestry was woven could be increased. Often both single and paired weft yarns occur on a piece since this was a means of enhancing the texture and enabling details of the composition, such as a person's hair, to be depicted with greater subtlety. These characteristics may also have been features of tapestries produced in England in the 13th and 14th centuries which are, at present, only known from documents. Ordinances of 1331 governing tapicers working in London decreed that only good wool of England and Spain was to be used in armorial

Fig 43 Tapestry weave with unlinked slits

tapestries, and in 1370 this was extended to all forms of tapestry with the additional proviso that English wool was not to be mixed with Spanish wool (Consitt 1933, 69 and 71). It is evident that these regulations were taken seriously since in 1374 Katherine Duchewoman was found guilty of weaving a tapestry coster (wall hanging) with a linen warp, instead of a wool warp, at her house at Finch Lane in the City and the coster was, therefore, ordered to be burnt, although in this case it was agreed that the judgement should not be executed (Riley 1868, 375–6).

Tapestry furnishings were popular in London throughout the 14th century, with wealthy citizens following the lead set by the royal court, which exploited all opportunities for the lavish display of textiles. In 1317 Edward II paid £30 to Thomas de Hebenhith, a London mercer, for a wool hanging portraying the king and earls, which was hung in Westminster Hall on festivals such as Christmas and Easter (Stapleton 1836, 344), and when Jean II, King of France, was paraded through the City as a prisoner of war in 1357, the streets were hung with tapestries depicting battle scenes (Thomson 1973, 55). Among a number of tapestries owned by Isabella of France, wife of Edward II, on her death in 1358 were a banker (bench cover) depicting the Nativity and two wallhangings of the history of the Apocalypse (King 1977, 161). Bogo de Clare, a corrupt and worldly churchman with a large London-based wardrobe and household, also had a number of tapestry bankers including one decorated with the arms of England which cost 20s. in 1284–5 (Guiseppi 1920, 30). It is not specified where any of these tapestries were made. There are indications, however, that tapestry weaving was already well established in London during the 13th century. Richard de Berking, Abbot of Westminster, who died in 1246, left two tapestry curtains, which were described in 16th- and 17th-century records as 'arras-work', for hanging in the abbey choir (Robinson 1909, 24–30; Binski forthcoming). One curtain showed scenes from the life of Edward the Confessor, who had been a great patron of the abbey and whose shrine there was a place of pilgrimage, and the other the life of Christ. The choice of St Edward as a subject suggests that the curtains were woven locally, although they could have been commissioned from a continental workshop.

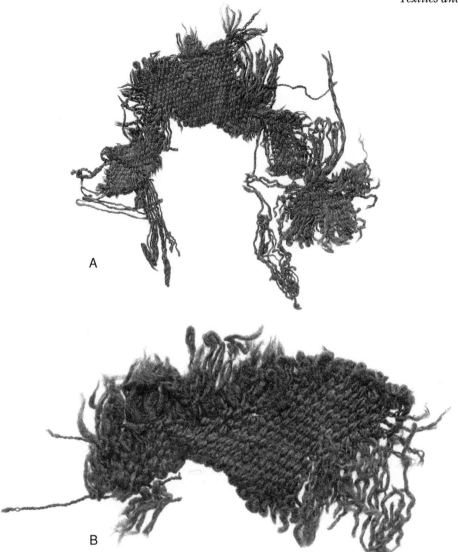

A

B

Fig 44 Wool tapestry, No 312, from a late 14th-century deposit. The warp is shown horizontally as this is how it would have been viewed. (A) Scale 1:2, (B) scale 1:1

Records imply that there were tapestry weavers working in London during the 13th and 14th centuries (Consitt 1933, 69) but only a small number of these artisans may have specialised in figurative pieces which would have demanded a considerable amount of time and skill to weave. The term tapicer was not applied only to weavers who produced tapestries in the modern sense.

Striped and plain fabrics which could be painted or embroidered were also among their products; all these textiles were presumably weft-faced and mainly used worsted yarn. Thus, in addition to many magnificent tapestries which belonged to Thomas, Duke of Gloucester, at the time of his disgrace in 1397, were eight pieces of black tapestry powdered with white roses *'viii peces de Tapitz de Tapicerie noir poudrez de blanc roses'* (Dillon & St John Hope 1897, 289). Parisian documents of the late 13th and early 14th centuries emphasise the distinction there by referring to three different groups of tapicer; *'tapissiers Sarazinois, tapissiers*

Nostrez' and *'tapissiers de la haute lisse'* (Weibel 1951, 4; Weigert 1962, 31–2).

Bequests of tapestries are included in the wills of Londoners during the 14th century. While precise descriptions are usually lacking, pieces woven with birds and animals as well as those bearing armorial or pseudo-armorial devices such as fleur-de-lis were among those owned in the 1380s (Cal Wills II, 249, 262, 265), and these can be assumed not to have been painted cloths. Tapestries with figurative compositions were also possessed by the more affluent; thus in 1361 William Brangewayn, a vintner, bequeathed to his son a dorser (hanging) depicting King Richard and Hector of Troy (Cal Wills II, 40—41). Meanwhile a tapestry identified as being a London product *fait à Loundres'* occurs in the will of the Earl of Arundel who died in 1392. This tapestry had red roses and the armorial bearings of the earl and his son on a blue ground (Thomson 1973, 81).

No motifs can be made out among the excavated pieces of tapestry, although outlines of motifs are preserved on some fragments at the point where the colours changed (Figs 44–46). As fewer colours of yarn would have been needed for the simpler armorial and bird patterns, it is probable that the small fragments derive from wool tapestries of this type. By contrast, 12 to 15 shades of colour appear to have been used for the set of Apocalypse tapestries commissioned by Louis, Duc d'Anjou in 1376 and preserved today in Angers, north-west France (Kendrick 1924, 4, 48).

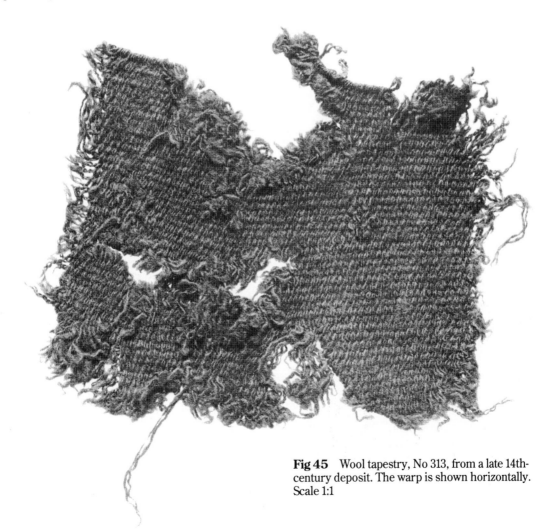

Fig 45 Wool tapestry, No 313, from a late 14th-century deposit. The warp is shown horizontally. Scale 1:1

Selected catalogue II

Last quarter 14th century

312 Dimensions: (i) h 150mm, w 150mm; (ii) h
   55mm, w 90mm
   Warp: wool, dark blackish-brown (natural pig-
       ment), Z/S-ply, 4 ends per cm
   Weft: (i)wool, reddish-brown (madder), S-spun
       (ii)wool, mid-brown, S-spun
       9 pairs per cm
   Fig 44

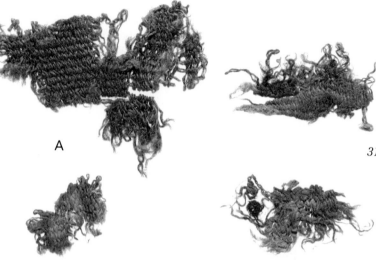

A

313 Dimensions: (i) h 170mm, w 150mm; (ii) h
   105mm, w 120mm; (iii) h 29mm, w 40mm
   Warp: wool, mid-brown, Z/S-ply, 5 ends per cm
   Weft: wool, mid-brown (madder), S-spun,
       13 pairs per cm
   Fig 45

314 Dimensions: (i) h 35mm, w 55mm; (ii) h 20mm,
   w 40mm; (iii) h 20mm, w 35mm; (iv) 20mm, w
   22mm; (v) h 40mm, w 58mm
   Warp: wool, light to mid-brown, Z/S-ply,
       5–6 ends per cm
   Weft: (i) wool, mid-brown, Z-spun
       (ii) wool, pinkish-brown, Z-spun
       (iii) wool, dark purple, finer than (1), (ii)
           and (iv), Z-spun
       (iv) wool, purplish-brown, S-spun
       15–18 pairs per cm
   Fig 46A

315 Dimensions: h 90mm, w 90mm
   Warp: wool, mid-brown, Z/S-ply, 5 ends per cm
   Weft: (i) wool, mid-brown, S-spun
       (ii) wool, reddish-brown, S-spun
       (iii) wool, purplish-brown, S-spun
       16 pairs per cm
   Fig 46B

Fig 46 Wool tapestries: (A) No 314, (B) No 315, from a late 14th-century deposit. The warp is shown horizontally. Scale 1:1

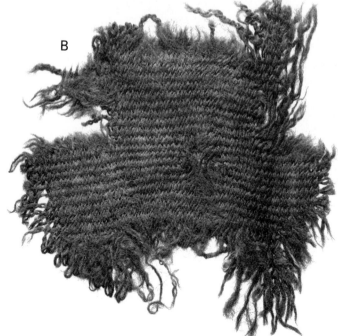

B

Knitting

Two groups of knitted fragments were found within the late 14th-century deposit at BC72 and further fragments were recovered from 14th-century waterfront deposits at FRE78 and BIG82. These are among the earliest examples of wool knitting found in northern Europe and are of considerable interest and importance.

One item (No 316, Pl 13A) consists of two small fragments worked from red (madder-dyed) two-ply yarn in an even stocking-stitch. There are approximately 2 stitches and 4 rows per cm. This formed a soft and flexible fabric and, although slightly matted through use or burial in the soil, it does not appear to have been heavily fulled or to have had a nap brushed up on the outer surface. It could have come from a garment like a child's vest or sleeve rather than from a piece of headwear, where fulling to keep out the rain became usual in later periods.

The second group of fragments (No 317) are

Goathair textiles

Little attention has been given to the role of goats in the economy of medieval England. The work of archaeologists is, however, beginning to reveal evidence that is not easily obtainable from written sources. Goatskin, known as cordwain, was sometimes used for shoes worn in London during the 11th to 13th centuries (Grew & Neergaard 1988, 44; Pritchard 1991, 222) and it appears also to have been common for shoes made on the Continent at the same period (Waateringe 1984, 29, fig 15). While there is a considerable weight of documentary evidence to show that cordwain was imported into England from Spain in the 13th and early 14th centuries (Childs 1978, 104, 136–7), the position is less clear for the 11th and 12th centuries and local supplies may have offered an initial stimulus to its use.

Hair was another important goat product. Correspondence shows that while Boniface was working in Germany during the 740s he sent a cloak of silk mixed with goat hair to Daniel, Bishop of Winchester, and blankets made from goathair to Hwaetbert, Abbot of Monkwearmouth-Jarrow (Budny 1984, 89, 93). Evidence from London points to the use of coarse textiles made from goathair between the 11th and 17th centuries and, although this volume is only concerned with textiles from the years 1150 to 1450, the other pieces show that this was not a new type of product nor was it to be superseded for many centuries. Unlike goatskin, the supply of hair did not depend on the slaughter of animals. Hair is shed naturally by goats in the spring, the coarse hairs of the outer coat preceding the shedding of the fine wool of the undercoat (Ryder 1966, 298, fig 2). It is, therefore, possible to collect the different types of hair separately, and accordingly they need not be intermingled when made into cloth. This characteristic of goathair appears to have been exploited in the making of the cloths described here. All are woven from thick two-ply yarn which is composed chiefly of kemp hairs. It is noticeable, however, that when these cloths degrade in anaerobic conditions the hairs lose their scale patterns and a mass of woollier fibres often results, which can at first be mistaken for a very loosely compacted felt.

Processing goathair

The methods of processing and spinning goathair were not necessarily the same as those used for sheep's wool, since the fibres are not alike in their scale formation, and goathair, which lacks crimp, does not cling together as easily as wool. No information on this subject appears to have been found in English records of the medieval period and so one has to turn to ethnographic studies for clues. A study undertaken on the spinning of goathair for the manufacture of tents in Syria in the 1960s revealed that, to ensure it remains water repellent, the hair was not washed at any stage before weaving; instead the raw fibres were cleaned by prolonged beating on the floor of a workshop (Hald 1981, 20–21). It has been suggested by Scandinavian writers that hair may usually have been spun into yarn with a spinning hook rather than with a drop spindle fitted with a whorl (Nordland 1961, 124–7; Schjølberg 1984, 88). This hook was made either from a single piece of wood, bone or metal, or from two pieces fastened together to form a cross (Nordland 1961, figs 73–5). A twisted end of hair was attached to the hook or cross which was continuously turned with one hand while the other hand drew out strands of raw fibre.

An alternative method of spinning goathair used today by Bedouin women in the Near East combines the use of a spindle with rolling the yarn against the thigh while seated. A length of hair is drawn out from a rove, which is held in the left hand, and rolled against the thigh with the right hand as the spindle is twisted in a clockwise direction with its tip resting on the ground. The spun thread is then wound round the shaft of the spindle below the whorl which is made from two cross-pieces of wood. Although this method is slow, it is well suited to spinning hair.

Table 8   Goathair cloths in tabby weave from medieval London

Cat. No	Dimensions h	w(mm)	Spin direction warp/weft	No of threads per cm warp/weft		Selvedge
Early 13th century (1200–1230)						
431	150	100	S/Z-ply S/Z-ply	2–3	2–3	—
432	120	95	S/Z-ply S/Z-ply	3	2–3	*
	120	100				
433	180	55	S/Z-ply S/Z-ply	2	2	*
	(largest fragment)					
434	120	60	S/Z-ply S/Z-ply	2	2	—
	(largest fragment)					
415	140	110	S/Z-ply S/Z-ply	3	2–3	—
Mid-13th century (1230–1260)						
435	150	150	S/Z-ply S/Z-ply	2–3	2–3	—
	(largest fragment)					
436	185	147	S/Z-ply S/Z-ply	2–3	2–3	*
416	80	55	S/Z-ply S/Z-ply	2	2	—
	(largest fragment)					
Late 13th to mid-14th century (1270–1350)						
437	60	30	S/Z-ply S/Z-ply	2–3	2	—
445	590	350	S/Z-ply S/Z-ply	3–5	3–5	* (Fig 53)
446	120	50	S/Z-ply S/Z-ply	3	3	—
Late 14th century (1380–1400)						
319	70	50	Z/S-ply Z/S-ply	2	2	—
439	160	125	S/Z-ply S/Z-ply	2	2	*

NB: — signifies no selvedge preserved; * selvedge present

The degree of twist given to the yarn used in the goathair cloths from medieval London was not great, and to stop the yarn from unwinding and as a strengthening measure the hair was usually plied with 3–6 twists per cm. This resulted in a fairly coarse thread, c.2–4mm in diameter. All the cloths listed here are woven from plied yarns and with one exception they are Z-plied from two S-twisted yarns (Table 8). The exception is a piece (No 319) from a deposit which dates to the late 14th century. It is one of the latest among the goathair cloths included here and could, therefore, mark a chronological difference. Excavations in Bergen, Norway, however, yielded 99 examples of the former type and 79 examples of the latter which were generally woven from finer

and better prepared yarn (Schjølberg 1984, 82–3). This, it was argued, could reflect a difference in place of manufacture.

The cloths from London are consistent in having a tabby binding and five out of the 13 examples preserve part of a simple selvedge (Nos 432, 433, 436, 439, 445, Table 8, Fig 53A) – a high proportion for a group of textiles. One cloth also has a series of looped ends forming a fringe, 30mm in length (Fig 53B). Further evidence about the size of these cloths comes from a complete loomwidth, of a similar fabric, which was recovered from an early 17th-century deposit beside the Thames at Southwark. It is 830mm (32⅝ins) wide and nearly 2m in length (one end is incomplete). It can therefore be inferred that these coarse

A

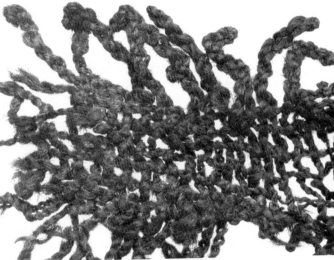

Fig 53 Goathair cloth, No 445, from mid 14th-century London: (A) detail of weave and selvedge, (B) detail of fringe. Scale 1:1

B

fabrics were woven in relatively narrow widths by one person on a simple frame or loom, which was probably positioned vertically.

Use of goathair textiles

The wide distribution of textiles of this type throughout northern Europe has emerged from recent studies of textile assemblages (e.g. Schjølberg 1984, 88; Walton 1988, 83). They are frequently present in waterfront deposits as these examples from 13th- and 14th-century London demonstrate, and there is a strong possibility that the cloth was used as a packaging material for merchandise, in a similar way to coarse wadmal (Hoffmann 1964, 364–5, fn 49). This was not, however, the only use of the cloth. Numerous fragments were found in a wattle-lined pit in London dating to the late 11th or early 12th century

(Pritchard 1984, 47, 59), where they may have fulfilled a particular function which is as yet unknown. Other cloths of this type have been recorded from five graves in Lund, Sweden, which are dated to the second half of the 11th century (Lindström 1976, 284), where they appear to have been used as covers or shrouds, and they are sometimes present in graves dating from the 11th to 14th centuries in England. These include a burial from the Cathedral green, Winchester, and another in a stone coffin at St Budoc's Church, Oxford (Crowfoot 1990, 476). This seems to reflect a bias towards monastic sites and has given rise to the suggestion that the cloth could have been used for hairshirts. Wrapping the dead in hairshirts was not confined to monks and clerics, John Atte Bataylle, a London weaver, for example, willed in 1352 that his body should be buried in this way (i.e. *in cilicio*) (Cal Wills I, 664).

A cloth of a similar weight and weave used for wrapping a corpse buried at St Mary's Priory, Thetford, was identified as wool rather than goathair (Carter & Henshall 1957, 102–3). The fleece is of a coarse hairy type similar to so-called carpet wool today, and includes natural brown coloured fibres. Hence, wool may sometimes have been substituted for goathair and points to another regional difference in origin for some of these cloths.

Linen textiles

The quantity of linen textiles from archaeological deposits in London is disappointingly small because of generally unfavourable local soil conditions. A number of charred pieces were recovered from a 12th-century deposit at Aldermanbury in the City (No 414), and although the fibres have not been positively identified as flax, the fact that the threads have preserved their form when burnt suggests that they were a vegetable fibre and not wool which is highly combustible. Other fragments (Nos 409 and 413) were preserved within layers of cess dating to the second half of the 13th century and the late 14th century at MLK76, and these scraps were probably used as sanitary towels and lavatory paper, functions for which moss and snippets of woollen cloth were also employed (Greig 1981, 281). Another piece of linen, which was recovered from an early 15th-century waterfront revetment dump at TL74, is partly coated in a black substance, possibly pitch, which enabled the cloth to survive in damp burial conditions (No 403).

All but one of these cloths are similar in weave, texture and quality, having been woven in a balanced tabby binding from Z-spun yarn (Table 9, Fig 54). They may have been bleached, but this

Table 9 Linen textiles from medieval London

Cat. No.	Dimensions h	w(mm)	Spin direction warp/weft	No of threads per cm warp/weft
Second half 12th century				
414	20	15 (largest fragment)	Z/Z	c. 15/12 (Fig 56)
Second half 13th century				
409	56	34 (largest fragment)	Z/Z	22/19–21
Last quarter 14th century				
413	6	9 (largest fragment)	Z/Z	c. 20/19
First half 15th century				
403	52	40 (largest fragment)	Z/Z	22/22 (Fig 54)

has not been confirmed analytically and unbleached flaxen cloth was also widely used. Linen of this medium grade must have been very common and underwear, bedlinen, headcoverings and aprons would often have been made from it (Fig 55).

Self-patterned weaves

Only the few small burnt fragments offer a little insight into the wide range of self-patterned linen fabrics available in medieval London for use as tablecloths, napkins, towels, and pillow covers. The cloth appears to be a type of huckaback with warp floats on one face and weft floats on the other (Fig 56), a fabric which remains to this day popular for towels because of its ability to absorb moisture. No similar cloths dating to the 12th century have been traced, although it is possible that pieces are preserved in continental treasuries for

Fig 54 Fragments of plain linen, No 403, from an early 15th-century deposit. Scale 1:1

Fig 55 Women revealing their underclothes, *c.*1340 (after *The Romance of Alexander,* MS Bodl 264, f.98)

Fig 56 Charred fragment of a huckaback cloth, probably linen, No 414, from a 12th-century deposit. Scale 2:1

An indication of the variety of self-patterned weaves produced in London in the later middle ages is provided by guild regulations which were written down in 1456 — 'crosse werk', 'crosse diamounde', 'smale knottes', 'cheynes yn werk', 'catrylettes', and 'damask knottes with the chapelettes' are among the types itemised (Consitt 1933, 206–7). Napery and towels of 'Paris work' are also specified showing that by the middle of the 15th century the name signified quality or texture rather than place of origin. There is little doubt, therefore, that if linen was more fully represented in the archaeological record a greater number of patterned cloths would be found to increase our understanding of this branch of the industry.

self-patterned linen has a long European history. The 'shroud of St Bathild' (died *c.*680) in Chelles, northern France, has bands of huckaback bordering a main web of tabby with a looped pile but this is considered to be a much older cloth (Laporte 1988, 100–1, fig 22). Fragments preserved from Anglo-Saxon burials include herringbone, lozenge and rosette twills, some probably imports, others perhaps made by the same weavers who produced fine four-shed worsteds (Crowfoot 1983, 422, 424, 439–41; Crowfoot forthcoming A), and a cloth in a honeycomb weave was recovered from a 10th-century deposit in York (Walton 1989, 353, fig 146, pl XXVa). Similar and more elaborate patterns have been recorded from graves on the Continent, particularly in the territory of the Alamanni in the central and southern Rhineland (Hundt 1980, 151–60; Hundt 1983, 207–11; Bender Jørgensen 1986, 356; Bender Jørgensen 1987, 112–4; Bender Jørgensen 1988, 117–8, fig 26.3), a region that has remained famous for its high quality linen.

Finishing

Although examples of linen cloths are rare from medieval deposits in London, an implement associated with the finishing and laundering of linen that is well represented is the linen smoother, or calender, made from glass. This was used to impart a gloss to linen, a process that was repeated after the fabric was washed as well as when it was new, and for pressing seams. The task of laundering linen was not insignificant in medieval England, for clean, carefully pressed, white linen was regarded as a status symbol and many households were prepared to pay for the services of a laundress, who was usually paid annually. Isabella, wife of Edward II, for example, employed two laundresses (*lotrices*) during 1311–12, of whom one, Joan, laundered the queen's napery and the other, Matilda, cared for the linen of the Queen's Chapel (Blackley & Hermansen 1971, 98–9, 108–9).

Silk textiles

England had no silk cloth weaving industry of its own during the medieval period, although unsuccessful attempts may have been made to establish one and a failed venture recorded at Westminster in the reign of Edward IV (Dale 1932–4, 332) may not have been an isolated example. The country was thus dependent upon gifts and consignments from abroad and accordingly shifts in international relations were as important as changes in taste in determining what was available.

Silk in Roman Britain and Anglo-Saxon England

The earliest example of a silk fabric known from Britain dates to the second quarter of the 3rd century AD when the country was under Roman rule. It is a geometric twill damask from the grave of a one-year-old child, who was buried in a lead sarcophagus embellished with Dionysiac figures and pecten shells, at Holborough, Kent (Wild 1965, 246). The cloth, described by classical writers as *scutulatus* on account of its checkered appearance, ranks as one of the earliest patterned silks woven in western Europe. A well known product of Latin workshops, it was listed in the Edict of Diocletian (AD 301), which stipulated that a weaver of the cloth was entitled to a minimum daily wage plus keep of 50 *denarii*, twice the earnings of a weaver in plain silk (Wild 1964, 265). Only one other silk cloth is known from Roman Britain, a lightweight, unpatterned piece from a 4th-century grave at Colchester, a town which then ranked close to London in importance. The cloth, woven from grège (gummed) silk, is considered likely to have come from China (Wild 1984, 20), possibly as the result of bales of cloth being used as currency by merchants from the Far East. Evidence for this practice was obtained from Aurel Stein's excavations at the garrison town of Loulan on the route of the Silk Road to Chinese Turkestan, where a roll of silk cloth dating to the 2nd century was found inscribed in Chinese characters as weighing 708.75 g (25 ozs) and possessing a value of 618 monetary units (Stein 1921, 373–4).

The disintegration and collapse of the Roman empire affected long-distance networks of supply and, although certain commodities from lands bordering the Mediterranean reached the petty kingdoms of Britain, little if any silk seems to have arrived during the 5th and 6th centuries. Indeed, the most elaborately furnished graves in Kent, the kingdom which maintained closest ties with the Continent, lack silk fabrics, unless the strips of gold brocading from women's headdresses could have come from silk braids (Crowfoot & Hawkes 1967, 57). Neither the Taplow barrow burial in Buckinghamshire nor the Sutton Hoo ship burial in Suffolk with their spectacular remains of material wealth yielded any fragments of silk cloth or embroidery, and a few threads of silk, perhaps part of an embroidery on linen, found inside a metal relic box in a child's grave at Updown cemetery, Kent (Crowfoot 1983, 412), is the first archaeological evidence for the presence of silk in 7th-century England, a period when written sources indicate an influx of silk cloth.

One reason for the increased volume of silk fabrics reaching England was the spread of Christianity, which led to improved communications with Rome where supplies of silk cloth were plentiful. Bede records in his *Historia Ecclesiastica gentis Anglorum* that in persuading Edwin, King of Northumbria (616–632), to accept the Christian faith, Pope Boniface V sent him a Byzantine robe (Sherley-Price 1955, 118), which it can be assumed was probably made from, or embroidered in, silk. Rich patrons were also inspired to donate to the church the costliest of worldly goods. Alcuin of York, an 8th-century scholar, refers to gifts of silk wallhangings interwoven with gold that Oswald, King of Northumbria (633–641), presented to the churches he had founded (Dodwell 1982, 129). The demand for silk cloth was not, however, confined to ecclesiastical patronage and by *c.*686 Aldhelm, a West Saxon churchman, described men and women as wearing tunics with silk-trimmed sleeves (Dodwell 1982, 145; Owen-Crocker 1986, 88–90).

Despite these documentary references, the number of early-medieval silk textiles preserved in England is very small. This may be due in part to the pillage of the Vikings, Normans and Protestant zealots, to outbreaks of fire, and to the melting down of gold thread for bullion. The best known are those associated with the relics of St Cuthbert preserved in Durham Cathedral, which span the 7th to early 12th centuries and include fragments of at least 10 different fabrics, in addition to embroideries and braids. They are, to date, supplemented by only one excavated piece dating to before the late 9th century, a cut circle of unpatterned cloth, found among a late 7th- or early 8th-century metalworker's hoard containing other continental items, from Tattersall Thorpe, Lincolnshire (Crowfoot forthcoming B).

In view of the sparse quantity of silk cloths preserved in England dating to the 8th century, it is curious to find that pieces of two silk cloths on the Continent have at times been claimed as Anglo-Saxon. Both are by historical tradition associated with 8th-century English missionaries, sent to convert pagan areas of northern Europe. One cloth, reputed to have been used to wrap the relics of St Lebwin (died *c.*770) and now in the Museum Het Catharijneconvent, Utrecht, depicts the figure of a squat man in trousers with inturned feet and out-turned hands between two half-sectioned trees bedecked with blossom and foliage (Fig 57; Visser 1935). The pattern in white, pale green and brown on a faded yellow or tan ground is oriented towards the selvedge in the manner of many early cloths (King 1981, 96–7), and perhaps was part of a border repeated along all four sides of the cloth. It is a loosely woven 1.2 weft-faced compound twill with a main warp of single ends, except where the ends were occasionally entered double or even in triplicate.

The other cloth, part of the so-called *casula* of St Harlindis and St Relindis, who were sisters and abbesses supposedly consecrated by St Willibrord and St Boniface respectively, forms one of the treasures of the church of St Catherine at Maaseik, Belgium. The cloth, also woven in a 1.2 weft-faced compound twill, has a pattern woven in olive green on a reddish-purple ground composed of rows of circles in the centre of which a king is enthroned holding a sceptre or cross, and is accompanied by the inscription DA/VID in two lines of capitals (Fig 58; Budny 1984, 75–6, fig 2, pl

Fig 57 Patterned silk woven in central Asia and associated with the relics of St Lebwin. Height of fragment 340mm. (Museum Het Catharijneconvent, Utrecht)

I; Budny & Tweddle 1984, 72, pl III; Budny & Tweddle 1985, 367–70, pls LVIII, LXVIb).

Both cloths are crude figurative pieces of a standard of design and execution far below that produced in imperial Byzantine workshops. They are, however, the products of two different centres situated many hundreds of miles apart. The Lebwin cloth, with its silk yarn lacking in any appreciable twist, pale colouring caused by the use of fugitive dyes, and oriental figurative pattern, can be identified with a group of textiles classified as

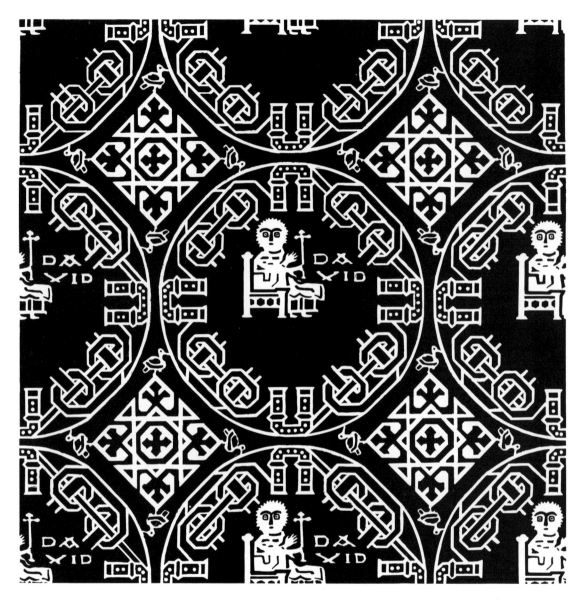

Fig 58   Reconstruction of the pattern on the David silk

Zandanījī II (Shepherd 1981, 107, 119–20), the name referring to a village near Bukhara which is inscribed on one of the cloths. These were produced in workshops in Sogdia (modern Uzbekistan), central Asia, a remote spot close to a path of the Silk Road, which thereby provided a route of communication with the west. Central Asia was, indeed, the source of many silk cloths recorded from early-medieval Europe including England; three of the textiles in St Cuthbert's tomb come from this region (Granger-Taylor 1989A, 311–2), and so too, it seems, does the earliest patterned silk cloth preserved from London (Pritchard 1984, 71). By contrast, the David silk with its Latin inscription was probably produced in western Europe (Budny & Tweddle 1985, 370), but it is extremely unlikely that the workshop was situated in England.

The establishment of a bishopric in London from AD 604 would have attracted gifts of silk furnishings to the City's churches, and in particular to St Paul's Cathedral. No references to any early examples have been traced, but by the early 10th century, when the town's centre of population had shifted back to within the City walls, there is documentary evidence for silken vestments in the will of Theodred, Bishop of London (Dodwell 1982, 152). He apparently bought a white and a yellow chasuble when he visited Pavia in northern Italy during the first half of the 10th century. There are also fragments of silk cloth. These were recovered during the excavation of a 10th-century building and sequence of pits at Milk Street, in the west of the City, in 1976, and comprise six items (Pritchard 1984, 59–63). Four are flat weaves, consisting of two tabby-woven cloths with Z-twisted warp yarn and weft yarn lacking any appreciable twist, a tabby-woven ribbon made partly from grège silk and a 1.2 weft-faced compound twill with the ends of both the main warp and binding warp lacking in twist and with weft threads of red, white and blue. The production centres for these cloths are not limited to one country. The first two, neither of which appear to have been dyed, were perhaps woven in small urban workshops within the Byzantine empire. The ribbon, which would also have been relatively cheap to produce since the yarn is not highly processed, is difficult to assign, but may have been woven somewhere further east because of the absence of twist in the warp. Meanwhile the patterned cloth to which the ribbon was stitched was probably the product of a workshop in central Asia. The other two silk items preserved from 10th-century London are part of a plied cord and braid which were probably manufactured locally from imported thread. These random survivals from London emphasise the long distances over which silk commodities were frequently transported and reveal that silk was available in some quantity in English towns during the 10th century. Other towns, notably York and Winchester, reinforce this impression for they have also yielded a small number of patterned and plain silk fabrics from 10th- and 11th-century deposits (Walton 1989A, 360–61; Crowfoot 1990, 473–4). It is, however, only when the tombs of prelates or the nobility are opened that patterned cloths occur in greater numbers, in accordance with materials preserved in treasuries and shrines.

Neither source, therefore, provides a full representation of the range of silks in circulation; instead they complement each other.

More than one type of loom was employed for weaving the early silk stuffs supplied to England. The drawloom, known to have been in use by the 3rd century AD, was the most complex device (see p 23). Closely associated with this loom in the early-medieval period was the weft-faced compound twill, popularly known as 'samite', which exploited the lustrous quality of silk to advantage by creating a smooth, glossy surface of long weft floats. The earliest examples have only one main end in proportion to each binding end. By the late 8th and early 9th centuries the use of double (or paired) main ends became a common feature of cloths manufactured within Byzantium, the superb 'Earth and Ocean' silk, which was presented to the shrine of St Cuthbert, possibly by King Athelstan in 934, or by King Edmund in 944, up to a century after it was made, being just one of many examples (Flanagan 1956, 57; Higgins 1989, 336–7; Granger-Taylor 1989B, 341; Granger-Taylor 1989C, 155, 162–3). This change has been attributed to the introduction of a wider loom, developed to produce heavier and more luxuriant multi-coloured cloths (Muthesius 1984, 146) as raw silk became more available in the west, and to the use of two rollers for the warp instead of only one, which enabled the tension on the main warp and binding warp to be adjusted separately. A main warp of paired ends was not, however, the prerogative of the Byzantine world and centres in central Asia also produced weft-faced compound twills with this characteristic from at least the 8th century (Shepherd 1981, 119–22). Significant differences in the manner in which the yarn was treated, twisted and dyed, in addition to stylistic qualities, nevertheless, help to distinguish the products of centres in Asia and Mediterranean lands, although sometimes no local peculiarities can as yet be detected to help identify the whereabouts of manufacture. Indeed, widely dispersed workshops in Islamic countries frequently came under the control of a single ruler causing patterns to be copied and assimilated within a surprisingly short space of time.

Less common than samite were geometric and figured twill damasks, whose beauty depended upon subtle pattern effects of contrasting light and dull areas rather than a brilliant palette of colours.

They, like weft-faced compound twills, were a late classical inheritance and it appears both were woven in the same centres, since certain small geometric patterns are common to both types of cloth (Schmedding 1978, 158). Both twill damasks and samite found their way to China, where they were imitated on local looms, but while the weft-faced compound twill remained popular in the west, twill damasks were produced in diminishing numbers by the 8th century and did not return to widespread favour until the late 13th century when they were imported from the Far East at the time of the Pax Mongolica (see p 99).

Another form of cloth construction represented among early-medieval silk textiles in England is the weft-patterned tabby, of which a dalmatic preserved among the relics of St Cuthbert was made (Flanagan 1956, 449–505; Granger-Taylor 1989A, 303–10). The two weft-patterned tabbies used in the dalmatic have geometric patterns formed by the pattern weft being bound by every sixth warp end (Flanagan 1956, 500). The weave is technically less accomplished than drawloom woven cloths and was probably produced on a horizontal loom which had an extra warp roller, a rod controlling preselected ends (every sixth end in this instance), and a series of pattern sticks (Jonghe & Tavernier 1978, 82). Silk weft-patterned tabbies, like many damasks, tended to be monochrome. A later, and more complex, type of weft-patterned tabby is included among the textiles from London (No 458).

By the 10th century new types of monochrome patterned silk fabrics were being produced. These were compound weaves known today as lampas which evolved from weavers experimenting with different bindings on the drawloom. At the same period new types of compound twill began to circulate including a group known as 'incised' twills from the way that the pattern appears to be engraved on the surface of the cloth. This effect was achieved by having two weft yarns of a similar, or almost similar, colour which when they changed position from the face to the reverse side of the cloth caused a break to appear, outlining a pattern in the smooth web. No incised twill has so far been identified from among the few 10th and 11th-century textiles preserved from English contexts — although numerous examples occur in tombs, treasuries and inside bookcovers on the Continent — but an early example of a short-lived

type of lampas, which is technically and stylistically closely related to incised twills, has been recovered from a site in London (No 459).

Another variety of compound twill produced at this period is often referred to as a 'proto-lampas' or 'proto-damask' from the appearance of the contrasting texture of the pattern and the ground. These silks were also produced in monochrome and often have similar patterns to those on incised twills and early lampas-woven cloths. Three fragments of one of these proto-damask cloths were recovered from the tomb of Edward the Confessor (died 1066) when it was opened in Westminster Abbey in 1685 during preparations for the coronation of James II (Dodwell 1982, 162). They are preserved today in the Victoria and Albert Museum and although the fragments are very small the pattern can be reconstructed (Fig 59) from similar patterned cloths recovered from the graves of many 11th- and 12th-century German potentates including Pope Clement II (died 1047) (Müller-Christensen 1960, 65–8, figs 31–8), Archbishop Arnold I of Trier (died 1183) (Kendrick 1925, 42, 52, no 1023; Wilckens 1987, 65, fig 4), and Philip of Swabia (died 1208) (Müller-Christensen *et al*. 1972, figs 1512–13). From this distribution it can be inferred that these textiles were originally diplomatic gifts, and it has been argued that King Edward received his as a coronation gift from a Byzantine emperor in 1043 (Ciggaar 1982, 90).

Sources of supply in the 12th to 14th centuries

Byzantium was a renowned centre of silk weaving in the early-medieval period but its importance as a source of supply to England diminished even before the fall of Constantinople in 1204, giving way to the products of Islamic Spain. A cloth patterned with what appears to be a pair of large dove-like birds, which was recovered from a deposit in London dating to *c*.1330–40, is the only patterned fabric catalogued here for which a Byzantine origin can possibly be argued (No 139), although a source in Spain is perhaps more probable.

The 12th and 13th centuries were marked by an increasing use of metal thread in silk cloths. Often this was used as a brocading thread to emphasise

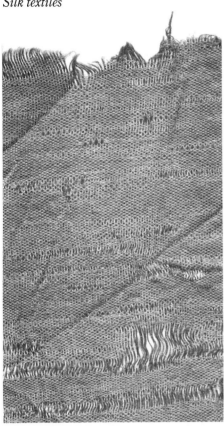

Figure 62 Shot silk cloth woven from yarn without any twist, No 320, from a late 14th-century deposit. There are twice as many threads per cm in one system. Scale 2:1

Fig 63 Silk cloths woven from Z-twisted warp yarn and weft yarn without appreciable twist, Nos 326 and 327, from a late 14th-century deposit. They have been stitched together with the warp of one piece running vertically and that of the other horizontally; the stripes on the cloths are due to the twist in the warp (see Fig 124A for a detail of the seam). Scale 1:4

much subtler effect and this led to the term 'changeable' being applied to shot taffeta and sarsinet in the 15th century.

Tabbies woven from Z-twisted warp yarn and weft yarn lacking appreciable twist

Most of the tabby-woven silks included here have a warp yarn which is Z-twisted and a weft yarn that lacks any appreciable twist (Figs 63 and 64). There are four from late 13th-century deposits and 46 from 14th-century deposits. All are lightweight fabrics usually with a slightly greater number of ends per cm than picks, and some have a more open texture than others. The warp yarn is generally finer than the weft, because of the twist put into it. Seventeen of these textiles preserve one of their selvedges (Table 10). All are strengthened with at least one edge cord. Next to an edge cord

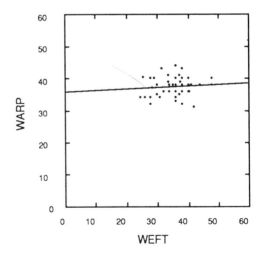

Fig 64 Scatter diagram showing the thread density of silk tabbies woven from Z-twisted warp yarn and weft yarn without twist based on 48 examples

Table 10 Selvedges on silk tabbies woven from
Z-twisted warp yarn and weft yarn without twist

Cat. No	No of threads per cm warp/weft	Description of selvedge
Late 13th century		
417	?/28	edge cord of *c.* 4 ends, 1 pair of ends and 8 singles in 1mm.
418	38/38	edge cord of *c.* 8 ends
419	38/44	edge cord of 4 ends and 8 singles in 1mm
Second quarter 14th century		
33	34/28	edge cord of 4 ends, 1 pair of ends and 6 singles in 1mm
69	36/40	edge cord of 13 ends
134	38/30	edge cord of 6 ends and 8 singles in 2mm
135	38/41	edge cord of 4 ends and 4 singles in 1mm
447	31/42	edge cord of *c.* 8 ends and 6 singles in 1mm
448	38–42/28	edge cord of *c.* 6 ends, cord of 3 ends, 1 pair of ends and 28 singles in 5mm
Last quarter 14th century		
322	35/30	15 pairs of ends in 4mm
323	36/32	8 edge cords of 2–3 ends in 3mm (Pl 14A)
324	38/34	2 edge cords of 6 ends
325	36/38	5 edge cords of 2–4 ends (Fig 65)
326	38/35	5 edge cords of 2 ends, 2 singles, 1 pair of ends (Figs 63, 124A)
327	40/36	2 edge cords of 8–10 ends (Figs 63, 124A)
328	40/29	8 edge cords of 2–3 ends (i.e. 3,2,2,2,3,3,2,3)
Unstratified		
395	38/48	incomplete (Fig 143B)

Fig 65 Silk cloth woven from Z-twisted warp yarn
and weft yarn without any appreciable twist, No 325,
from a late 14th-century deposit. (A) cloth, note the
slubs in the weft, scale 1:1, (B) detail of selvedge,
scale 5:1

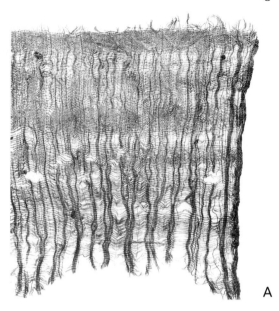

A

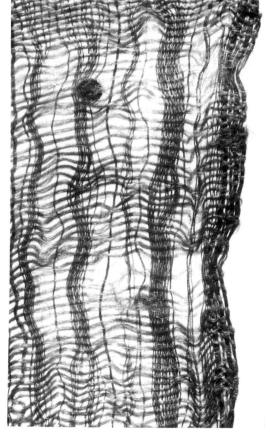

B

is usually a narrow width of very closely spaced ends, occasionally with a pair of ends in between (e.g. No 417). Sometimes a selvedge has a second cord or, more often, a sequence of cords used for reinforcement (Nos 323–328, Table 10, Fig 65, Pl 14A). The latter are more common on cloths discarded in the late 14th century in London, but, at present, the number of textiles is too small to prove that this has any significance either for the date or place of manufacture. The cloths from late 13th- and 14th-century London deposits are, nevertheless, distinguishable from those in use in England during the 10th and 11th centuries which were frequently made into headdresses. These are not as fine as the later medieval fabrics and have reinforced selvedges made from a series of paired ends, which often number around 40 pairs (Muthesius 1982B, 132–6; Pritchard 1984, 60–61; Walton 1989A, 360–63).

Sixteen cloths were tested for dyes including two facings that remained stitched to woollen fabrics. Three proved to have been dyed with the insect dye kermes, three with madder, including one which was combined with a yellow dye, and two with unidentified dyestuffs, one possibly a lichen giving a bluish-purple dye and the other a red dye. Eight gave negative results, and seven of these are stained the golden-brown which in silk fabrics is often indicative of undyed cloth. Despite the discoloration that these textiles have undergone in the soil, enough of the original tint is preserved to provide a guide to their colours. Two of the cloths dyed with kermes appear to have been pale pinkish-mauve rather than a deeper shade of red; the hue of the third piece is less easy to determine but it was probably a darker tint. The cloths dyed with madder also show variations of colour intensity ranging from tomato-red (No 323, Pl 14A) to dark crimson. Unlike patterned silks at this period, some of these plain cloths may have been piece dyed (King & King 1988, 75).

Most cloths of this type found in London preserve traces of stitching and they appear often to have been used as linings or facings to woollen garments. Thus the silk facings for buttonholes (Nos 32–34, 64, 67, 68, 159, Figs 135–138), 142, 163), a buttoned edge (No 395, Fig 143B), eyelets (No 329, Fig 138), an armhole (No 78, Fig 131) and a neck opening (No 50, Pl 2B) are all of this type, as are two linings covered with rows of stitching (Nos 35, 136, Figs 151, 152). The colour of these

silk facings and linings is consistently golden-yellow or pale brown and it is doubtful if any were dyed; two examples tested yielded negative results (Nos 33, 67). Contemporary inventories and wardrobe accounts indicate that it was common among the upper classes for a garment to be lined with a silk fabric, such as tartaryn or taffeta, which was dyed a similar colour to the rest of the garment. Linings of a contrasting colour also found favour and among the long gowns listed as belonging to Thomas, Duke of Gloucester, at the time of his downfall in 1397 was one of blue cloth lined with white tartaryn which was valued at 23s. 8d. (Dillon & St John Hope 1897, 304).

Tabbies woven from Z-twisted yarn

Eight silk tabbies from late 14th-century deposits in London are woven from yarn that is all Z-spun. The yarn has a heavy twist giving the cloth the appearance of crêpe. None of the silk yarn appears to have been dyed but this remains to be confirmed by dye analysis since only one has been tested. The fabrics have a thread density of between 48 and 60 ends and 42 and 52 picks per cm although the openness of the web has caused the threads to bunch together in areas. Selvedges are preserved on two pieces and both are characterised by a series of paired ends, 26 pairs in a width of 6.5mm on one cloth and 70 pairs in a width of 14mm on the other which was folded double and hemmed (No 331, Fig 66).

Fig 66 Silk cloth woven from Z-twisted yarn, No 331, from a late 14th-century deposit. The selvedge consists of paired ends and has been folded double to form a hem. Scale 1:1

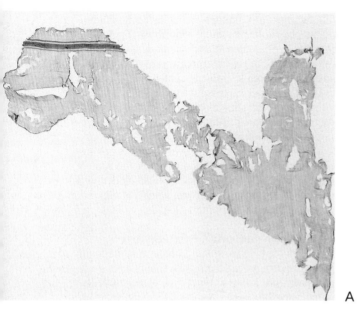

A

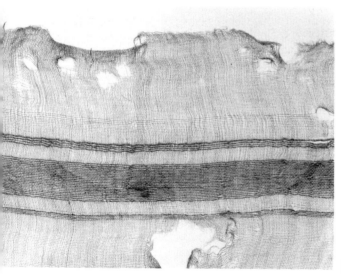

B

Fig 67   Silk tabby with self-patterned bands No 332: from a late 14th-century deposit: (A) cloth, scale 1:4, (B) detail, scale 2:1

dence for their use as head veils since tiny scraps of a cloth of this type are preserved along the edge of a contemporary silk-bound wire headdress frame (Egan & Pritchard 1991, fig 195). A veil made from similar tightly twisted Z-spun yarn is associated with a reliquary of the Virgin Mary in the church of St Verena, Zurzach, Switzerland, and appears to correspond with one referred to in an inventory of 1347 (Schmedding 1978, 310–11, no 295). This cloth, which measures 720mm x 235mm, was at one time considered to have been woven from byssus, a filament obtained from a species of mollusc (*Pinna nobilis*) common in the Mediterranean which was referred to by Arab merchants as 'sea-wool' (Geijer 1979, 13). Analysis, however, indicated that the fibre is silk, like those discussed here. Similar lightweight veils in balanced tabby bindings have been identified from other ecclesiastical centres in Switzerland (Schmedding 1978, 194, 197, 290–91, nos 167, 172, 274), and these include one which preserves its complete loomwidth of 460mm (18 ins). Other veils woven from Z-spun yarn with loomwidths of between 210mm and 230mm are preserved from late 10th- and 11th-century deposits in Dublin (Heckett 1987, 161; Pritchard 1988, 156) but none of them are as fine as the cloths from 14th-century London.

Tabby-woven cloths with self-patterned bands

Three of the lightest and finest silk tabbies are patterned with a series of weft-faced bands. Two of the pieces have three bands, a wide one flanked by two narrower ones near one end, and the third was probably similar with one narrow band now missing (Figs 67, 68, 129). These bands would probably have been repeated at the opposite end of the cloth, and as well as being decorative they would have marked the border of the fabric when it was on the loom. The main weave is woven from very fine yarn with a slight Z-twist. while the bands are woven from thicker yarn which has some slubs in it. One piece (No 334) apparently had traces of gold on the main weave when it was excavated but these are no longer in evidence. The similarity of these textiles suggests that they were woven in a workshop which specialised in their output.

In view of the open texture of the cloth, which makes it transparent, it is not surprising that none of these silks appears to have been used as a garment facing, in contrast to many of the fabrics that are Z-spun in the warp only. Instead there is evi-

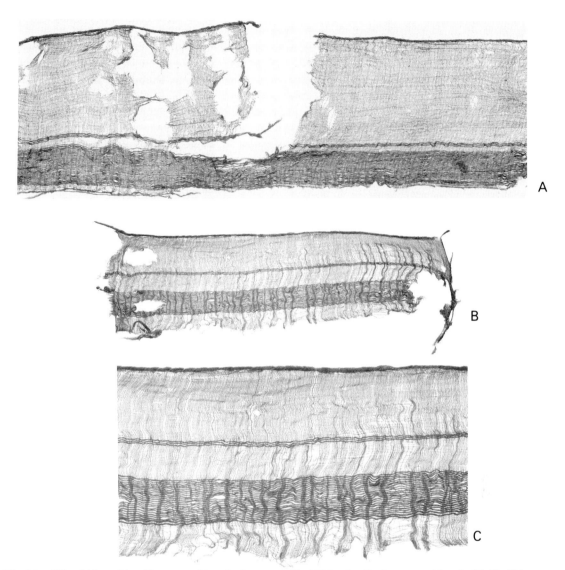

Fig 68   Silk tabbies with self-patterned bands, from a late 14th-century deposit: (A) No 333, scale 1:1 (see Fig 129 for detail of weave and hem), (B) No 334, scale 1:1, (C) detail, scale 2:1

Selected catalogue III

Last quarter 14th century
332 Dimensions: h 280mm, w 350mm
    Warp: silk, slight Z-twist, 58–62 ends per cm
    Weft: (i) silk, slight Z-twist, 52 picks per cm
         (ii) silk, slight Z-twist, coarser than (i),
            44 picks per cm

Pattern: 14mm main weave
    4 throws weft (ii)
    10 throws weft (i)
    23 throws (5mm) weft (ii)
    10 throws weft (i)
    4 throws weft (ii)
Fig 67

333 Dimensions: h 43mm, w 170mm
  Warp: silk, Z-twist, 58–61 ends per cm
  Weft: (i) silk, Z-twist, 65–72 picks per cm
       (ii) silk, slight Z-twist, coarser than (i),
          34 picks per cm
  Pattern: 28mm main weave
       3 throws weft (ii)
       11 throws weft (i)
       34 throws (10mm) weft (ii)
       11 throws weft (i)
       2 throws weft (ii) (incomplete)
  Figs 68A, 129

334 Dimensions: h 27mm, w 98mm
  Warp: silk, Z-twist, 62 ends per cm
  Weft: (i) silk, slight Z-twist, 60 picks per cm
       (ii) silk, slight Z-twist, coarser than (i),
          42 picks per cm
  Pattern: 10mm main weave
       3 throws weft (ii)
       24 throws (4.5mm) weft (i)
       24 throws (6mm) weft (ii)
       22 throws weft (i) (incomplete)
  Fig 68B and C

Tabby-woven cloth with band in 1.3 twill

Striped silk cloths became increasingly popular in western Europe throughout the 13th century. They ranged from narrow pinstripes in alternating colours to wide bands patterned with animals and Kufic or Naskhi script incorporating metal thread and as many as six different colours of silk yarn. The luxuriance of these fabrics meant that in Spain, where a large number were woven, the Christian kings issued decrees prohibiting them to be worn by all but the highest ranking persons (May 1957, 108). Many striped materials were thick cloths woven in compound twill, but thinner pieces were also produced, and these have withstood deterioration less successfully.

One fragment of a thin silk cloth with transverse stripes was recovered from a late 14th-century deposit in London. The main weave in a tabby binding has faded to a pale pinkish-mauve tint, while the band, 23mm deep, is composed of three weft-faced twill stripes woven in white silk thread (Fig 69, Pl 14B). Two other stripes alternated with the twill-patterned ones but their character is uncertain owing to the decay of the weft threads in

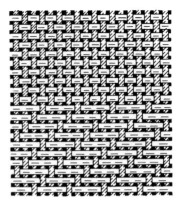

Fig 69 Weave diagram of a tabby-woven cloth patterned with a band in 1.3 twill, No 335, from a late 14th-century deposit

both these areas. The likelihood is that they were woven in metal thread or a cellulose fibre, probably flax, but an alternative possibility is that the mordant used to dye the thread may have weakened the yarn and made it more susceptible to photochemical decay. That the missing yarn was metallic or coloured seems probable owing to its juxtaposition with white silk and this argues against the use of linen thread, which was frequently left undyed. As will be described below, similar cloths preserved in treasuries often include green stripes or have a green ground. Since this colour was frequently produced using an iron mordant, which is notorious for causing silk fibres to disintegrate, it is suggested that the missing yarn could have been green silk.

Horizontal bands woven in 1.3 twill were a feature of many lightweight silk cloths in the 14th century, although few in cathedral treasuries associated with relics can be closely dated. Examples of cloths similar to the London one include part of a reliquary cover in the Abbey of St Maurice, Switzerland. It is of almost identical weight and has twill-woven bands in five colours — blue, pale green, white, red and yellow, extending to a width of 30mm on a red tabby ground (Schmedding 1978, 195, no 169). In addition, among the medieval furnishings and vestments from the Marienkirche, Gdansk, is a chasuble in a white Chinese twill damask lined with a violet silk patterned with twill bands in white, pale red and green; another silk lining has a sequence of white, blue and red twill bands on a green ground (Mannowsky 1938, V, 27, 34, nos 73, 123, fig 25). A further cloth, which was used to edge a funeral pall from this church in Gdansk, has a green tabby ground patterned with white, pale blue, red and yellow bands 55mm wide woven in 1.3 warp-chevron twill (Mannowsky 1938, V, 16, no 11, fig 25). As for fragments from town excavations, a piece was recovered from a deposit in Lübeck provisionally dated to the 15th century (Tidow 1987, 194, fig 2). An example preserved in the library of Canterbury Cathedral is rather differently coloured since it has a brown, white and red band 23mm wide in 1.3 weft-chevron twill on a yellow tabby ground (Robinson & Urquhart 1934, 181, no 10d). A characteristic of these cloths, which can be more easily discerned from the examples which have not been buried in the soil, is the subtle shot appearance of the main weave caused by using a main weft of a slightly different tint from that of the warp.

The importance of such striped silk cloth should not be overlooked, even though only one fragment has been recovered from the London excavations, since cloths of this character may have acted as a design source for the distinctive horizontal striped wool cloths found in greater abundance in 14th-century deposits in the City (see p 52–68). Striped silk fabrics were often used as linings for secular clothing as well as vestments in northern Europe and for furnishings, particularly bedhangings. These hangings are often described as torn in inventories, presumably from the strain put on the silk fibres (Dillon & St John Hope 1897, 54). The fragment from London therefore serves as a valuable pointer to what some of these striped fabrics actually looked like.

Selected catalogue IV

Last quarter 14th century
335 Dimensions: h 75mm, w 30mm. Cut, rectangular fragment
Weave: tabby with a weft-faced band in 1.3 twill, Z-diagonal
Warp: silk, faded mauve, Z-twist, 38 ends per cm
Weft: (i) silk, faded mauve, no visible twist, 32 picks per cm
      (ii) silk, natural white, no visible twist, *c*.40 picks per cm
      (iii) (decayed)

Width of band: 23mm
Pattern: 18 throws (4mm) white
      5 mm (decayed)
    21 throws (5mm) white
      5 mm (decayed)
    16 throws (4mm) white
Pl 14B

Weft-patterned tabby

Two fragments of a lightweight silk cloth woven in weft-patterned tabby were found in the fill of a cesspit dating to the second half of the 14th century at Dukes Place. The cloth appears to have one warp and two wefts, one forming the ground and the other the pattern (Figs 70, 71). The length of the weft floats are irregular and it is uncertain whether the piece was woven on a drawloom or on a loom with multiple pattern rods. The development of cloths with this type of weave has been traced from late classical antiquity to the medieval period (Flanagan 1956, 497–9; Jonghe & Tavernier 1978), but the multiplicity of different types of weft-patterned tabbies in the 11th, 12th and 13th centuries has not been examined in any depth. Here the small scale pattern, which consists of a saltire cross infilled with tiny lozenges, has a repeat only 20mm in width and height. The yarn is not of a consistently high quality and occasionally there are slubs in the ground weft. Similar weft-patterned tabbies, including cloths brocaded in gold thread with inscriptions in Arabic, have been attributed to workshops in Spain (Nockert & Lundwall 1986, 71, no 28).

Selected catalogue V

Second half 14th century
458 Dimensions: (i) h 145mm, w 57mm; (ii) h 60mm, w 45mm. Both ragged
Weave: tabby with supplementary pattern weft
Repeat: h 20mm, w 20mm
Warp: Silk, Z-twist, 45 ends per cm
Wefts: proportion, 1:1
Ground weft: silk, no visible twist, 44 picks per cm
Pattern weft: silk, no visible twist, 44 passes per cm
Dyestuffs: warp and ground weft, ? indigotin and a red dyestuff (too weak to identify)
Figs 70, 71

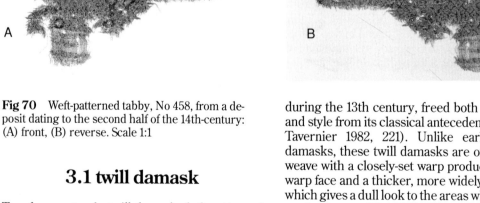

A   B

Fig 70   Weft-patterned tabby, No 458, from a deposit dating to the second half of the 14th-century: (A) front, (B) reverse. Scale 1:1

3.1 twill damask

Two fragments of a twill damask cloth patterned with small, stylised peonies (Fig 72A), were recovered from the deposit at BC72 dating to the second quarter of the 14th century. The cloth belongs to a type of damask which evolved in China during the 13th century, freed both in technique and style from its classical antecedents (Jonghe & Tavernier 1982, 221). Unlike earlier western damasks, these twill damasks are of unbalanced weave with a closely-set warp producing a glossy warp face and a thicker, more widely spaced weft which gives a dull look to the areas where the weft predominates (Fig 72B). There is no apparent consistency in the cloths as to whether the warp or the weft areas form the pattern; on the London cloth the warp face of the twill forms the ground.

At least 16 of these cloths are known from

A

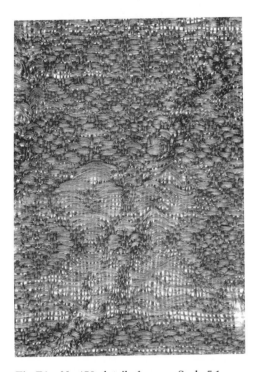

Fig 71 No 458, detail of weave. Scale 5:1

B

Fig 72 3.1 twill damask with a pattern of peonies, No 138, from a deposit dating to the second quarter of the 14th century: (A) front, with hem along bottom edge, (B) detail of weave, scale 5:1

northern Europe. One, in reddish-purple silk patterned with cloud scrolls symbolising immortality, was made into a dalmatic for the Holy Roman Emperor, and is preserved in the Weltliche Schatzkammer, Vienna (Jonghe & Tavernier 1982, 217, fig 16, 228, fig 33). Others were used for chasubles, altar frontals and reliquary bags in churches and cathedrals in Finland, Sweden, Poland, Germany, The Netherlands and Belgium. Only two other examples with English associations have been recognised. One, formerly in St Leonard's Church, Catworth, Huntingdonshire, is an orphrey made from a buff-coloured damask, and is embroidered in *opus anglicanum* with heraldic shields displaying the arms of Clinton and Leybourne (Christie 1938, 164; Jonghe & Tavernier 1982, 216, 230, table 3). These arms enable the orphrey to be linked with William de Clinton, a boyhood companion of Edward III, who married Juliana de Leybourne in 1329. The other, incorporated into the back of an orphrey embroidered in a style which can be dated to c.1330 to 1350 (King 1963, 46, no 101), is also a faded buff colour, and is patterned with sprays of flowers, probably peonies. Both pieces, therefore, provide corroborative evidence for the presence of such cloth in England during the first half of the 14th century.

Evidence from China for the production of the cloth in the 13th century comes from the tomb of Huang Sheng, a 17-year-old girl who died in 1243. She was the daughter of the supervisor of foreign trade in Quanzhou, Fujian (Fukien) Province, and the wife of a minor member of the imperial family. Because of her high status she was buried in lavish style with a complete wardrobe of clothes and household items. Among the enormous variety of silk goods were twill damasks including one patterned with peonies and another with branches of plum blossom (Fujian Sheng Bowuguan 1982, pls 54, 55).

The patterns of the damasks with mythical birds and beasts of the Orient, cloud scrolls and assorted flowers and foliage frequently disposed in an asymmetrical manner, offer a vivid contrast to textiles produced in Europe in the late 13th and early 14th centuries. The peonies represented on the London textile have an unrealistic wavy outline of curling leaves, a form of ornament that persisted for many centuries in the Far East (Rawson 1984, 85–6) and which was used as decoration on wide range of artefacts, including metalwork, lacquerwork and porcelain, as well as on embroidered and woven textiles. The colours of the oriental cloths also display a different palette from those produced in western centres, and the tints of pink, turquoise, orange and green were to have almost as an important influence on the colouring of textiles, particularly those produced in Italian cities from the second quarter of the 14th century, as the exotic patterns were to have on cloth design. Dye tests indicated the presence of two dyestuffs on the twill damask from London, a red dye and a yellow one. The red dye is madder,

while the plant from which the yellow dye was extracted remains unidentified. All the yarn appears to have been dyed alike for the London cloth, presumably resulting in an orange-red hue. There are, however, some examples of these damasks woven from warp and weft yarn of contrasting colours which throw up the pattern more clearly.

The presence of such an exotic silk in 14th-century London is not surprising. The establishment of the Mongol empire in Asia not only led to the reopening of trade routes with the Far East during the 13th century but also inspired a vogue for oriental dress, particularly among Italian princes as shown by the exotic burial robes of Cangrande della Scala, the overlord of Verona (died 1329) (Magagnato 1983). The impact of renewed contact with the east was less marked in England although it impressed the popular imagination sufficiently for William Langland, a 14th-century satirist, to portray Charity in his book *Piers Ploughman* as preferring 'clean rich robes of cobweb lawn and cloth of Tartary' (Goodridge 1966, 186, book XV), while at a tournament held in Cheapside in 1331 Edward III and his courtiers were dressed in the style of Tartars *'et ad similitudinem Tartarorum larvati'* (Safford 1928, 112). *Pannus de Tars*, a name implying cloth of an Asian origin, had been bought for the Great Wardrobe on several occasions before this event (Monnas 1989, 294, 302) and it is specified also in some 14th-century wills and inventories, including the will of William le Peyntour de Derby, a London notary, who bequeathed a small psalter covered with cloth of Tars to his daughter's son, Antonine, in 1354 (Cal Wills II, 681). Significantly, on three occasions in the opening decade of the 14th century, Tartar princes ruling in the western dominions of the Mongol empire sent envoys to Europe to gain support in a bid to drive the Mamelukes out of Palestine. These Mongol ambassadors were received at the English court by Edward I in 1300 and 1303, and by Edward II in 1307 (Hornstein 1941, 413–14). Clearly these diplomatic missions provided an opportunity for silk cloths from the Far East to be exchanged as gifts along with porcelain, which is also encountered in English households of the 14th century (Whitehouse 1972, 66).

Selected catalogue VI

Fig 74   1.2 weft-
faced compound twill
patterned with a pair
of birds wearing col-
lars, No 139, from a
deposit dating to the
second quarter of the
14th century: (A)
front, (B) detail of
weave, scale 5:1

Second quarter 14th century

138 Dimensions: (i) h 62mm, w 140mm; (ii) h 27mm,
  w 32mm. Both fragments have traces of a
  single-folded hem sewn with two-ply silk
  thread along one edge
  Weave: 3.1 twill damask. Ground 3.1 twill, S-diag-
  onal; pattern 1.3 twill, Z-diagonal
  Warp: silk, stained dark reddish-brown, strong
  Z-twist, 80 ends per cm. Decoupure 4 ends
  Weft: silk, stained dark-reddish brown, no visible
  twist, 27 picks per cm. Decoupure 2 picks
  Dyestuffs: madder and an unidentified yellow dye
  Fig 72

1.2 weft-faced compound twills

The three 1.2 weft-faced compound twills included
in this study were found in deposits dating to the
14th century. Two patterned pieces were recovered from a deposit of the second quarter of
the 14th century and a plain fabric from a deposit
of *c.*1380–1400. All three cloths have a main warp
of doubled silk thread (Fig 73) but otherwise they
have little in common.

A

Fig 73   Structure of a 1.2 weft-faced compound twill
with paired main ends shown from the front; the upper section shows an expanded view

The oldest is probably a piece patterned with a
pair of birds (No 139, Fig 74). Only part of the
repeat is preserved showing the outline of a bird,
possibly a dove or a parrot, in profile with its mir-

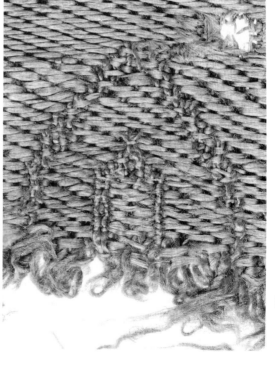

B

ror image beside it. From this it can be deduced that pairs of facing birds, more than 90mm in height, were woven in horizontal rows across the cloth. The original colours of the silk yarns have faded but the bird's pouting breast retains a tinge of pink, and a green or yellow band encircles its eye and forms a collar round its neck. The wing

and tail feathers are less distinct but the bird is clearly perched in a sitting position. It is not known whether the birds were enclosed within a frame or roundel, for although these were common they were not universal (see, for example, Chartraire 1911, 389, no 43; Herrmann & Langenstein 1987, 216–17, no M143).

Large bird patterns were popular in the 10th to early 14th centuries and they occur in many different types of binding. Examples bound in weft-faced compound twill include a large number of eagle silks such as those preserved in Brixen Cathedral, Austria, and the shroud of St Germain

Fig 75   Detail of 1.2 weft-faced compound twill woven from silk and silver thread, No 140, from a deposit dating to the second quarter of the 14th century. Scale 5:1

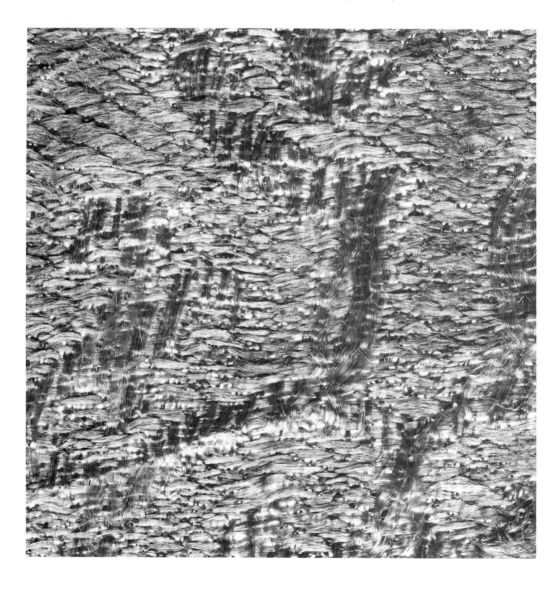

at Auxerre, France (Kendrick 1925, 38–9), which were mass-produced in Byzantium for gifts to the German emperor and his court. Pairs of large, facing birds were also common on Spanish cloths in the 12th century (Shepherd 1957, 378; Muthesius 1982A, 82–3) and others have been attributed to Sicily. The original source of the London fragment is, therefore, uncertain.

The other patterned piece was originally a sumptuous cloth of silver (No 140, Pl 15A). The metal thread in which the pattern was woven was used as a continuous weft throughout the web and was not restricted to small areas of brocading. Very little of this thread is preserved but tiny fragments are visible under magnification. Analysis of the surface of the thread by XRF shows that the metal is silver, *c.*98% pure with *c.*2% copper and only traces of gold, lead and zinc. The thin strips of silver appear to have been S-twisted round a core which has disintegrated in the soil. This suggests that the core was a cellulose fibre, probably linen or hemp. Two other pattern wefts were used in the cloth. One, perhaps originally purple, formed the ground and a finer thread outlined the silver pattern. The silk yarn used for the main warp and binding warp is extremely fine and lacks any appreciable twist (Fig 75).

Only a small part of the pattern is preserved, from which it can be estimated that the repeat was greater than 125mm in height and breadth. It consists of stylised palmettes placed one above another enclosed within circular frames from which sprout trefoil tendrils. A second plant motif is missing but there is no evidence for any animal or figurative elements within the design.

No close parallel to this cloth has been traced but the details of its construction and pattern enable its time and whereabouts of production to be narrowed down. The use of a continuous pattern weft of silver suggests that it is unlikely to have been woven before the 12th century, although the lack of surviving textiles may give a false bias; cloths of silver are recorded in much earlier inventories, including the *Liber Pontificalis*, which records gifts of cloth of silver woven in Islamic Spain that were presented to Pope Gregory IV (827–844) (May 1957, 3). While metal thread was easily traded, silver thread is less often mentioned than gold thread. Silver mines in Spain meant that there was no genuine shortage of the metal despite a so-called 'silver famine' (Watson 1967, 2–7),

and weavers were not dependent on melted bullion. Warp yarn without twist was not common among textiles woven in the west and rules out a Byzantine source for it, but it appears sometimes to have been used by Arab weavers in the 12th century and also in newly established weaving centres in Italy where standards of production varied considerably (Tietzel 1984, nos 12, 14, 18, 19, 27, 29, 34). The plant scroll pattern of the cloth shows Islamic influence. It is reminiscent of stucco decoration, carved ivories and metalwork from the palace of Abd al-Rahman III at Madinat al-Zahra, southern Spain, which was built in 936 and was influenced by Syrian models (Talbot-Rice 1975, pl 76; Smith 1976, no 486). Similar stylised palmettes were often used to decorate the borders of medallions on polychrome samites and other patterned silks woven in Byzantium as well as in Islamic centres in the 11th and early 12th centuries (e.g. Falke 1913, I, nos 193, 194, 197, 199; Shepherd 1951, 75), but the ornament was long-lived and on its own is not a useful dating feature. Overall the evidence points to an Islamic workshop operating in the 12th or early 13th centuries and probably situated in southern Spain.

The third 1.2 weft-faced compound twill is an unpatterned strip of cloth that appears to have been used as a garter (No 336, Fig 76). The smooth surface of the cloth, the result of it having a high density of weft threads, meant that similar materials were popular as ground fabrics for embroidery in England until the early 14th century when velvet was preferred.

Selected catalogue VII

Second quarter 14th century
139 Dimensions: h 150mm, w 56mm. Rectangular
    fragment with cut edges
    Weave: 1.2 weft-faced compound twill, at least 2
      pattern wefts, S-diagonal
    Warp: proportions, one pair of main ends to each
      binding end
    Main warp: silk, strong Z-twist, 15 pairs per cm
    Binding warp: silk, strong Z-twist, 15 ends per cm
    Weft: (i) silk, pale pink, no visible twist
        (ii) silk, greenish-yellow, no visible twist
        34–35 passes per cm
    Fig 74

140 Dimensions: h 135mm, w 55mm. Rectangular
       fragment with cut edges
       Weave: 1.2 weft-faced compound twill, three pat-
       tern wefts, S-diagonal
       Warp: proportions, one pair of main ends to each
       binding end
       Main warp: silk, no visible twist, 12 pairs per cm
       Binding warp: silk, no visible twist, 12 ends per
       cm
       Weft: (i) silk, no visible twist
             (ii) silk, no visible twist, finer than (i)
             (iii) silver filé, S-twisted round a core of a
                   cellulose fibre
             21 passes per cm
       Fig 75, Pl 15A

Fig 76   Unpatterned 1.2 weft-faced compound twill
used as a garter, No 336, from a late 14th-century deposit. Scale 3:4

336 Dimensions: (i) h 10mm, w 430mm; (ii) h 7mm, w
       65mm, sewn to (i) and tied in a knot
       Weave: 1.2 weft-faced compound twill, S-diagonal
       Warp: proportions, one pair of main ends to each
       binding end
       Main warp: silk, Z-twist, golden-brown, 19 pairs
       per cm
       Binding warp: silk, Z-twist, golden-brown, 19 ends
       per cm
       Weft: silk, no visible twist, pale crimson, 50 passes
       per cm
       Fig 76

1.3 weft-faced compound twill

One delicate silk tissue is woven in a distinctive 1.3
compound twill (No 398, Fig 77). Wide-spaced
single main warp ends give the cloth its lightweight texture while the gum was removed from
the weft yarn in such a manner as to make it
slightly fluffy. Five small pieces of the cloth have
been stitched together with silk thread which is
single rather than plied (see p152) to form what
originally appears to have been the top section of a
pouch. The opening has a single folded edge and
was finished with two tablets that were given quarter turns. Across one of the five silk scraps runs a
horizontal band bound in tabby which uses a pattern weft of a darker orange-brown hue (Fig 77B).
Like the paler-coloured weft used for the rest of
the cloth, the orange-brown yarn gave a negative
result when tested for dyes. A peculiar feature of
the band is that the tabby weave is bound by the
threads of the main warp as well as by those of the
binding warp (Fig 78). Apart from the band which
may be part of a starting border, the cloth does not
appear to be patterned but this may simply reflect
the small size of the fragments.

Lightweight cloths woven in a similar 1.3 weft-
faced compound twill, have been recorded from
various church treasuries and museum collections on the Continent (Errera 1927, nos 15, 21;

Fig 77   1.3 weft-faced compound twill with single
main ends and a band in tabby weave, No 398, from a
late 13th-century deposit: (A) pieces of the cloth
made into a pouch and finished with a tablet-woven
edge, scale 1:1, (B) detail of tabby-woven band, scale
5:1

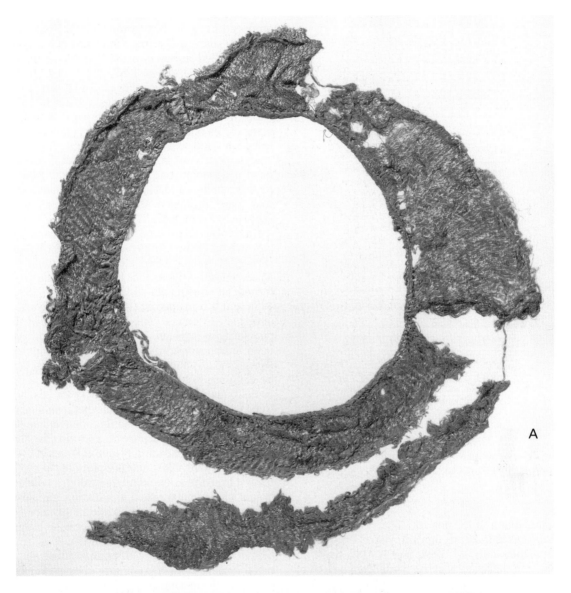

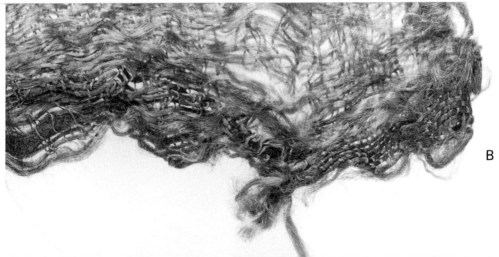

Fig 78 Weave of No 398 shown from the front; the upper section shows an expanded view

Schmedding 1978, nos 31, 156a, 156b, 249–53; Wilckens 1981, 287–8, figs 3, 4; Tietzel 1984, nos 4, 15; Ceulmans *et al.* 1988, nos 17, 18), while in England there is a seal bag made from a cloth of this type, which is attached to a letter dating to between 1144 and 1168, preserved in Westminster Abbey (WAM 2455). All the cloths have approximately 13 to 16 main ends per cm and 13 to 16 binding ends per cm, and many have a Z-diagonal to the wale of the twill as on the example from London. The colours used for them are pale red, yellow, white and blue and many appear to have faded. In addition the example excavated in London shows that weft bands were sometimes introduced in a contrasting binding as well as in contrasting colours.

It has been argued that cloths of this type were produced in Spain (Schmedding 1978, 265) and that they share similarities with a distinctive type of cloth called *pannus de arista* in medieval documents (Desrosiers *et al.* 1989, 223, fn 10). *Arista* was a classical Latin term for an ear of corn; during the medieval period it was applied to fishbones, and the relevance of the word was that many cloths of this type have a herringbone patterned ground weave (King 1968, 29). A recent study of cloths of arista suggests that a special form of drawloom, one without shafts, was used in their production and it appears that a similar loom may have produced these 1.3 twills as well (Desrosiers *et al.* 1989, 220–21, fn 10).

Cloth of arista is recorded in England from the last quarter of the 12th century — Gilbert Foliot, Bishop of London (died 1188), gave two pieces patterned with griffons to St Paul's Cathedral to be turned into vestments (Sparrow Simpson 1887, 495), and it remained in use at court for liveries until 1330 (Monnas 1989, 291). The peak of its popularity in England, however, appears to have been in the second quarter of the 13th century (King 1968, 27) and details of its use and cost can be glimpsed from court rolls of this period. Two cloths bought from Adam de Basing for 26s. 5d. were used to make and embellish various vestments including a chasuble, amice, stole, maniples, cuffs and orphreys, and also for the border of a hat for Edward, Prince of Wales in 1247 (CLR, 1245–1251, 123). Another piece of the cloth bought from the same Adam de Basing, a London draper who often supplied silk textiles and vestments to Henry III, cost 14s., while an unspecified number of cloths purchased from Gerard le Bas in 1250 cost £14 8s, (CLR, 1245–1251, 194, 286). Textiles from English and Scottish excavations show that the use of cloth of arista spread beyond court circles. A drawstring pouch thrown away in the medieval town ditch at Aldersgate and recovered during building work in 1932 is made from a cloth of arista patterned with swans, fleur-de-lis and triple-towered castles on a lattice-patterned ground (Ward Perkins 1940, 161, fig 49), and three fragments of another cloth with pairs of addorsed birds on a lozenge-patterned ground were found at Kirk Close, Perth (Muthesius 1987, 167–71, no 29). Loosely woven 1.3 weft-faced compound twills appear to have a corresponding date range and the disposal of the tattered London pouch in the third quarter of the 13th century indicates that these fabrics were not as hardwearing as many other figured cloths.

Selected catalogue VIII

Late 13th century
398 Dimensions: (i) h 40mm, w 78mm; (ii) h 25mm, w 45mm; (iii) h 100mm, w 20mm; (iv) h 110mm, w 20mm; (v) h 30mm, w 130mm. All five pieces have been sewn together. An opening at one end, diameter 85mm, is reinforced with a tablet-woven edge made with two 4-hole tablets given $^1/_4$ turns
   Weave: 1.3 weft-faced compound twill, Z-diagonal, with a band of tabby
   Warp: proportions, one main end to each binding end
   Main warp: silk, strong Z-twist, 16 ends per cm
   Binding warp: silk, strong Z-twist, 16 ends per cm
   Weft: (i) and (ii) silk, no visible twist, pale golden brown, 21 passes per cm
   (iii) silk, no visible twist, orange-brown
   Dyestuffs: weft (i), (ii) and (iii) negative
   Fig 77

Lampas weaves

It is uncertain where in the Middle or Near East lampas weaves originated, although the technique had certainly evolved in Arab workshops by the late 10th century, and highly accomplished cloths associated with the royal workshops of the Buyids in Iran (932–1055) can be dated by their inscriptions (Shepherd 1954, 55; Guicherd 1963, 26). It is probable that the cloth construction was from the start intended for the weaving of silk since it subtly exploited the lustrous quality of the fibre by contrasting the pattern with that of the ground. This was achieved by bringing the main warp to the surface of the cloth, instead of leaving it concealed within the material as was the practice with weft-faced compound twills, and by introducing a ground weft, which interlaced with the main warp or ground warp according to the requirements of the pattern. As with the production of weft-faced compound twills and twill damasks in 6th-century Europe, certain silk-weaving centres tended to reproduce the same patterns in

samite and lampas-woven fabrics in the 11th century, usually in monochrome white, ivory, yellow, green or more rarely purple. One purple cloth has proved to be dyed with a shellfish purple, similar to the famed Tyrian purple of antiquity, suggesting a Syrian source for that particular example (Schmedding 1978, 181, no 153). By the end of the 11th century a more colourful range of lampas cloths was being woven in western Europe, principally Sicily and Spain, and metal thread was introduced to highlight details of the patterns, particularly the heads and feet of birds and beasts, instead of being added as embroidery after the cloth was woven. Monochrome fabrics, nevertheless, continued to be produced, especially on looms in Islamic Spain.

Many combinations of weaves could be used for lampas cloth. A group of monochrome silk cloths dating to around the late 11th century have a pattern in a 1.2 twill on a tabby ground (e.g. Vial 1963, 29; Schmedding 1978, nos 18, 94, 153). Other early examples were often woven with a glossy weft-faced pattern bound in tabby on a smooth warp-faced tabby ground, a style which is sometimes called 'diasper' after what appears to have been the medieval Latin term for the cloth (King 1960, 42, 45). However, even within this particular type of lampas a wide variety of different weights of cloth could be produced depending upon the thicknesses of the different warp and weft yarns, the proportion of main ends to binding ends and their spacing. At present no examples of the cloth appear to be preserved from 11th-century England but they can occasionally be identified from written records. Thus a white silk, cloth patterned with birds and trees in roundels (*'diaspero albo plano orbiculariter operata avibus et arboribus in orbicularibus'*) was made into a chasuble for Hugo de Orivalle, Bishop of London (1075–1084/5), and was apparently still in use nearly two centuries later when it came to be listed in an inventory compiled in 1245 (Sparrow Simpson 1887, 482).

Longevity of use is also a feature of the earliest type of cloth in a lampas weave excavated from London (No 459, Figs 79–81). This was recovered in nine tattered fragments from the fill of a cesspit dated by its associated pottery to the second half of the 14th century. The pit was situated in the precincts of Holy Trinity Priory (founded in 1108), one of the richest ecclesiastical foundations in

Fig 79 (A) and (B) Cloth patterned with intersecting circles, plant ornament and Kufic lettering, No 459, from a depositing dating to the second half of the

14th century. The shaded areas on the reconstruction (C) mark the extent of the fragments

London, and, from the fine quality of the cloth, there can be little doubt that the textile had formerly been used for a vestment. Indeed, it is because a number of continental bishops were buried in vestments made from similar cloths that the date of production of the London textile can be narrowed down to the late 11th or 12th century.

The weave is an unusual type of lampas, having a pattern in a warp-faced tabby on a weft-faced 1.2 twill ground (Fig 81A). It is in a non-reversible

double weave and the reverse face has the appearance of an unpatterned 1.2 twill, neither the main warp or the pattern weft being visible (Fig 81B). In order to produce this effect two ground wefts of identical colour and thickness were used. The main warp, which is composed of paired ends, comes to the surface on the front of the cloth forming a pattern in outline. The pattern weft bound by the main warp also emerges on the surface along the line of the pattern but it is so fine

c

that it is barely visible except under magnification.

The cloth's pattern is composed of intersecting circles, each one surrounding an eight-pointed star with radiating acanthus palmettes. Debased Kufic letters, which can be read either as *Allah* or *baraka* (blessing) lie between the outer points of the star, and the remaining spaces are infilled with stylised plant ornament (Fig 79). The subtlety of the patterning on the London textile has been diminished by its worn and stained ap-

pearance, but fortunately its superb workmanship can be appreciated from other cloths of similar pattern and weave. These include the pale pinkish-white mantle of St Gertrude of Nivelles in Belgium, fragments of which are preserved in the Kunstgewerbe Museum of Schloss-Charlotten-burg, Berlin (Lessing 1913, I, fig 124a). Other cloths with comparable geometric patterns are preserved in La Colegiata de Santa Maria, Tudela Navarre (Maldonado 1978, pl 52), Quedlinburg,

A

B

Fig 81   Detail of weave of cloth No 459: (A) front,
(B) reverse. Scale 5:1

Fig 80   Two small strips of cloth No 459

Lower Saxony, the church of St Servatius, Maastricht, the latter two both woven with a grey pattern on a crimson ground (Pl 15B; Muthesius forthcoming), the Abbey of St Foy, Conques, central France (No 53/N/433, Anna Muthesius pers comm), Bamberg Cathedral, Germany, where the dalmatic in which Bishop Otto II (died 1196) was buried was made from the cloth (Müller-Christensen 1960, pls 104–15), Bremen Cathedral, where Archbishop Bezelis/Alebrand (died 1043)

Map 2: Distribution throughout western Europe of double weave cloths similar to No 459

was interred wearing a vestment made from a fabric similar to the example in Bamberg (Nockert & Lundwall 1986, 46), and in Angers Cathedral, France, where the shroud of Bishop Ulger (died 1148) is another cloth of this type (Shepherd 1967, 3098–9, fn 18; Shepherd 1974, 50). While these patterns are not identical to that on the cloth from London, the motifs remain confined to geometric and plant ornament rather than including animal or figurative elements. These abstract patterns, combined with the use of Kufic letters, enable the cloths to be attributed to an Islamic workshop. The plant ornament and the subtle patterning drawn in outline belong to a

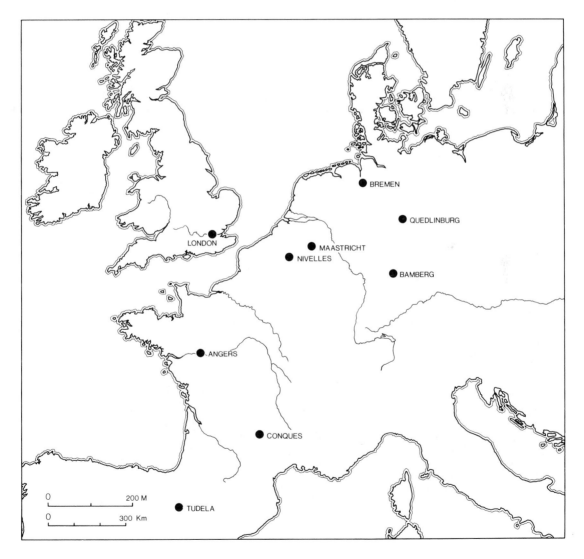

school of 'incised' twills many of which appear to have been produced in Syria *c.*1000 (Müller-Christensen, 1960, 59–63). Palmettes radiating from an eight-pointed star can be seen, for example, in the yellow incised twill used for the burial chasuble of St Bernard (died 1153) at Xanten, Germany (Lessing 1913, I, fig 59b) and in the cloth from London. The lettering, particularly that in a band running across the sleeve of Otto II's dalmatic, bears a close resemblance to that on the so-called 'lion-strangler' silk from the tomb of St Bernard Calvo, Bishop of Vich, Catalonia (died 1243), as well as to that on the 'imitation Baghdad' silk from Burgo de Osma in Soria province, Spain (Shepherd 1957, pls 4B, 4C). Both of these cloths were almost certainly produced in Islamic Spain while it was under the rule of the Almoravids in the first half of the 12th century.

The evidence suggests, therefore, that the cloth found at Dukes Place was the product of a leading workshop operating in Spain in the 11th and early 12th centuries. All examples are associated with richly endowed ecclesiastical centres and the inference must be that the cloths were gifts from rich benefactors. The donor could per-

haps have been the king or queen in the case of Holy Trinity Priory, which maintained close royal connections throughout the first half of the 12th century and two of King Stephen's children were buried in the church (Hodgett 1971, 3). To narrow the date of the gift down further, it may be assumed that the cloth was presented to the priory after the fire of 1132 which destroyed the church and most of the conventual buildings, as well as much of the rest of the City (Hodgett 1971, 3).

Surviving specimens of silk cloths in lampas weave from the first half of the 13th century indicate that the tabby on tabby binding was popular throughout many generations. Examples with English associations include a chasuble and dalmatic from among the burial robes of Hubert Walter, Archbishop of Canterbury, who died in 1205. Both materials are a monochrome yellow patterned with rows of medallions enclosing pairs of birds, and were formerly enlivened with a brocading thread of silver that has since tarnished (Muthesius 1982A, 81–2). As with the cloth from London described above, Islamic Spain was probably the source of these two textiles. These silken fabrics apart, 12th- and 13th-century cloths in lampas weave are scarce from medieval England, but this is probably an accident of survival rather than a true reflection of the period. Evidence from the Continent shows that the tabby on tabby lampas construction continued to be popular in Europe into the 14th century. The influence of silks from Iran and the Far East, however, in-

Fig 82   Silk cloth, No 337, from a late 14th-century deposit: a lampas with a tabby ground and tabby pattern (three single main ends to one binding end), (A) front, (B) detail of weave. Scale 5:1

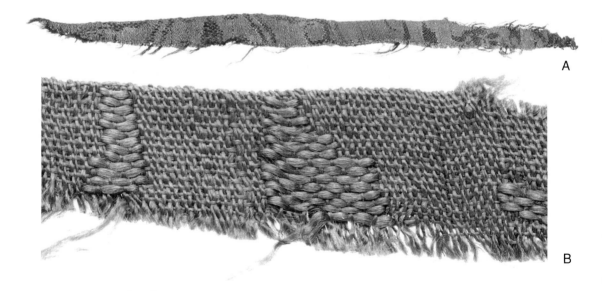

A

B

creased the output of lampas weaves with a ground bound in warp-faced twill or satin, and by the end of the 14th century the production of the tabby on tabby lampas appears to have ceased (King 1960, 43, 45).

There are pieces of three cloths woven in lampas with a tabby pattern on a tabby ground from London all of which come from late 14th-century deposits (Nos 337–339). They are woven with three main ends to one binding end and have, on average, 45 main ends to 15 binding ends per cm. The two narrower strips have single main ends, except occasionally where mistakes have occurred in entering the warp and the ends are paired (Fig 82). A larger strip used for a pouch has paired main ends, which would appear to have been more common to judge by the number of examples that are preserved today (e.g. Tietzel 1984, nos 42–70), but this sample may be misleading. The range of colour employed on the London cloths was limited, only one pattern weft being used to contrast with a darker coloured ground on each of the three pieces. Traces of colouring are preserved on the cloth used for a pouch; the pattern appears to have been woven in white on a red or purple ground. A recent study of the regulations governing silk weaving in Lucca, which were drawn up in 1376 and 1381, has identified textiles of the type used for the pouch as *'camucha di una et di du sete'* (King & King 1988, 69). The other two cloths were probably also varieties of *camuchas*, for the term included a range of different weights and grades of cloth. These fabrics are generally referred to as 'camaca' or 'camoca' in contemporary English documents, and an inventory compiled in 1388 of vestments in Westminster Abbey, for example, includes three dalmatics of white camaca patterned with animals reclining among flowers (*'camaca albi coloris cum bestijs infra flores cubantibus'*) (Legg 1890, 224).

The patterns on the London cloths are less easy to determine than their technical characteristics. Two of the strips have been cut across the width of the cloth, while the third, which was cut lengthwise, has been stitched inside out. The narrowest piece shows part of a fleur-de-lis within a circular frame surrounded by small leaves and flowers (Fig 82). The folded piece also appears to have a small-scale pattern of foliage (Fig 83). A larger part of the pattern on the cloth purse is preserved (Fig 84). It consists of a row of hexagons alternat-

Fig 83 Silk cloth, No 338, from a late 14th-century deposit. Scale 1:1

Fig 84   (A) Pouch made from a silk lampas-woven cloth and stitched together with a tablet-woven edging, No 339, from a late 14th-century deposit. The handle is a fingerloop braid. Note the warp of the cloth is shown horizontally. (B) Reconstruction of the pattern on the cloth used for the pouch

A

B

ing with a row of eight-pointed stars edged with a grid of small squares. Within the hexagons are sprays of flowers intertwined with beasts or birds, repeated in reverse in alternate hexagons. Vertical panels containing two pseudo-heraldic devices, one of lozenges and the other of waved chevrons, lie between each hexagon while the motif enclosed within the star is incomplete and only groups of rays radiating in three directions remain.

The small plant patterns of the two thin strips recall the 'tiny patterns' with leaves and animals strewn across the cloth which one scholar has argued were influenced by Chinese models (Wardwell 1976–7, 186). Well-dated examples of these patterned fabrics are rare but one woven in a lampas binding with a tabby pattern on a tabby ground and made into a chasuble is embroidered with the arms of Blanche of Navarre (1349–1398) (Chartraire 1911, 459–60; Falke 1913, II, fig 281; King & King 1988, 69, 76, fn 1). Inventories indicate that small scale patterns were common between 1360 and 1390 (Wardwell 1976–7, 186), a period that neatly coincides with the date of the two London offcuts, although by the 1380s many pieces would already have looked old-fashioned.

The same late 14th-century deposit in London yielded fragments of five lampas-woven silk cloths with patterns bound in tabby on a warp-faced twill ground. One is a strip cut from a selvedge whereas the others are patterned remnants. At least one fragment has traces of stitching showing that it must have been used before it was discarded (No 341). The patterned cloths are generally comparable in weight and quality with approximately 45 paired main ends to 15 single binding ends per cm and a S-diagonal to the twill. The yarn is Z-twisted for the main warp while that of the binding warp is not twisted. Occasionally mistakes can be observed in the entering of the main ends with one, three, or four ends sometimes occurring instead of just two (Fig 88B), but overall these errors would not have detracted from the general appearance of the cloths. These examples are also similar technically to many cloths documented in other collections showing that guild regulations, which were concerned with maintaining standards in the silk-weaving industry, were strictly complied with.

The cloths are interesting stylistically, particularly as none of the patterns appears to have been recorded before. Owing to the small size of the surviving fragments, however, only one of the patterns can be fully reconstructed. This pattern, which is woven in yellow or white on a faded pinkish-purple ground, has a spray of three flowers with a scroll of Naskhi or pseudo-Arabic lettering partly unfurled on either side (No 340, Fig 85). The height of the repeat is 170mm and the width *c*.30mm. This makes it an extremely narrow repeat for a cloth of this character, but even more remarkable is the small area of the pattern in relation to the large expanse of the ground. The cloth was clearly relatively cheap and this impression gained from the pattern is reinforced by the type of dyestuff used for the main warp (none of the other yarns have been dye tested) which has been identified as a lichen purple. Written sources indicate that this would have been orchil, the name given to a genus of lichens including *Rocella tinctoria* L. and *R. fuciformis* which are native to the shores of the Mediterranean. These lichens enjoyed a renewed popularity in silk dyeing in Italy from the early 14th century through the enterprise of a Florentine merchant who apparently reintroduced them commercially after travelling in the Levant (Kok 1966, 252–3). Initially orchil produced a vivid purple tint but exposure to light caused its colour to fade very rapidly and it was, therefore, often combined with other dyes, madder and indigo for example (Roover 1966, 243). Here, however, no other dyestuff was detected.

Scrolls of pseudo-Arabic characters were a popular motif on Italian fabrics during the 14th century. In this they copied cloths of Islamic origin where Kufic and later Naskhi script often formed part of the patterning. On Islamic textiles the letters are arranged in bands, or as part of a roundel, ogee, or motif such as a tree trunk, palmette or bird's plumage, instead of forming scrolls (see Figs 60 and 79). No Italian examples appear to be associated with lampas bindings which have a tabby ground weave or can be dated earlier than the middle of the 14th century, although the evidence for dating is limited (see, for example, Wardwell 1976–7, 191–3). Unlike the pattern on the London offcut, many cloths with lettered scrolls have very lively patterns which reveal a plethora of cross-cultural influences — Chinese, Persian and Saracen as well as west European. One example, which was made into a chasuble for the Marienkirche, Gdansk (founded 1343), has a

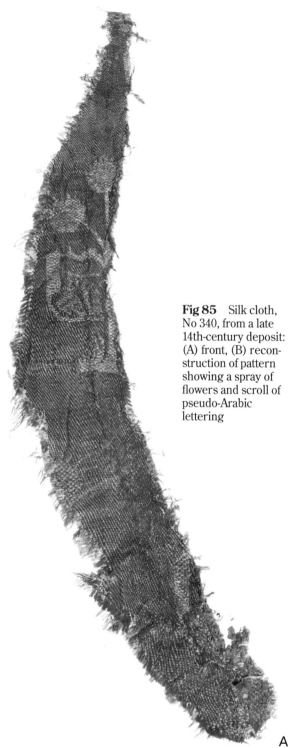

Fig 85 Silk cloth, No 340, from a late 14th-century deposit: (A) front, (B) reconstruction of pattern showing a spray of flowers and scroll of pseudo-Arabic lettering

B

A

panther with a monkey chained to its back leaping from the edge of a scroll while birds fly towards it, below the scroll an elephant sits on a small wagon which is pushed by a monkey or dwarf in a hat while another monkey tweaks the ear of the elephant which is holding a feather in its mouth (Mannowsky 1931, I, no 12, figs 16, 17; Santangelo 1964, 30, fig 18). Despite the elaborate pattern of this cloth, its symmetrical layout on a point repeat harness resembles that of the London cloth, although the chasuble fabric has two different rows of motifs instead of only one. A closely related fabric, now in Stralsund Museum (on the Baltic coast), Germany, has two scrolls of pseudo-Arabic lettering, one intertwined with a monkey holding a dog and the other intertwined with a fierce beast with a bird perched on its rump (Falke 1913, II, fig 438; Roover 1950, 2927). This pattern has a straight repeat rather than a point repeat and demonstrates the enormous capacity for variety that prevailed in the Italian silk weaving industry

Fig 86 Silk cloth, No 341, from a late 14th-century deposit

Fig 87 Reconstruction of pattern on a silk lampas cloth woven in Italy during the mid-14th century (after Lessing 1913, II, fig 140a). The pattern has a straight repeat and it is woven with a pattern bound in tabby on a 2.1 twill ground

during the 14th and early 15th centuries. This is emphasised by a recent study on silk design in Italy at this period, one Lucchese designer, for example, signed a contract in 1424 to supply a small workshop of four weavers in Genoa with at least 60 new designs a year for two years (Monnas 1987, 419).

The other London cloths are closer to the bizarre examples just described in their amount of patterning and, accordingly, they have larger repeats. One long, narrow strip shows an exotic crested bird turned sideways perched under a hat with knotted tie-strings and an ostrich feather plume (No 341, Fig 86). Similar feathers are typical of many whimsical patterns produced in Italy in the second half of the 14th century and many of these cloths were woven in a similar lampas binding with a warp-faced 2.1 twill ground (e.g. Fig 87; Tietzel 1984, 282–4, no 84).

Another cloth from London, a triangular offcut, shows a series of sinuous rays and the edges of

Fig 88 Silk cloth, No 342, in lampas weave with a pattern bound in tabby on a 2.1 twill ground, from a late 14th-century deposit: (A) front, (B) detail of weave, scale 5:1

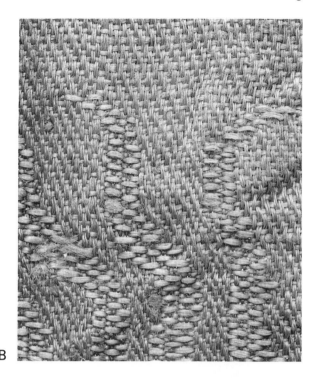

B

A

Fig 89 Reconstruction of pattern on an Italian silk lampas-woven cloth (after Falke, 1913, II, fig 491)

meandering trilobe leaves on a faded red or purple ground (No 342, Fig 88). The disposition of the rays enables the pattern to be compared with that on a chasuble from the Marienkirche, Gdansk, and on smaller fragments in the Victoria and Albert Museum, Germanisches Nationalmuseum, Nuremberg, and Deutches Textilmuseum, Krefeld (Mannowsky 1931, I, no 46, figs 63, 64; Wilckens 1958, 22, no 29, fig 7; Tietzel 1984, 323–5, no 100). This pattern consists of a lion with a 'peacock tail' clutching a bird in its claws; a pair of wings, or hunter's lure, is attached to the lion by a cord and six-link chain and on one wing stands a griffon with its tail between its legs, looking backwards at the lion hovering above (Fig 89). A variation of this pattern, also woven on a background of trilobe leaves, has a similar lion clasping a gazelle as its prey, while overhead flies a

Fig 90   Silk cloth, No 343, from a
late 14th-century deposit

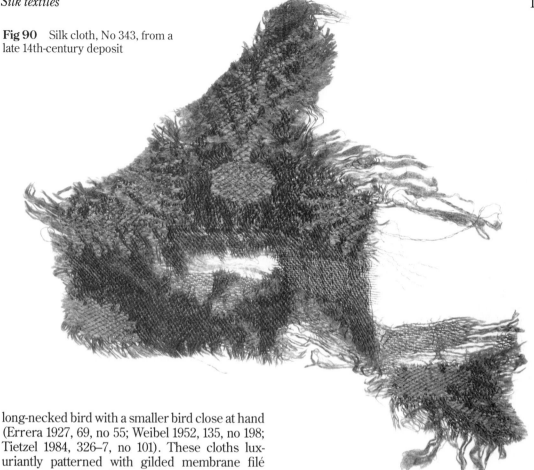

long-necked bird with a smaller bird close at hand
(Errera 1927, 69, no 55; Weibel 1952, 135, no 198;
Tietzel 1984, 326–7, no 101). These cloths lux-
uriantly patterned with gilded membrane filé
thread are attributed to an Italian workshop probably based in Lucca and operating around the
second and third quarters of the 14th century.
The stylistic similarity of the London piece suggests it was also produced there, or at any rate the
pattern can be traced to the hand of a designer of
the same school. The absence of metal thread in
the London cloth indicates that it was not one of
the more expensive varieties of *baudekins* (King &
King 1988, 68–70) but it appears that, unless a
design was a special commission, similar patterns
were adapted to different grades of cloth rather
than being exclusive to one type.

A fourth example — another offcut — preserves only the central portion of its pattern (No
343, Fig 90). A plant motif is flanked by two others
with identical spiky outlines suggesting that it was
mounted on a point repeat harness.

An inventory of vestments in Westminster
Abbey, which was taken in 1388 and therefore
very close in date to when the fabrics were thrown

out as rubbish in the East Watergate, shows that
cloths with fanciful patterns were not an unusual
sight in the metropolis in the last quarter of the
14th century. Cloths of gold patterned with lions
chained to boughs (*'leonibus ligatis ad ramos au-
reos cathenis'*), golden cranes standing on
branches which the birds hold in their beaks with
other animals grazing under trees (*'gruibus aureis
super blodio stantibus ramos in rostris habentibus et
alijs bestijs sub arboribus pascentibus'*), pairs of de-
formed birds in quadrangles interspersed with
crowns and golden fish (*'bestijs deformibus binis
infra quadrangulis coronis et piscibus aureis inter-
textis'*), flying falcons with little lions sitting in between them (*'falconibus volantibus et parvis leonibus
sedentibus intermixtis'*), and golden swans, tied by
their necks to trees, standing in little boats (*'signis
deauratis stantibus in naviculis ad arbores col-

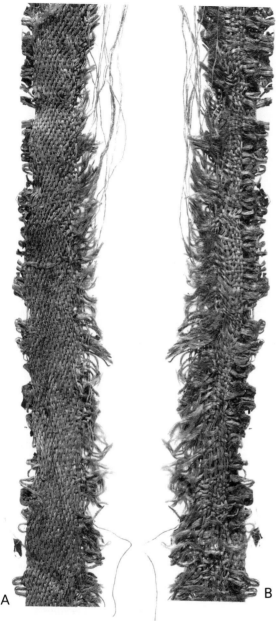

Fig 91 Detail of selvedge on lampas cloth, No 344, from a late 14th-century deposit: (A) front, (B) reverse. The two cellulose fibre edge cords are badly decayed. Scale 2:1

ligatis'), are just a few of those listed in the inventory (Legg 1890, 229, 261–3).

The character of the selvedge shows that it too conformed to guild regulations in force in Italian weaving centres. It is approximately 10mm wide and woven in 2.1 twill with a Z-diagonal (No 344, Fig 91). The silk ends are paired and consist of a pale coloured yarn, perhaps originally yellow or white, and the edge is reinforced with two plied cords of a cellulosic fibre — probably linen. The number of edge cords is significant. Florentine regulations specified the use of a single linen cord in lampas-woven silks in 1344; in 1352 this was changed to a maximum of two linen cords and this continued to be a requirement into the second half of the 15th century (Monnas 1989, 38–40). This does not mean that the selvedge considered here was cut from a Florentine cloth woven in 1352 or sometime later but it is a possibility. Other selvedges recorded on lampas-woven silk cloths dating to the 14th and early 15th centuries usually have either two or three linen cords followed by silk ends of a different colour to the main web (e.g. Tietzel 1984, nos 82, 98, 100–1; Monnas 1989, 40) but a few all-silk selvedges also occur (Tietzel 1984, no 99). It is not possible to reconstruct the precise character of the weave from the selvedge, although it can be deduced that the ground weave was warp-faced 2.1 twill as the binding of the selvedge and of the ground weave on Italian lampas fabrics were usually similar.

Selected catalogue IX

Second half 14th century

459 Dimensions: nine fragments, largest (i) h 156mm, w 185mm; (ii) h 145mm, w 40mm; (iii) h 115mm, w 100mm; (iv) h 87mm, w 94mm. Six of the fragments preserve traces of a seam, 4–6mm wide

Weave: lampas with a double cloth ground. The pattern is formed by one continuous weft bound in tabby on a 1.2 ground, Z-diagonal

Height of repeat *c.*105mm, width of repeat *c.*90mm

Warp: proportions, one pair of main ends to each binding end

Main warp: silk, strong Z-twist, paired, 23 pairs per cm

Binding warp: silk, strong Z-twist, single, 23 ends per cm

Warp decoupure: 1 pair of main ends

Weft: proportions, 1:1

Ground weft: silk, no visible twist

Pattern weft: silk, no visible twist, much finer than ground weft

Weft decoupure: 1 pass
42 passes per cm
Dyestuffs: negative
Figs 79–81

Last quarter 14th century

337 Dimensions: h 14mm, w 210mm. Cut strip, folded in two lengthwise
Weave: lampas, the pattern formed by one continuous weft of silk bound in tabby on a tabby ground.
Warp: proportions, 3:1
Main warp: silk, strong Z-twist, single and occasionally paired, 45 ends per cm
Binding warp: silk, no visible twist, single, 15 ends per cm
Warp decoupure: 2 main ends
Weft: proportions, 1:1
Ground weft: silk, no visible twist
Pattern weft: silk, no visible twist, thicker than ground weft
Weft decoupure: 1 pass
12 passes per 5mm (i.e. 24 per cm)
Fig 82

338 Dimensions: h 105mm, w 19mm. Cut strip, tapering to a point folded in two and stitched down the centre with running-stitches, in 2-ply sewing thread, 8 stitches per 5mm
Weave: lampas, the pattern formed by one continous weft of silk bound in tabby on a tabby ground
Warp: proportions, 3:1
Main warp: silk, strong Z-twist, single, 45 ends per cm
Binding warp: silk, no visible twist, single, 15 ends per cm
Warp decoupure: 2 main ends
Weft: proportions, 1:1
Ground weft: silk, no visible twist
Pattern weft: silk, thicker than ground weft, no visible twist
Weft decoupure: 1 pass
20 passes per 10mm
Fig 83

339 Dimensions: h 60mm, w 135mm. Folded double and sewn into a square, unlined bag. The bag is finished with a tablet-woven braid, made with 30 tablets, along the two cut edges and round the opening, ending in a tassel at both bottom corners. Two unreinforced holes have been made in one corner at the top, on either side, and a five-loop finger braid slotted through to form a small handle
Weave: lampas, the pattern formed by one continuous weft of silk bound in tabby on a tabby ground
Width of repeat 88mm
Warp: proportions, 3:1
Main warp: silk, faded pink, strong Z-twist, paired, 48 pairs per cm
Binding warp: silk, no visible twist, single, 16 per cm
Warp decoupure: 2 pairs of main ends
Weft: proportions, 1:1
Ground weft: silk, faded pink, no visible twist
Pattern weft: silk, ? white, thicker than ground weft, no visible twist
Weft decoupure: 1 pass
21 passes per cm
Fig 84

340 Dimensions: h 233mm, w 27mm. Cut strip with curved edges
Weave: lampas with double cloth ground. Pattern formed by one continuous weft bound in tabby on a 2.1 twill ground, S-diagonal
Height of repeat 170mm, width of repeat *c.*30mm
Warp: proportions, 3:1
Main warp: silk, faded pink (lichen purple), strong Z-twist, paired and occasionally single, 48 pairs per cm
Binding warp: silk, no visible twist, single, 16 ends per cm
Warp decoupure: 2 pairs of main ends
Weft: proportion, 1:1
Ground weft: silk, faded pink, no visible twist
Pattern weft: silk, slightly thicker than ground weft, no visible twist
Weft decoupure: 1 pass
19–21 passes per cm
Fig 85

341 Dimensions: h 202mm, w 13mm. Cut, ragged fragment with evidence of stitching
Weave: lampas with double cloth ground. Pattern formed by one continuous weft bound in tabby on a 2.1 twill ground, S-diagonal
Warp: proportions, 3:1
Main warp: silk, Z-twist, paired, *c.*45 pairs per cm
Binding warp: silk, no visible twist, single, 15 ends per cm
Warp decoupure: 2 pairs of main ends
Weft: proportions, 1:1
Ground weft: silk, no visible twist
Pattern weft: silk, thicker than ground weft, no visible twist
Weft decoupure: 1 pass
22 passes per 10mm
Fig 86

342 Dimensions: h 122mm, w 26mm. Cut, triangular
    fragment
    Weave: lampas with double cloth ground. Pattern
       formed by at least one continuous weft bound
       in tabby on a 2.1 twill ground, S-diagonal
    Warp: proportions, 3:1
       Main warp: silk, faded purple, strong Z-twist,
          paired with a few in threes or fours, 45 pairs
          per cm
       Binding warp: silk, pale brown, no visible twist,
          single, 15 ends per cm
       Warp decoupure: 2 pairs of main ends
    Weft: proportions, 1:1
       Ground weft: silk, no visible twist
       Pattern weft: silk, no visible twist, thicker than
          ground weft
       Weft decoupure: 1 pass
       28–29 passes per 10mm
    Fig 88

343 Dimensions: h 93mm, w 80mm. Cut, ragged
    fragment
    Weave: lampas with double cloth ground. Pattern
       formed by one or more continuous wefts
       bound in tabby on a 2.1 twill ground, S-diagonal
    Warp: proportions, 3:1
       Main warp: silk, strong Z-twist, both paired and
          single, 45 per cm
       Binding warp: silk, no visible twist, 15 ends per
          cm
       Warp decoupure: 2 pairs of main ends
    Weft: proportions, 1:1
       Ground weft: silk, no visible twist
       Pattern weft: silk, thicker than ground weft, no
          visible twist
       Weft decoupure: 1 pass
       19–21 passes per cm
    Fig 90

344 Dimensions: h 300mm, w 12mm. Strip cut from
    selvedge
    Weave: lampas with double cloth ground. Pattern
       formed by one continuous and at least one in-
       terrupted weft, bound in tabby on a 2.1 twill
       ground
    Warp: proportions, 3:1
       Main warp: silk, strong Z-twist, mainly paired,
          40 pairs of ends per cm
       Binding warp: silk, strong Z-twist, paired
       Warp decoupure: uncertain, no pattern
          preserved
    Weft: proportion, 1:1
       Ground weft: silk, no visible twist
       Pattern wefts: (i) Continuous, silk, no visible
               twist

            (ii) Interrupted, silk, no visible
               twist finer than (i)
    Weft decoupure: uncertain, no pattern
       preserved
    18–19 passes per cm
    Selvedge: 2 plant fibre (? linen) cords Z/S-ply, pat-
       tern wefts extend to edge cord, ground weft
       only to inner cord, Z-diagonal
    Fig 91

Satin

Satin-woven silks first appear in London deposits of the late 14th century. The cloth was, however, introduced into England no later than the last quarter of the 13th century. The earliest dated example known from this country is a blue satin which was used for a set of embroidered vestments made between 1270 and 1294 of which only a cut down chasuble, known as the Clare chasuble, is preserved (Christie 1938, no 44; King 1963, no 30, 19–20).

By the late 14th century, garments including doublets, tunics, hanselyns and sloppes cut from satin were fashionable. It was also used for furnishings, including cushions and bedhangings, as well as for girdles and garters. According to written records the colours favoured in England as this period were white, black, blue, red, *blodei* and green. In addition, the cloth was frequently enlivened with embroidery executed in gold or silver-gilt thread, or powdered with small motifs in gold leaf. Painted decoration was sometimes applied as a cheaper alternative. The term 'double satin' also occasionally occurs in accounts; for example in 1391–2 eight ells of double red satin were supplied for 'one paltok', 'one doublett' and the sleeves of a paltok (Wylie 1898, 160). Florentine sources indicate that this was not a wider cloth but a thicker and heavier one woven by men rather than women (Roover 1966, 247; King & King 1988, 74–5).

Further descriptive details of the silk fabric can now be added by reference to the four examples of 14th-century satin recovered from London. All are five-end satins (Fig 92), woven from warp yarn with a strong Z-twist and weft yarn lacking any appreciable twist. They are warp-faced, the ratio of warp to weft threads ranging from 1.5:1 to 2:1.

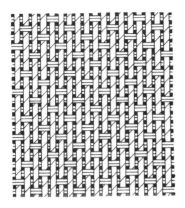

Fig 92 Five-end satin, warp face

This density is lower than is customary nowadays and consequently the cloth possessed a looser texture. Only one of the satins was with certainty dyed. It is now a pale salmon-pink with a contrasting yellowish-white selvedge 6mm wide, which consists of a series of paired ends (interspersed with an occasional single end or groups of four or five ends) similar to that of the main web (Pl 16A). The pink yarn was dyed in the thread with madder while the yarn for the selvedge would have been prepared separately in common with patterned cloths of the period. This coloured satin is also distinctive for its use of paired ends, a feature more characteristic of heavier compound weaves.

Another of the cloths, a narrow strip, preserves part of its starting border (No 346, Fig 93). This border was folded inwards to form a hem and was, therefore, hidden from view; that it was used at all demonstrates the thrifty use of the fabric. This and another trimming of satin (No 345, Fig 153B) were applied inside out.

Fig 93 Five-end satin, No 346, showing starting border, from a late 14th-century deposit. The warp face is obscured by the folded edges. Scale 2:1

Selected catalogue X

Last quarter 14th century

345 Dimensions: (i) h 17mm, w 160mm; (b) h 160mm, w 23mm. Cut strips
Weave: 5-end satin, decochement of 3, S-diagonal
Warp: silk, golden-brown, strong Z-twist, 60 ends per cm
Weft: silk, golden-brown, no visible twist, 28–30 picks per cm
Fig 153

346 Dimensions: h 160mm, w 23mm. Cut strip
Weave: 5-end satin, decochement of 2, Z-diagonal
Warp: silk, golden-brown, strong Z-twist, 58–60 ends per cm
Weft: silk, golden-brown, no visible twist, 40–42 picks per cm
Starting border: h 2mm (incomplete)
Fig 93

347 Dimensions: (i) h 64mm, w 43mm; (ii) h 55mm, w 24mm. Two fragments of similar cloth joined by a seam
Weave: 5-end satin, decochement of 3, S-diagonal
Warp: silk, pale brown, strong Z-twist, 54 ends per cm
Weft: silk, pale brown, no visible twist, 30 picks per cm
Fig 124B

348 Dimensions: (i) h 45mm, w 195mm; (ii) h 50mm, w 130mm. Both pieces were cut but the edges have become frayed
Weave: 5-end satin, decochement of 3, S-diagonal
Warp: silk, pink (madder), strong Z-twist, 48 paired ends per cm.
Weft: silk, pink (madder), no visible twist, 30 picks per cm
Selvedge: silk, yellowish-white, strong Z-twist, w 6mm
Pl 16A

A

B

Satin damask

Damasks bound in satin were a later development than twill damasks, which they generally supplanted. Originating in the Far East, they began to be copied in the west, notably in Mameluke Egypt, Spain and the Italian city states, during the 14th century. This may have been in indirect consequence of the resettlement of weavers in the wake of the Mongol conquests but, at present, little is known about the early development of the cloth's production in the west. As the manufacture of satin damasks became widespread from the second half of the 14th century onwards it is often not possible to distinguish precisely where particular pieces were produced, although by the 16th century at least some cloths made in Spain were woven with the warp face of the damask forming the pattern and not the background (Digby 1939, 222).

A narrow strip of a satin damask recovered from Swan Lane, London, has a pattern of a pomegranate surrounded by stylised foliage (Fig 94A and B). Here the glossy warp face of the damask forms the ground on the front of the cloth (Fig 94C). It is woven in a five-end binding with approximately three times as many ends as picks, and, in order to achieve this density of threads, a very fine warp yarn with a S-twist was used. The S-twist of the warp yarn marks a break from the tradition of Z-twisted yarn which can be traced back to the very beginning of silk-weaving in the west, although there are exceptions to this. The change would appear to be associated with a technological development in silk throwing — possibly the diffusion of water-powered throwing mills such as are known to have been operating in Lucca, north-west Italy, during the 14th century (Roover 1950, 2917–18), following improvements

in reeling and throwing silk which reputedly took place in nearby Bologna during the latter part of the 13th century (Born 1939, 995; Lopez 1952, 76). This development can be compared to the greater use of S-twisted warp yarn in the English cloth industry in the late 14th century, which is linked to the adoption of the spinning wheel (see p45).

It is unfortunate that the date of the deposit from which this cloth was recovered is uncertain. Stylistically the piece could date to either the 15th or 16th century, but once a corpus of satin damasks has been compiled it should be possible to assess its date more accurately. Similarly, it should be possible to reconstruct the pattern unit of the London cloth since damasks, and velvets, with patterns of this type were produced in large quantities and many are preserved in museums and church treasuries. The large scale of the patterns meant that it was common for only one repeat to be woven across the width of the cloth on a point repeat harness. This resulted in fabrics often less than 609.5mm (24ins) wide. Three satin damasks, for example, which were made into a doublet in the 16th century and which are technically similar to the cloth from London have loomwidths of approximately 550mm (21^5/$_8$ins), 555mm (21^3/$_4$ins), and 585mm, (23ins), (Flury–Lemberg 1988, 228–9, 481, no 45), the latter being roughly the equivalent of one *braccio* in certain Italian cities, including Florence (Monnas 1989, 36). Widths prescribed for monochrome damasks in 15th-century Italian silk-weaving statutes were wider than these and this helps to distinguish earlier cloths from later examples.

The relatively narrow width of the cloth and the use of only one warp and one weft meant that it could be woven more quickly than wider, compound fabrics such as samite and those with lampas bindings. This helps to explain why satin

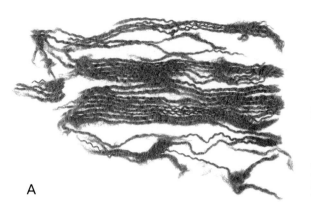

A

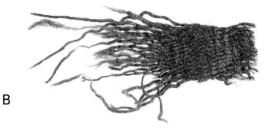

B

Fig 97   Wool and ?linen union cloths from late 14th-century deposits: (A) balanced weave No 354, (B) weft-faced No 355. Scale 1:1

the weft, but by contrast to Nos 353 and 354, the wool yarns are Z-spun and cloth is weft-faced with a ratio of warp to weft threads ranging from 1:3 to 1:4.5 (4 threads per cm in the warp and 12–18 threads per cm in the weft) (Fig 97B). This weft-

faced fabric is patterned with horizontal bands of red and yellow, the yellow yarn being slightly finer in diameter. The character of this piece suggests that it, too, could have been used as a rug, bedcover or hanging.

Narrow wares

The manufacture of braids was an important craft in medieval Europe. Domestic output was considerable, and workshops were established under the patronage of the court and church where elaborate pieces incorporating costly metal thread could be commissioned. London had probably become the main centre of the industry in England by the late 12th or 13th century, for large quantities of silk and metal thread were imported to meet the demands of embroiderers, many of whom resided in the City. Braid-making was closely associated with embroidery but developed independently and until the 16th century remained chiefly the preserve of women, who not only made the goods but frequently handled supplies of silk thread, dealing directly with foreign merchants (Dale 1932/4, 327–9).

Braids from the London excavations fall into four groups categorised by how they were made — tablet woven, fingerlooped, plaited and tabby woven. The first three methods enable both flat and tubular braids to be produced and a range is represented here. Silk thread was preferred since its great natural strength and elasticity made it the most adaptable, but worsted yarn and linen were also used. As a further strengthening measure the silk thread was usually plied and then used double or in groups of threes, fours or fives, these processes forming part of the routine tasks undertaken by silkwomen and their apprentices. Metal thread was more sparingly used but it was incorporated as a supplementary pattern weft in two of the tablet-woven braids described here. In both XRF analysis indicates that the metal is silver with a very minor amount of copper (not gilded silver or silvered copper alloy). In one instance (No 420) the strip of precious metal was wound round a core of silk, on the other (No 356) probably round a core of linen thread which has rotted in the riverside environment where it lay buried. The metal may have been applied as silver leaf to a substrate of animal gut (membrane) but this is uncertain. Another tablet-woven braid (No 441) combines worsted and silk thread in the warp but generally only one type of fibre is used throughout each braid described here.

Tablet-woven braids

The technique of tablet-weaving was practised in England at least as far back as the Iron Age (Henshall 1950, 150) and the recovery of a bone tablet pierced with four holes from a deposit in London dating to the second half of the 1st century AD (Museum of London, Department of Urban Archaeology excavations at 5–12 Fenchurch Street, FEN 83 acc no 981) shows that the skill was already known very early in the City's history. Wool and linen thread were used for braids in early Anglo-Saxon England, but pattern brocading could be carried out with other fibres; hair, possibly from horsetails, was identified on wool bands from the graves of chieftains at Evebø and Snartemo in west Norway (Dedekam 1924/5, 22; Magnus 1984, 300) and may possibly have been used for similar decoration on braids found in early graves — perhaps of the 5th century — at Snape, Suffolk (Crowfoot forthcoming C). Metal, in the form of flat cut strips of gold foil, was used to brocade patterns on wool braids at Taplow Barrow (Crowfoot 1983, 475–6, fig 336) and for decoration on women's hairbands in 6th-century Kentish graves (Crowfoot & Hawkes 1967). The growth in imported silk thread from the middle of the 7th century led to silk tablet-woven braids becoming highly desirable in England. This development coincided with a change in the type of metal thread used, flat strips of gold, or silver, now being spirally twisted round a core of silk or flax, or more exceptionally, round a core of horsetail hair (see Budny & Tweddle 1984, 76).

The art of tablet-weaving attained a high level of accomplishment in England over the course of many centuries. Among the best known are the braids sewn to the embroidered stole and maniple which were commissioned by Queen Ælfflaed between 909 and 916 and were subsequently presented to the shrine of St Cuthbert, probably by King Aethelstan, Ælfflaed's stepson, in 934 (Battiscombe 1956, 13). These braids include pieces patterned with birds, lions and acanthus sprays (Crowfoot 1939, 57–80; Crowfoot

1956, 433–45), which appear to have been woven to preconceived designs rather than freely improvised by the weaver (Crowfoot 1956, 451). Braids with geometric patterns, like one example from London (Pl 13B), were more commonplace and so are more difficult to date stylistically. Many are still preserved sewn to vestments, but they would also have trimmed clothing worn by much of the populace, status being defined by the lavishness of the metal thread, the type of fibres used, the colours the yarn was dyed, the complexity of the pattern, and the width of the braid. It was this form of weaving that many royal ladies seem to have pursued as a pastime. Eleanor (died 1214), a daughter of Henry II, is reputed to have made a stole which is interwoven with her name while she lived in Spain after her marriage to Alfonso VIII of Castile, and this is preserved in the Colegiato de San Isidoro, Leon (May 1957, 98). This tradition was continued by her descendant, Eleanor of Castile, who married Edward I and sought solace in weaving during her last illness in the autumn of 1290 (Parsons 1977, 12). Noblewomen emulated royalty in weaving braids but the output of these aristocrats was negligible compared with that of nuns, and women whose livelihood depended upon it.

A silk thread from what may have been a tablet-woven braid was recovered from the floor of a 10th-century building at Milk Street (Pritchard 1984, 63 pl IVC), but the earliest archaeological deposit in the City from which a clearly identifiable tablet-woven braid has been recovered dates to the second half of the 13th century. In this narrow silk braid, 4mm wide, silver thread was used to create a surface pattern of circles alternating with rectangles, in the centre of which is a cross made from the ground weave (No 420, Fig 98). The metal thread passes to the reverse of the braid at this point, a practice that sometimes means both sides are to be seen. A similar braid, brocaded with crosses in silver-gilt thread on a ground of green silk, was used to edge an embroidered silk mesh hairnet which was recovered from the tomb of a 13th-century landgrave of Hesse in the church of St Elisabeth, Marburg, Germany and which is now in the Germanisches Nationalmuseum, Nuremberg (Hampe 1901, 50–51, no 2980), and perhaps the London braid served the same purpose although no stitch holes are apparent along either edge. Two linen tablet-

A   B

Fig 98 Silk tablet-woven braid brocaded with silver thread and made with nine tablets, No 420, from a late 13th-century deposit: (A) front, (B) reverse. Scale 2:1

woven *cingula* from among the large group of liturgical vestments from the Marienkirche, Gdansk, are similarly brocaded at intervals with small cross and rosette patterns on a four-hole ground weave (Mannowsky 1938, V, 15, no 213, fig 139). These are merely a very few of the relatively simple braids produced in the 13th and 14th centuries where the ground weave was left partly exposed.

A wider silver braid recovered from a late 14th-century deposit (No 356, Pl 13B) was probably more than a hundred years old by the time it was discarded. Here, as in most metal-brocaded braids, the metal thread conceals most of the ground weave except at the edges where the brocading thread returns and only shows briefly on the reverse. The warp ends used for the two edge tablets on either side of the braid are silk but those forming the rest of the ground, which would have been hidden, have disintegrated suggesting that they were a cellulosic fibre. Despite

Fig 99 Silk tablet-woven filet stitched to a false plait of hair, No 142, from a deposit dating to the second quarter of the 14th century: (A) complete item, scale 1:3, (B) detail of braid, scale 1:1

A   B

appears that they were used as hair filets, girdles and, perhaps, spur leathers.

A tablet-woven braid used in styling the hair is sewn to a plaited hairpiece (No 142, Fig 99). The braid itself is unpatterned but pairs of stitch holes indicate that ornaments, probably of octofoil form, were originally attached to it at intervals. The stitching of the ornaments is revealing since in some centres, such as Paris, regulations required bezants and ornaments of precious metal to be stitched, rather than riveted, on to silk (Newton 1980, 36). Jewelled hairbands or filets can be seen in many 14th-century depictions of fashionable ladies. In the 1340s filets were worn with vertical plaits held in place beside both cheeks, and it was probably to this fashion that the tablet-woven braid and hairpiece belong.

Tablet-woven girdles could be highly decorative as well as very strong and flexible. Many elaborate examples can be cited from medieval Europe, including the so-called sword belt of the Infante Don Fernando de la Cerda (died 1275) ornamented with pearls, sapphires and enamelwork (Gómez–Moreno 1946, 22, no 84, pls 135, 136; Collin 1956, 6–11; Fingerlin 1971, 331–2, no 61, figs 368–9). Another geometrically-patterned girdle garnished with fittings in silver and silver gilt, which is now in the National Museum of Denmark, is sometimes claimed to have belonged to Eric of Pomerania (died 1459), who became King of Norway and then also King of Sweden and Denmark in the late 14th century (Fingerlin 1971, 362, no 126, fig 409). A belt from the funeral achievements of the Black Prince in Canterbury Cathe-

the poor preservation of the braid, it appears that all the tablets were threaded through four holes.

The six flat braids made wholly from silk thread are sturdier than those brocaded with metal thread since each element is composed of a greater number of strands doubled and quadrupled. These braids were produced in double-faced weaves rather than having a right and a wrong side and, instead of being applied to another fabric, probably functioned on their own. There are four examples from 14th-century deposits in London and two from deposits dating to around the second quarter of the 15th century; it

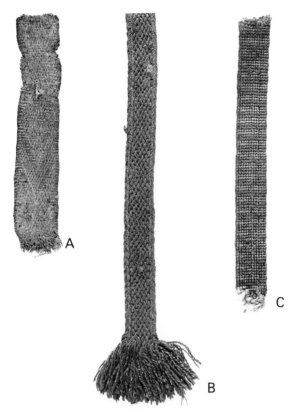

Fig 100   Silk tablet-woven braids from mid 14th-century deposits, (A) No 143, (B) No 450, (C) No 451. Scale 1:1

dral is tablet woven (Alexander & Binski 1987, 481, no 632) but little of its former splendour now remains. Furthermore, it can be deduced that many silk girdles bequeathed by Londoners in the 14th and 15th centuries were made by this technique. Patterned tablet-woven spur leathers were also common in medieval Europe. A pair from the

tomb of Sancho IV (died 1319) in Toledo Cathedral are patterned with triple-towered castles, the arms of Castile (Museo de Santa Cruz 1984, 136, no 60), and others include those from the tomb of Fernando de la Cerda (Gómez–Moreno 1946, pl 140; Carretero 1988, 37).

Three of the silk tablet-woven braids from 14th-century London could have been either girdles or spur leathers since their narrow width of 8.5mm to 12mm would have been appropriate for either purpose. Two have lozenge patterns, one possibly monochrome (No 450, Fig 100B) and the other with at least two colours (No 143, Fig 100A). The third is patterned with alternating bands of faded pink and yellow or white and has three brass bar-mounts riveted to it (No 451, Fig 100C).

Cheaper girdles were made from worsted thread; the stock of a haberdasher's shop in London in 1378 included a black wool girdle valued at 2d. (Riley 1868, 422). An example of an all-worsted tablet-woven girdle from a late 14th-century deposit is preserved with its buckle attached but too little of it remains to establish its overall design (No 357, Fig 101). Another from a contemporary late 14th-century deposit combines worsted threads with a small amount of silk arranged to produce a striped pattern (No 441, Fig 102).

Fig 101   Worsted tablet-woven girdle attached to a buckle frame, No 357, from a late 14th-century deposit. Scale 1:1

Fig 102   Worsted and silk tablet-woven girdle, No 441, from a late 14th-century deposit. Scale 1:1

Fig 103   Silk tablet-woven girdle which was pre-served inside a strap-end, No 423, from a deposit dating to the first half of the 15th century. Scale 5:1

Fig 104   Silk tablet-woven girdle, No 404, from a deposit dating to the first half of the 15th century. Scale 2:1

Only the worsted yarn appears to have been dyed, a red weft contrasting with the near black hue of the wool warp. The weft would have shown along the edges and in the central stripe where the silk ends were threaded through four holes and twisted in a different sequence to the rest of the pack.

Two tablet-woven girdles from 15th-century deposits in London, one preserved within a copper alloy strap end to which it was originally riveted (No 423, Fig 103) and the other bearing traces of three rivet holes, probably also from a strap end (No 404, Fig 104), reveal a change in style, for they have a smooth surface lacking in colour effects or patterning. This change is also evident from visual sources, from which it can be seen that women began to wear wider girdles above the natural waistline in subdued monochrome colours which often resemble satin, velvet or satin damask. Written sources reinforce this impression, especially the Statute of Apparel passed in 1463 during the reign of Edward IV, which refers to 'corses wrought like to velvet or to satin branched' (Statutes of the Realm, 3 Ed. IV c.5). By analysing the braids it can be seen that weavers were able to adapt the technique of tablet weaving to meet the challenge of simulating satin, velvet and satin damask just as in earlier centuries they had simulated samite. This development is illustrated even better by three tablet-woven girdles from the Continent; one a girdle from the tomb of Prince Sigismondo Pandolfo Malatesta (died 1468) in Rimini, Italy (Vial 1971; Flury–Lemberg 1988, 454–7, 471, figs 957–61, no 24) and another supposedly from a hoard of treasure recovered at Chalcis, Euboea, off the coast of Greece (Fingerlin 1971, 377–8, no 174) both of which are patterned with bands of cut pile velvet and gold loops on a tablet-woven ground, whereas another, in the Germanisches Nationalmuseum, Nuremberg, simulates satin damask (Fingerlin 1971, 418–21, no 356).

Table 11 Tubular tablet-woven braids

Cat. No	Fibre	Dimensions		No of tablets
		l	d(mm)	
First half 14th century				
451	silk	(i) 1735	1	12
		(ii) 620	1	
Last quarter 14th century				
358	silk	(i) 118	2	12 (Fig 106)
		(ii) 66	2	
359	silk	265	2	12 (Fig 105A)
360	silk	(i) 260	2.5	12
		(ii) 40	2.5	
361	silk	620	3	16
144	wool	65	6	5
362	wool	65	3	3 (Fig 105B)

There are also seven tubular tablet-woven braids, of which five are silk and two worsted, from 14th-century deposits in London (Table 11). They differ from flat braids in that the weft was always passed through the same side, thereby forming a tube when the weft was pulled tight. This often caused the braid to twist on its own axis, as can be observed from a braid which is patterned with alternating groups of dark and light coloured threads (No 359, Fig 105A), and also from a shorter worsted braid (No 362, Fig 105B). The silk tubular braids were worked on 12 to 16 two-hole tablets which were threaded in an identical direction and given half turns forwards after each passage of the weft. The worsted braids, by contrast, appear to have been worked with a smaller number of four-hole tablets which were given quarter turns. A rather similar braid attaching a seal to a Scottish charter dated 1 August 1294 has an attractive pattern of stripes and dots produced by using silk threads of four different colours (Henshall 1964, 161–2, no 5, fig 2G pl XXIIIC).

These tubular braids were put to many uses. Eight amber beads from a rosary still threaded on a string made from one such silken braid were recovered from the late 14th-century dock infill at BC72 (No 358, Fig 106; see also Mead 1977, pl 6; Egan & Pritchard 1991, no 1489, pl 8H), others

Fig 105 Tubular tablet-woven braids, (A) silk, No 359, (B) wool, No 362. Scale 1:1

were used for lacing up garments, tying hose to the breech girdle, making purse strings or appending wax seals to documents, especially grants in perpetuity (PRO 1968, 15–17). A similar tablet-weaving technique was often used to bind cut edges on garments, particularly sleeve openings (Figs 133–137, 142, 163, Pl 1), or on seal bags and purses (Figs 77, 84A, Pl 16B), including pouches made from leather as well as cloth. Cloth pouches tended to be finished with a greater number of tablets than leather pouches, presumably because the edges of the former were likely to fray. The small pouch made from a strip of lampas-woven silk was, for example, finished with 30 tablets threaded through two holes (Fig 84A). A drawstring leather pouch in the collections of the Museum of London (MOL acc no 20732), by contrast, was finished with just two four-hole threaded tablets and this edging also helped to

hold in place a narrow silk facing round its opening. A similar edging produced with two tablets is preserved on a fragmentary silk pouch made from a loosely woven weft-faced compound twill and here a 4–6mm width of cloth was firstly folded inwards to provide a firmer edge (Fig 77).

Selected catalogue XII:

Flat tablet-woven braids

Second half 13th century

420 Dimensions: l 318mm (in 8 fragments), w 4mm
     Pattern unit: 13mm (30 picks)
     Warp: silk, mid-brown (negative), Z/S-ply

Fig 106 Rosary consisting of a tubular tablet-woven silk braid strung with amber beads, No 358, from a late 14th-century deposit. Scale 2:1

Weft: silk, mid-brown (negative), Z/S-ply, 22–23 picks per cm
Pattern weft: silver filé, S-twisted round silk core
Weave: 9 four-hole tablets, alternately S and Z threaded. After throwing the ground weft the tablets were given a ¹/₄ turn in the same direction
Fig 98

First half 14th century

142 Dimensions: (i) l 150mm, w 10mm; (ii) l 90mm, w 10mm. (i) is sewn to a plaited hairpiece. At intervals of *c.*10mm along the braid there are

groups of holes indicating that ornaments were formerly attached to the braid

Warp: silk, golden-brown (negative), Z/S-ply

Weft: silk, golden-brown, Z/S-ply, 46 picks per cm

Weave: 26 tablets, the 2 edge tablets on either side were four-holed, threaded in a S-direction, and given continuous $\frac{1}{4}$ turns forward after the weft was thrown. The centre 22 tablets were two-holed and given $\frac{1}{4}$ turn backwards followed after the next pick by $\frac{1}{4}$ turn forwards to produce a tabby weave

Fig 99; (Egan & Pritchard 1991, fig 192)

143 Dimensions: l 64mm, w 12mm

Warp: silk, pale brown, Z/S-ply

Weft: silk, pale brown, Z/S-ply, 25–26 picks per cm

Weave: 33 or 35 four-holed tablets, double-faced weave with lozenge pattern

Fig 100

449 Dimensions: (i) l 132mm, w 8.5mm; (ii) l 118mm, w 8.5mm; (iii) l 79mm, w 8.5mm. (i) has a small hole near its central axis perhaps for a buckle pin, and (ii) has three brass bar mounts riveted to it spanning the width of the braid

Warp: (i) silk, yellowish-brown, Z/S-ply;
(ii) silk, pinkish brown, Z/S-ply (i) and (ii) both used double except for the two edge tablets where the ends are grouped in 4s

Weft: silk, yellowish-brown, Z/S-ply, 14 picks per cm

Weave: 12 four-hole tablets grouped in threes being threaded SSSZZZSSSZZZ. The tablets were threaded with the same two colours of silk inserted in corresponding holes and were continuously given a $\frac{1}{4}$ turn in the same direction with the weft being thrown before each $\frac{1}{4}$ turn. One reverse of pack occurs on fragment (i). The pattern is similar on both faces except for a reversal of the colouring

Fig 100C; (Staniland 1975, 167; Egan & Pritchard 1991, fig 30)

450 Dimensions: l 220mm, w 8.5mm. Cut at each end. Weight 2.1gm

Warp: silk, dark reddish-brown (negative), Z/S-ply, used in 4s

Weft: silk, dark reddish-brown (negative), Z/S-ply, 24 picks per cm

Weave: 12 four-holed tablets. The 2 edge tablets (i.e. one on each side) were continuously given a $\frac{1}{4}$ turn forwards, 4 alternate tablets in the centre were given two $\frac{1}{4}$ turns forward followed by two $\frac{1}{4}$ turns backwards while the other four alternate tablets were turned in op-

position. This resulted in a double-faced weave with a diagonal twill effect

Fig 100B; (Staniland 1975, 167)

Last quarter 14th century

356 Dimensions: l 37mm, w 30mm

Warp: silk, dark golden-brown (negative), Z/S-ply

Weft: silk, dark golden-brown, no appreciable twist, 14 picks per cm

Pattern weft: silver filé, S-twisted round a (?) plant fibre core

Weave: c.41 tablets, the 2 edge tablets on either side were four-holed, threaded in a S-direction on one side and a Z-direction on the other, and given continuous $\frac{1}{4}$ turns forwards after each pick. The centre tablets were manipulated to produce a geometric strapwork pattern

Pl 13B

357 Dimensions: l 15mm, w 18mm. Riveted to three-piece buckle ensemble

Warp: worsted, Z/S-ply

Weft: uncertain

Weave: uncertain

Fig 101; (Egan & Pritchard 1991, fig 30)

441 Dimensions: fragmentary, w c.18mm

Warp: (i) worsted, dark brown, Z/S-ply
(ii) silk, golden-brown, Z/S-ply

Weft: worsted, red (madder), Z/S-ply, 5 picks per cm

Weave: at least 36 tablets; 14 tablets on each side had two-hole threading and were given $\frac{1}{2}$ turns forwards to produce a tabby weave, all these were threaded with worsted thread except for the second and third tablets in from each edge which were threaded with silk; the centre eight tablets were threaded with silk through four holes and were given $\frac{1}{4}$ turns to produce a diagonal twill

Fig 102

First half 15th century

440 Dimensions: l 170mm, w 28mm

Warp: silk, reddish-brown (negative), Z/S-ply

Weft: silk, reddish brown (negative), Z/S-ply, 26 picks per cm

Weave: c.110 four-holed tablets alternately S and Z threaded given a continuous $\frac{1}{4}$ turn forwards after each pick and used in two packs

423 Dimensions: l 14.5mm, w 15.5mm

Warp: silk, brown but with traces of a crimson hue, Z/S-ply

Weft: silk, brown, Z/S-ply, 22 picks per cm

Weave: *c.*39 four-hole tablets alternately S and Z
threaded given continuous $^1/_4$ turns forwards
after each pick and used in two packs
Fig 103; (Egan & Pritchard 1991, fig 31)

Fingerloop braids

Braids made by the fingerloop method were also
extremely common in the medieval period, and 24
examples have been recovered from London deposits of the late 12th to early 15th centuries (Table
12). Two of these were used to edge knotted mesh
hairnets (Nos 399 and 145, Figs 119–121), and another as a purse string (No 339, Fig 84A). Others
could have been used for fastening clothing (see p
164). The techniques required threads to be
looped at one end in order to slip over the fingers,
while at the opposite end the threads were attached to a fixed point. A minimum of three loops
was essential, with an even number of loops being
placed on the fingers of one hand and usually an
odd number on the other. According to the manner in which the loops were manipulated, either a
flat or a tubular braid could be made (Fig 107;
Speiser 1983, 126–42). For more than seven loops
a second person was required since it was imprac-
tical to use the thumbs for hooking the loops from
one hand to the other. Braids in excess of an arm's
length also needed the help of an assistant to
transport the shed to the opposite end of the
loops. Examples from London show that it was not
unusual to have at least two people working together, and as many as three would have been
necessary for a 20-loop braid recovered from the
late 14th-century dock infill at BC72 (Fig 108C).
Braids of 10 or more loops made by two people
had the advantage that they could be divided into
two tails along part of their length (Fig 108B),
which added to their versatility as purse strings.
Braids made with fewer loops sometimes had
plaited tails (e.g. No 365) and it is probable that
the knotted purse string associated with the fragmentary pouch (No 398) is another example.

A flat, 10-loop braid, 700mm in length, which is
preserved complete, weighs a mere 0.8gm (Fig
108A). It can, therefore, be estimated that at least
35 such braids could be made from one ounce of
silk (an ounce representing the usual measure by
which silk thread was sold). By contrast the
amount of silk required for a girdle could weigh at

Table 12   Fingerloop braids made from two-ply silk thread from medieval London

Cat. No	Dimensions l	w(mm)	No of loops	No of tails
Second half 12th century				
407	800	2.5	7	—
408	455	3.5	—	—
First quarter 13th century				
427	210	3	7	—
Last quarter 13th century				
399	320	3	7	— (Fig 120)
400	700	3	10	— (Fig 108A)
First half 14th century				
145	290	2	5	— (Fig 121)
146	180	3.5	5	—
147	320	2	5	—
148	250	3	5	—
149	70	2.5	5	—
452	(i) 230	3	7	—
	(ii) 165	3		—
453	(i) 420	4.5	10	2
	(ii) 210	4.5		—
	(iii) 120	4.5		—
454	175	4	10	2
Last quarter 14th century				
339	60	2.5	5	(Fig 84A)
363	2210	3.5	5	—
364	(i) 50	3.5	7	—
	(ii) 37	3.5		—
	(iii) 30	3.5		—
365	475	4	7	4
366	340	5	10	2
367	210	6	10	2
368	170	7	14	2
369	250	7.5	14	2
370	120	7	14	2 (Fig 108B)
371	70	10–11	20	— (Fig 108C)
First half 15th century				
405	85	10	14	2

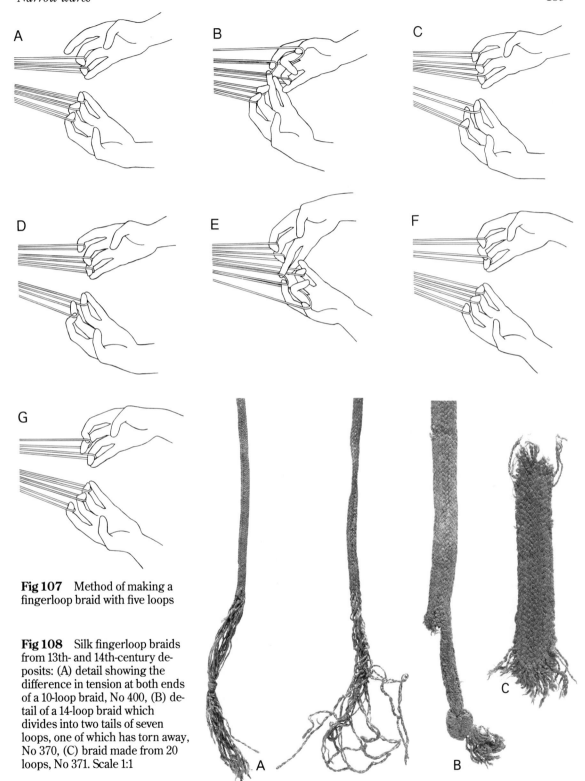

Fig 107 Method of making a
fingerloop braid with five loops

Fig 108 Silk fingerloop braids
from 13th- and 14th-century deposits: (A) detail showing the
difference in tension at both ends
of a 10-loop braid, No 400, (B) detail of a 14-loop braid which
divides into two tails of seven
loops, one of which has torn away,
No 370, (C) braid made from 20
loops, No 371. Scale 1:1

least 11ozs (Dale 1928, 82). Most of the fingerloop braids from London appear to have been monochrome. Apart from one crimson-coloured fragment (No 408), all are now shades of brown and no dyestuffs have been positively identified. However, threads of two hues forming alternating blocks of colour can be observed on one braid which has two loops of dark brown silk and three loops of a paler golden-brown (No 148). Fingerloop braids using silk threads of three and four different colours are known from cathedral treasuries, where they often form drawstrings to reliquary bags, and threads of another colour were sometimes added to the tassels; but, in contrast to tablet weaving, the technique precluded complex patterning.

Plaited braids

Plaiting was another ancient and widespread method for producing braids. When made from silk thread they resemble fingerloop braids both in their dimensions and elasticity, and they were equally quick to produce. As with fingerloop braids no equipment was necessary to make them, although in some regions today bobbins are tied to each element to improve the tension and rhythm of interlacing (Hald 1980, 240–42). Square braids made from eight elements are the most common plaited braids from medieval London, where they occur in deposits of the 13th and 14th centuries (Table 13, Fig 109), and a braid plaited from six elements was found in a late 13th-century deposit (No 421, Fig 110A). At least one

Table 13   Plaited braids made from two-ply silk thread

Cat. No	Dimensions l	d(mm)	No of elements
Last quarter 13th century			
398	120	2	2 tails of 3
401	280	2	8
421	(i) 220	2	6 (Fig 110A)
	(ii) 90	2	
First half 14th century			
150	120	2	8
151	65	2	8
152	(i) 170	2	8
	(ii) 175	2	
	(iii) 130	2	
455	210	2	8
456	230	1.5	8
457	185	2	8
Last quarter 14th century			
372	(i) 300	2	8
	(ii) 8	2	
373	355	1.5	8
374	160	1.5	8
375	(i) 515	2	8
	(ii) 235	2	
376	280	2	8
377	90	2	8
378	255	1.5	8
Unstratified			
425	126	2.5	8

Fig 109   Method of making a square plait with eight elements

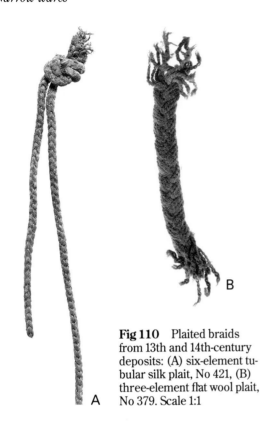

Fig 110 Plaited braids from 13th and 14th-century deposits: (A) six-element tubular silk plait, No 421, (B) three-element flat wool plait, No 379. Scale 1:1

silk braid appears to have been made from threads of more than one colour (No 457) and, as well as producing a pattern (Fig 109), the different colours helped the threads to be manipulated in the correct sequence.

The only plaited braid not made from silk thread is a flat, three-element plait of worsted thread (No 379, Fig 110B). Each element is made up of five two-ply threads which would have enabled the plait to withstand a considerable amount of tension.

Tabby-woven braids

Silk ribbons in tabby weave appear in English deposits of the 10th and 11th centuries (Pritchard 1984, 473, 481–2, no 36, pls IVB; Walton 1989A, 367–9; Crowfoot 1990, nos 1017–19, 1021, pls xxxviif, xxxviii a and b) but they do not reappear until the late 14th century, when they are generally woven from two-ply warp and weft yarn (Table 14). The earlier ribbons are not woven from plied thrown silk; instead, grège (undegummed) silk was common and the warp and/or weft yarn sometimes has a S-twist. This indicates that the

Table 14   Tabby-woven ribbons from late 14th- and early 15th-century deposits in London

Cat. No	Fibre	Dimensions l	w(mm)	Twist of yarn warp/weft	No of threads per cm warp/weft
Last quarter 14th century					
216	silk	20	10	Z/S-ply Z/S-ply	28/15 (Fig 144)
380	silk	260	9	Z/S-ply Z/S-ply	c. 30/30 (Fig 111A)
381	silk	8	8+	Z/S-ply Z/S-ply	c.32/34
219	silk	20	10	Z/S-ply Z/S-ply	36/22
382	silk	465	13	Z/S-ply Z/S-ply	38/13
383	silk	279	11	Z/S-ply Z/S-ply	43/18 (Fig 130)
384	silk	152	9	Z/S-ply Z/S-ply	48/13
385	silk	750	9	Z/S-ply Z/S-ply	50/16
386	silk	110	11	Z/S-ply Z/S-ply	50/18 (Fig 111B)
387	wool	(i) 85 (ii) 35	13 13	Z Z	28/12 (Fig 111C)
First half 15th century					
406	silk	325	12	Z/S-ply Z/S-ply	48/19

Fig 111 Tabby-woven ribbons:
(A) and (B) silk, Nos 380 and
386, (C) worsted, No 387. Scale
1:1

and have stitch holes and traces of sewing thread along each side (Nos 384, 385); two others are stitched to the wrist openings of buttoned sleeves (No 216, Fig 144, No 219); and another to the edge of a leather pouch (No 383, Fig 130). Indeed, the use of this braid as a binding in the late 14th century appears to mark the beginning of a shift away from tablet-woven edgings.

Garters

By the second quarter of the 14th century garters had become a sufficiently conspicuous item of male dress to be satirised in contemporary art. An early 14th-century embroidered orphrey shows one of Christ's flagellators wearing a garter (Christie 1938, no 72; King 1963, 33, no 58) and many examples are depicted in the *Luttrell Psalter, c.*1325–35 (Fig 112). Shortly afterwards garters became enshrined in popular imagination by the creation of the Order of the Garter, sometime between 1347 and 1349 (Nicolas 1846, 124–30). In earlier periods diagonally wound or cross-garters, such as those depicted in the Bayeux Tapestry, were popular since they enabled loose leg coverings to be held firmly in place. Narrow lengths of cloth, usually between 75mm and

ribbons have different places of origin, the earlier ones perhaps coming from small workshops situated in the Levant or central Asia, the later ones being locally produced in London from imported thread. As with other types of braid, worsted yarn was sometimes used instead of silk and one woven from single Z-spun worsted yarn, which was found in a late 14th-century deposit, is, like most of the silk ribbons of similar date, warp-faced (No 387, Fig 111C). No colour effects are visible whereas similar silk ribbons stitched to vestments show that many were made with multi-coloured stripes.

Some of the ribbons were used to bind cut edges. Two lengths are folded down the centre

Fig 112 Man wearing bejewelled garters *c.*1325–35 (after the *Luttrell Psalter*, BL Add MS f.158b)

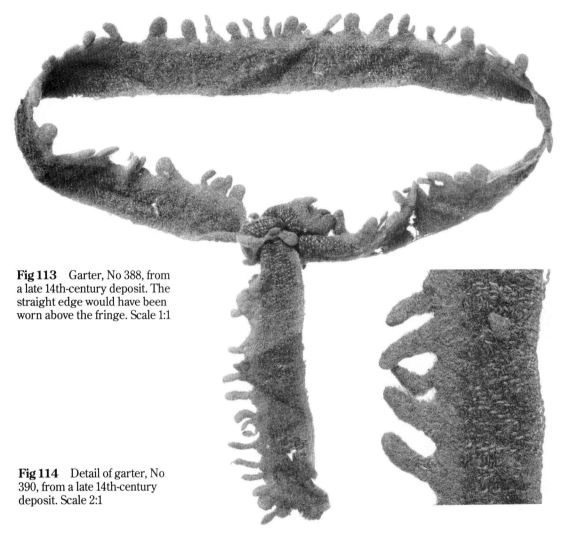

Fig 113 Garter, No 388, from a late 14th-century deposit. The straight edge would have been worn above the fringe. Scale 1:1

Fig 114 Detail of garter, No 390, from a late 14th-century deposit. Scale 2:1

100mm wide and generally woven from worsted yarn in four-shed broken chevron twill, have been identified as garters and are known from many north European settlements including 10th-century London (Pritchard 1984, 68–9, pl IIID). They appear to have been woven in long strips and then cut in two to provide a matching pair. Some of these, however, may have been used as leg bandages rather than as garters, and their width can be contrasted with the narrower garters, 18mm to 23mm wide, from 14th-century London. Despite the obvious interest taken in the colour and cut of hose in the 12th and 13th centuries, which is apparent from manuscript illuminations, little is known about what garters, if any, were worn at

this time. Their popularity in the 14th century, like that in the earlier Carolingian period, coincided with a shortening of men's tunics. Often slit in the front up to waist height (Newton 1980, 4), these caused the leg to be displayed more prominently than it had been for some centuries.

It is likely that women also wore garters which remained concealed beneath their full-length tunics. The excavation of the tomb of a Merovingian princess, possibly Queen Arnegunde, who was buried *c.*565–70 in the cathedral of St Denis, France, revealed that she was laid out wearing linen hose secured below both knees with leather cross-gartering garnished with silver buckles and strap ends (France-Lanord & Fleury

1962, 345, 354, fig 3; Werner 1964, 212–14, figs 11, 12).

Three purpose-made garters recovered from a late 14th-century deposit in London enable us to determine more precisely how they were made at this period. A long warp was set up on a narrow band loom. The best preserved of the London garters has 25 ends arranged in a sequence of four red ends, 18 black ends, three red ends (No 388, Fig 113). Fourteen of the black ends were entered through the heddles of the loom in pairs, which resulted in a stronger garter with a more elastic fit. When weaving commenced the weft passed backwards and forwards along one selvedge, but on the other side of the weft extended round a rod or cord beyond the web so that a fringe was created. After the full length of the garter was woven, the piece appears to have been left on the loom and the weft yarn, which remained attached to the last pick, was darned to and fro in the warp direction on the extended loops to the width desired for the scallop. The same length of thread was used for the next scallop by overstitching one edge of the completed scallop and then repeating the process previously described (Fig 115). The width and length of the scallops vary not only from garter to garter but also in the same piece, showing that it was done by eye without counting the threads. When the garter was worn the straight selvedge would usually have been placed at the top and the decorative scallops below. Colour effects which are present on all three garters were created by grouping together a series of different coloured ends to form narrow stripes, which would have run horizontally round the leg. Neither the starting or finishing edge is preserved on these London garters and so it is not known whether they had elaborate fringes. This method of making garters was laborious and time consuming. Consequently, it became common in later centuries to make two garters at once by weaving a wider loompiece which was cut in half lengthwise and then finished by hand.

Not all garters were purpose made and strips of cloth were sometimes recycled as garters. Examples from the late 14th century include a piece of samite (No 336, Fig 76) and possibly some knotted selvedges from woollen fabrics. The essential quality of all these pieces is that they are relatively strong.

Selected catalogue XIII

Last quarter 14th century
388 Dimensions: l *c.*270mm, w 22mm (including scallops 7mm deep)
     Weave: tabby
     Warp: (i) wool, red (madder), S-spun
              (ii) wool, black (madder), Z-spun, 11–12
              pairs per cm

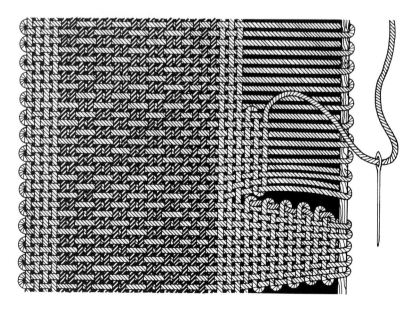

Fig 115 Method by which purpose-made garters may have been woven

Weft: wool, red (madder), Z-spun, 20–21 picks per
   cm
Pattern: 4 red ends, 7 pairs of black ends, 4
   single black ends, 3 red ends, *c.*10 darned in
   red threads forming scallop
Fig 113

389 Dimensions: l 220mm, w 18mm (including scal-
   lops up to 10mm deep)
Weave: tabby
Warp: (i) wool, red, S-spun
      (ii) wool, black, S-spun
      10 ends per cm
Weft: wool, red, S-spun, 8–9 picks per cm
Pattern: 6 black ends, *c.*14 darned in red threads
   forming scallop

390 Dimensions: l 95mm, w 23mm (including scallops
   8mm deep)
Weave: tabby
Warp: (i) wool, red, S-spun
      (ii) wool, black, Z-spun, 10 pairs per cm
Weft: wool, red, Z-spun, 20 picks per cm
Pattern: 4 red ends, 10 pairs of black ends, 4 red
   ends, *c.*12 darned in red threads forming
   scallop
Fig 114

Hairnets

Hairnets were also made in London from imported silk thread (Dale 1932/4, 331). Four
examples of knotted mesh hairnets have been recovered from excavations in the City: one from a
late 13th-century deposit, two from deposits
dating to the second quarter of the 14th century,
and a small fragment from the late 14th century.
The condition and size of the latest piece suggests
that it was already old at the time of deposition.
This accords with visual evidence which shows
that hairnets with a small knotted mesh declined
in popularity during the 14th century as female
hairstyles changed to reveal more of the hair, although nets often continued to be worn over the
back of the head. By contrast, when hairnets
again became conspicuous in the latter part of the
century their structure had altered and they appear to have consisted of a much larger, sturdier
mesh to which jewels could more easily be
attached.
   Examination of the four hairnets, which are

Fig 116   Typical female headdress including a hairnet *c.*1270–80 (after a prefatory miniature to a psalter,
St John's College, Cambridge MS K 26 f.231)

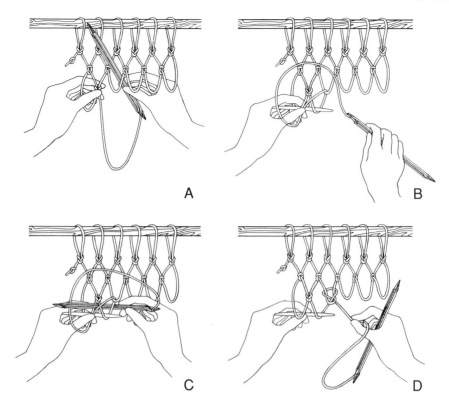

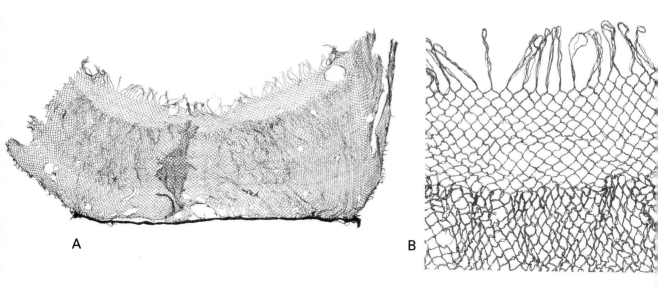

Fig 117   Method of making mesh hairnets

Fig 119   Silk mesh hairnet, No 399, from a late 13th-century deposit, and detail of loops and knotted mesh: (A) complete piece, scale 1:4, (B) detail, scale 1:1

structurally similar, provides an indication of the method by which they were produced (Fig 117). A series of loops was made from a lightly plied double thread. Rows of knotted mesh were then created with the aid of a narrow netting needle which, to judge from examples preserved from 14th- and

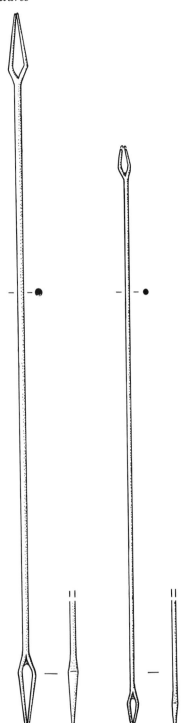

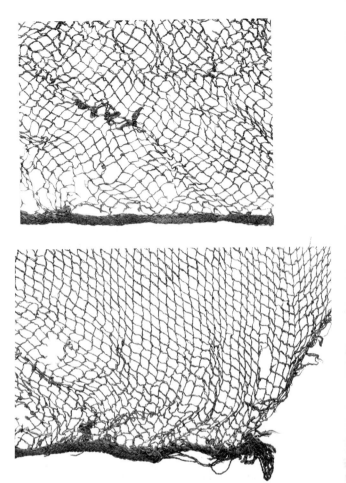

Fig 120 Details of a repair to the mesh and the fingerloop braid stitched to the lower edge of hairnet No 399. Scale 1:1

Fig 118 Copper alloy netting needles from deposits dating to late 14th century. Scale 1:1

early 15th-century deposits in London, were usually of copper alloy. These needles, which vary in length from 101mm to 147mm, were made from drawn wire and have an open eye at each end so that the silk thread could be wound on to the needle very easily (Fig 118). Sheet bend knots were usual, with the size of the mesh and the fineness of the thread varying from one hairnet to another (Figs 119–121). In order to ensure an even size of mesh, a small measuring stick, perhaps a short metal rod, was probably used as is the practice today in netmaking by hand (Sanctuary 1980, 14). On the 13th-century hairnet finer thread was

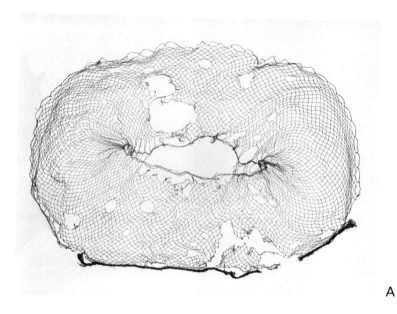

A

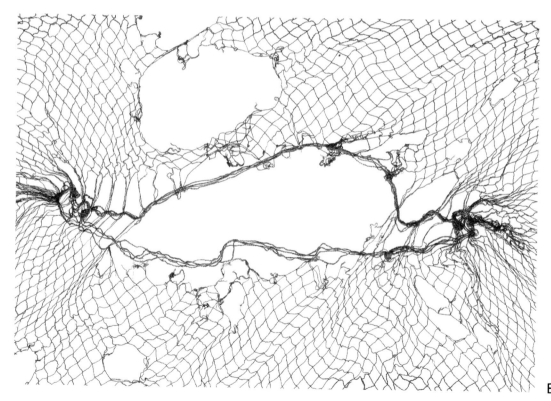

B

Fig 121 Silk mesh hairnet, No 145, including detail showing the shaping of the crown, from a deposit dating to the second quarter of the 14th century: (A) complete piece, scale 1:4, (B) detail, scale 3:4

used for the first 15 rows of the mesh at which point the number of knots was increased to extend the circumference (Fig 119). A similar feature is apparent on a hairnet excavated from a 14th-century deposit in Amsterdam (Vons-Comis 1982, 154) and this suggests that it was a fairly common practice. The most complete hairnet shows that it was made in the round and that the crown was shaped afterwards by passing a cord of four threads through the long loops at one end (Fig 121). The opposite end with shorter loops was finished by stitching the loops to a narrow silk braid. On the two London hairnets where this edging is preserved, a fingerloop braid has been attached with two-ply silk sewing thread (Fig 120). However, a knotted mesh hairnet from the grave of a 13th-century landgrave of Hesse which is preserved in the Germanisches Nationalmuseum, Nuremberg, has a narrow green silk tablet-woven braid, brocaded with crosses in silver-gilt thread, stitched round the edge (Hampe 1901, 50–1, no 2980). The mesh of this hairnet in Nuremberg is embellished with a chequered pattern of crosses darned in green and white silk. It appears, therefore, that simple knotted silk mesh hairnets were sometimes used as the foundation for much more elaborate cauls.

This method of making hairnets was by no means the only technique in use in the medieval period. A German painting dated *c*.1460 shows a woman seated by an upright post from which a net is tensioned (Wyss 1973, 121, fig 8). She works at the net with a needle in her right hand, but rather than beginning with a series of loops and working in the round the net increases in width each row.

Selected catalogue XIV

Last quarter 13th century
399 Dimensions: h *c*.155mm, l of lower edge 320mm
Thread: silk, Z/S-ply, dark brown
Mesh: 3mm square
7 loop fingerloop braid stitched to edge of mesh with golden brown two-ply (Z/S) silk sewing thread; l of braid 320mm
Figs 119,120

Second quarter 14th century
145 Dimensions: h *c*.110mm, circumference 970mm

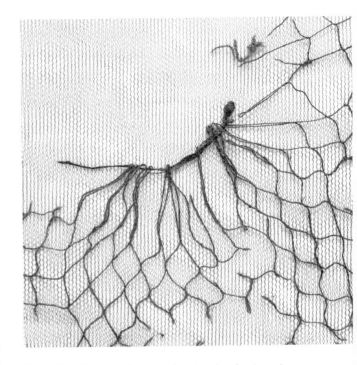

Fig 122   Silk mesh hairnet, showing the shaping of the crown, No 153, from a deposit dating to the second quarter of the 14th century. (The gauze enveloping the hairnet is a conservation measure.) Scale 1:1

Thread: silk, Z/S-ply, mid-brown
Mesh: 4mm square
Crown threaded with a cord of four Z/S-ply silk threads which passes through the long loops on alternate sides
5 loop fingerloop braid stitched to edge of mesh with dark brown two-ply (Z/S) silk sewing thread; l of braid 355mm
Fig 121

153 Dimensions: fragmentary
Thread: silk, Z/S-ply. golden-brown
Mesh: 9mm square
Crown threaded with a bichrome cord of four Z/S-ply silk threads, two are light golden-brown and the other two are dark brown
Fig 122

Last quarter 14th century
391 Dimensions: four small fragments
Thread: silk, Z/S-ply, pale golden-brown
Mesh: *c*.3mm square

Sewing techniques and tailoring

Careful examination of the textiles preserved from medieval London reveals a much greater range of evidence for sewing techniques than is immediately obvious. Furthermore, a fair number of the 14th-century fragments can be associated with items of clothing with a certain degree of confidence. Yet the very fact that the overwhelming majority of these textiles represent discarded scraps from worn clothing several or many years old at the time of deposition, makes such an exercise of identification hazardous and uncertain, and it is to be hoped that more light will be shed on the identification of some of the scraps as a direct result of this publication.

For the present some supporting evidence can be drawn from the extensive corpus of medieval clothing excavated in Scandinavia, from London's rich remains of 16th-century clothing fragments, and from more recent European excavations. At the other end of the scale is the fine array of surviving medieval embroidery, most especially the group attributed to English manufacture (*opus anglicanum*), much of which is believed to have been worked in the city of London (King 1963, 5). These embroideries demonstrate the high level of stitching skills which existed side by side with the tailoring needs in a major conurbation like medieval London.

Contemporary illuminations and sculptures have been much used in the study of medieval dress (Cunnington & Cunnington 1952; Evans 1952; Herald 1980; Scott 1980; Scott 1986), but these mostly give a generalised impression of clothing at the time: they rarely provide the details of construction and sewing techniques which particularly interest us in the late 20th century. Such images can certainly help to guide us to datings for the textiles excavated in London, evidence which in turn is corroborated by the dating evidence of associated artefacts from the same sites coupled with dendrochronology (tree-ring dating).

Documentary sources have been used much less by dress historians, with one or two exceptions (Goddard 1927; Evans 1952; Newton 1980).

Contemporary comment in the form of literature or chronicles needs to be judged with caution, full though they are of powerful images and details. Each contains an element of fact or interpreted fact. But how do we today identify these elements or judge the bias of a chronicler, probably a very conservative churchman, vehemently attacking some whim of fashion which he might himself eventually adopt through familiarity and the desire to conform?

Far more important as a factual source are the records relating to the making of garments at the time, most of which centre upon the Great Wardrobe of the English royal household. These accounts record the purchasing of cloths, silks, linen, furs, threads, braids, fringes, etc. from drapers, mercers and silkwomen in London, the subsequent treatment of some of the woollen cloths, and finally the distribution of these goods to the royal tailors and armourers who made the clothing and such other textile items as bed and room hangings, horse trappers and jousting gear, and flags and banners for the king and his family and friends (Staniland 1978; Staniland 1989). Information about the prices and range of materials which these accounts provide can be usefully associated with surviving textiles like those excavated in London and can help to extend our knowledge and understanding of what are now small brown scraps of cloth.

Other Great Wardrobe accounts detail the expenses claimed by the tailors and armourers for additional requisites and labour costs. The latter are particularly valuable for the information that they can provide about the time taken to make certain garments, the number of work people involved, and, on rare occasions, the actual names of the workforce. Thus we can see that men and women often worked alongside each other, the women receiving lower wages (about half) than their male counterparts. It is clear that the clothing of the rich incorporated many refinements and subtleties of finish which might not be found in the clothing of the less affluent. Nevertheless, the information that we can gather about the time taken to make certain types of garment in the 14th century is of great interest, and matching wages against manufacturing costs we can gain some idea of how long it took to put together certain garments in the 14th century:

a pair of hose	about half a day (*c.* 1½d.–2d. each)
a hood	a half to a whole day depending upon whether it was lined or not (2d.–3d. each)
a cloak	three to six days depending upon whether it was lined or not (1s.–2s. each)
a supertunic	three to six days depending upon whether it was lined or not (1s.–2s. each)
a tunic	one to six days depending upon complexity, lining, etc. (3d.–2s. each)

These records, albeit for an extremely wealthy household, provide a quantity of information which is either directly relevant to aspects of the excavated textiles or which illuminate such topics as use or cost. Where appropriate, therefore, reference to some of these accounts is included in the following commentary.

The general account of the evidence for sewing techniques and clothing construction which follows brings together information from the technical analyses originally made of the fragments together with a more recent study of them. This evidence, which is crucial to the history of the development of sewing and tailoring skills, has tended to be overlooked or obscured in the past but can lead to a richer understanding of sartorial attitudes in medieval times.

Sewing threads

As far as is known the sewing thread in general use in the later middle ages was linen, the spun fibres of the flax plant (*Linum usitatissimum*). Being cellulose this decomposes rapidly in wet conditions and is rarely found in north European archaeological excavations. Traces of stitching survive in textiles from BIG82 and BC72 in

Fig 123 Copper needlecase (missing cap) with an iron needle, which was found inside, from a late 14th-century deposit. Scale 1:1

London, mostly of an undetermined vegetable fibre believed to be flax; these occur in seams and hems, exactly where one might expect to find linen stitching (e.g. No 221, Fig 164A and B, No 246, Fig 170, and No 249, Fig 182A). Elsewhere the former presence of stitching is attested by a multiplicity of holes (e.g. No 136, Fig 152) and it is probably not unreasonable to assume that in most cases linen rather than silk thread has disappeared.

The Great Wardrobe accounts of the 14th century show that linen thread was used extensively in the various workshops supplying the court with clothing and other textile items. Naturally linen thread was used for sewing linen clothing and such other domestic items as towels, tablecloths or napkins; it was also used for quilting bed coverlets and mattresses. Some intricate linen embroidery of the 13th and 14th century survives in Germany (Schuette & Müller-Christensen 1963, XVII, 306–7, nos 142, 143, 146, 154–7, 168) and Switzerland (Schmedding 1978, 107–9, nos 100–103), but whether this technique played a significant role in England is less certain. The linen thread supplied to the Great Wardrobe in the 1330s cost between 2s. and 2s.8d. per lb and came not only in different thicknesses, but also in a variety of colours. The thread came either from the London mercers or from women who, like the better known silkwomen, also made linen tapes, braids, and cords.

There is little documentary evidence for cotton sewing thread in medieval England. Raw unspun cotton was certainly imported in the 13th and 14th centuries, and was used as wadding in jousting garments, and for stuffing bed mattresses and coverlets (Nicolas 1846, 33–4, 37, 44–9, 53); it cost 5d.–5½d. per lb in the 1330s. Plied cotton thread was used for the wicks of candles (Lysons 1812, 74; Blackley & Hermansen 1971, 94–5) causing the quality of artificial lighting to improve considerably (Mazzaoui 1981, 102–3). In 1392–5 a Great Wardrobe account records the purchase of 6lb of cotton thread at 12d. per lb from Alice Spicer (PRO E101/402/13), and there is some evidence that it was used in making clothes for Richard II.

Silk thread was used extensively in the sewing and ornamentation of royal clothing in the middle ages, a practice which is likely to have been followed by the aristocracy and rich merchant families. It is virtually the only sewing thread to have survived the damp, anaerobic conditions of London's waterfront sites. Most of the silk threads are two ply, each element being Z-twisted and then S-plied. Exceptions include the stitching of a pouch from a late 13th-century deposit and a hemmed edge of what was probably a veil where single threads of floss silk were used (No 398, Fig 77A, and No 331, Fig 66).

Silk thread is used for seams and hems on most surviving fragments of woven silk. The coarsest thread is found on Nos 326 and 327, where two pieces of fine silk tabby are joined by firm over-stitching (Fig 124A). Clearly here the sewer was more concerned with a firm join then with visual niceties, as this is not a very elegant piece of workmanship; it may be a later repair and probably comes from a lining of a garment. Elsewhere very fine two-ply thread is used for hemming or edge-whipping the extremely fine silk veils (Nos 332–334, Figs 67, 68, 129). Silk thread is also used for all the surviving complete buttonholes and eyelets (Figs 135–138, 142, 146, 163), for securing many of the buttons (Figs 141, 143, 144, 162), for decorative top-stitching (Figs 137, 142) and for decorative braids and edges worked directly on to the edges of sleeves and purses (Figs 77A, 84A, 135, 142, 163, Pl 16B).

Silk thread can also be found used upon woollen cloth, not only for ornamental purposes but also for buttonholes, hems, and seams. The preponderance of lost stitching among the London textile remains suggests that linen thread was usually used for the main seams, whereas the more expensive silk thread was probably reserved for visible and decorative stitching. This evidence helps to explain references to the dual use of linen and silk thread on various garments in the Great Wardrobe accounts which have been difficult to interpret hitherto. In 1333, for instance, a set of five garments of green cloth was presented to Queen Philippa for her Easter clothing, the making of which had required 1lb of linen thread and 3ozs of silk thread. On a pound to pound basis, silk thread was considerably more expensive than linen thread. The Great Wardrobe accounts of the 1330s show that linen thread often cost less than 3s. per lb (2d. per oz, for example), whereas silk thread cost in the region of 15s. to 20s. per lb. The silk thread was usually purchased from City mercers or Italian merchants and was available in a wide range of colours. White, black, yellow, blue, green, red, purple and flame are repeatedly specified, and these would have matched the dyes of the cloths and woven silks, although on occasion it is possible that contrasting colours might have been employed.

More Great Wardrobe accounts need to be examined to clarify the supply of goods like silk threads. At present only a little is known about London silkwomen before the middle of the 14th century, although extensive research has produced a quantity of information regarding their activities later in the 14th and in the 15th century (Dale 1932–4; Lacey 1987). They specialised in twisting silk thread and producing ribbons, cords, braids, fringes, tassels and other small silk goods.

Wool thread was also used to sew garments in the middle ages. A practice of considerable antiquity and one which appears to have been normal on wool clothing worn in London, and also in York, during the 10th and 11th centuries (Pritchard 1984, 58–9; Walton 1989A, 408), there is little documentary confirmation for it in 14th-century London. It would seem that by this time linen and silk threads probably predominated — at least, that is the impression one gets from the fragments. There can be little doubt, however, that the use of wool sewing thread must still have been widespread in the lower classes of society and it is this type of thread that was used on the 14th-century garments from Herjolfsnes, Greenland, which was a farming community (Østergård 1982, 271).

Only five examples of wool thread used for stitching purposes survive from London for this later medieval period. Three are associated with tabby-woven cloths, including one which is patterned with weft-faced bands (No 285). It is also inserted through the selvedge of a twill (No 158) and to stitch a fragmentary roll of twill cloth (No 156). The roll could have been used as a belt, but equally may have been a tie for fastening a cloak or mantle. The stitching thread is similar to the woven threads and it is possible that the thread was unravelled from the material. Wool thread made from worsted yarn (later known as crewel thread) occurs only occasionally in the Great Wardrobe accounts when it seems to have been used solely for embroidery motifs (Nicolas 1846, 33).

Sewing techniques

The original construction of clothing in northern Europe from animal skins no doubt brought about a set of sewing skills appropriate to fur and leather which were gradually modified for use with cloths woven from wool, linen, and, eventually, silken textiles. The repertoire of stitches used to join and finish textiles is not a large one but the mechanical process of analysing and listing stitching, seaming, hemming and other finishing techniques is a useful contribution to a broader understanding of the development of sewing and constructional skills in medieval and early modern Europe. In the following commentary sewing is translated from the point of view of a right-handed technician; it is very likely some stitching was carried out by left-handed sewers, but it has not been possible to identify this with certainty.

As we currently understand it, stitching was primarily a joining technique that was gradually extended in its use on woven textiles to embrace such practical refinements as hemming, gathering or decorative effects achieved by the application of bands, braids or fringes. Stitching also came to be used on its own to create decorative effects (embroidery).

Seams

Overstitching, or whipping two edges together, is a common technique for joining two pieces of fine leather or felt, allowing a flat, or almost flat, surface when the pieces are opened out, and being economical of precious material. It is most easily carried out with the two pieces face to face, but

can be worked with them flat and only the two requisite edges in contact. Such a method of joining is usually unsatisfactory for woven textiles, since fraying is likely to occur except where the edges are selvedges or where they are both folded.

The most obvious example of this method among the London textiles occurs in Nos 326 and 327 (Fig 124A). Two pieces of medium-weight tabby-woven silk are very firmly overstitched together, with a fairly coarse two-ply silk thread, along the selvedge of one piece and the folded edge of the other; the stitching is consistently even, and so by an experienced hand, but the sewing does not display the care for matching fineness of thread and smallness of stitch which is appropriate to such a silk and which is demonstrated on other finds in the group. It is not clear what purpose these fragments served; they were perhaps a lining of a garment, already recycled from some earlier use. The join appears not to have been opened out or to have had tensions placed upon it from each side, and as the method is an obvious way of joining edges of a purse or bag, for instance, this is another possible interpretation. The direction of the stitching, coupled with what seems to be a starting knot at the left-hand side, suggests that it was carried out from right to left, or with the work held in the left hand, in a direction away from the body. In recent times it has been more usual for right-handed sewers to work from left to right, or towards the body.

Another joining technique which may derive from leather working is that of *overlapped* edges, again rather less satisfactory on woven textiles because of fraying. This is a method where the folding of one or both edges will bring greater strength to the join, as in run-and-fell seams, for example. A small group of fragments from the late 14th century (Nos 236 and 238–242) display evidence of overlapped seams although all the stitching threads, presumably originally linen, have long since disappeared (Fig 125). The pattern of stitching holes coupled with the distribution of worn and unworn areas confirm this was the seam that was used. With one exception all these fragments appear to be the remains of the foot section of hose, where flat seams would be most comfortable; the double stitching technique would enable the seams to resist the greater pressure of wear experienced inside a shoe or boot. It

A

B

C

Fig 124 Seams formed by overstitching two edges together: (A) Nos 326 and 327 (both sides): the starting knot is shown at the top of the photograph and further rows of stitching holes can be seen on either side of the seam, (B) No 347, note the warp is shown horizontally. From late 14th-century deposits. (C) illustrates how (A) may have been stitched. Scale 1:1

approach is the same. One fragment (No 242) with much more deeply overlapping seams of 6–9mm does not appear to be from hose, and may be from another garment, although at present it is impossible to hazard what this might have been.

Today the most traditional form of seam is that where a line of stitching runs parallel with the two raw edges to be joined, and it has to be assumed

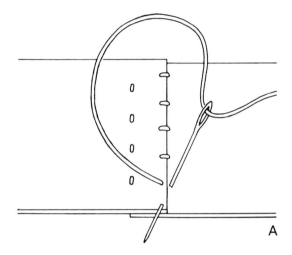

A

Fig 125 (A) Seam formed by overlapping edges usually found on foot sections of wool hose, (B) photograph showing stitch impressions and evidence of overlapped edge, No 215. Scale 1:1

B

would seem likely that the heat and dampness of the human foot created conditions where further shrinkage of the cloth took place: the raw edges along the seams now have an undulating appearance which has suggested 'pinking' or oversewing to earlier researchers, but in fact it is simply that the sewing thread remained in place whilst the surrounding threads of the cloth shrank. The usual overlap on these seams is 4–7mm, whilst the stitches are about 3mm long and placed at 3–4mm intervals. The stitching holes and associated depressions in the cloth show that a fairly upright hem-stitch was used along both raw edges. Fraying was thus minimised; furthermore the cloth would have been fulled before being manufactured into garments, a process which also reduced fraying. The special use of a seam of this kind on the foot sections of hose is confirmed by fragments of hose of 16th-century origin found in the City earlier this century. The stitching on some of these latter fragments is still intact and, although one edge is usually folded to give strength on the finer twilled cloth which superseded tabby-woven cloth hose, essentially the

that by the middle ages too this was the most usual method for joining textiles. Although a number of seams of this kind survive among the London textiles, the stitching threads have almost completely disappeared, leaving well-defined stitching holes. From this evidence it is possible to show that in the majority of cases a fairly fine *running-stitch* was usual for holding the two edges together (Fig 126A). The size of the stitch varies somewhat, as is to be expected, but it is usually

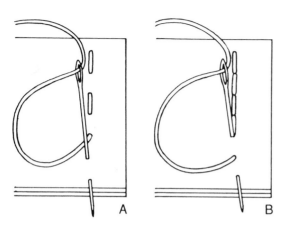
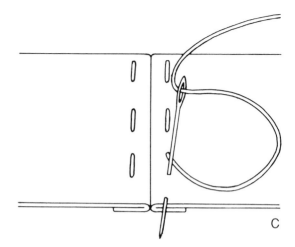
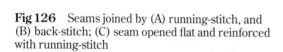

Fig 126   Seams joined by (A) running-stitch, and
(B) back-stitch; (C) seam opened flat and reinforced
with running-stitch

related to the fineness and flexibility of the cloth;
stitch lengths of 2–4mm have been recorded, 2–
3mm, being usual. Detailed microscopic examination of the holes and impressions left by the lost
stitches could very well produce more exact information about the sewing methods used.

A line of running-stitches has long been the
usual method of holding garment seams together
and is present in many examples of surviving
clothing of the 16th and 17th centuries onwards.
Where seams came under pressure, particularly
those employed in shaping garments to fit closely
to the human form, or in forming crucial joints
(armholes, for example), one of the variants of
back-stitch would have been more appropriate
(Fig 126B). There is no certain evidence of back-
stitched seams amongst the London textile fragments, but it is possible that the seams of bias-cut
hose may have been back-stitched to prevent
them coming apart during use. Added strength
was given to these seams through the use of a row
of running-stitches on each side of the seam,
worked through both seam allowance and outer
layer, parallel with and close to the seam (about 2–
3mm). This held the seam allowances underneath
flat (Fig 126C), a technique which is also found in
fragments of 16th-century hose in the Museum of
London collections.

Hems

Because the cut edges of woven fabrics usually
fray quite quickly as the result of friction, a number of stitching techniques have been developed
to control this process; they can involve various
methods of oversewing where friction is not considerable, or more particularly, at the edges of the
garment, single or double folds (hems) of material which greatly strengthen the edge. Whereas
today exposed raw edges are invariably strengthened in some way, certainly at garment edges, it is
likely that in past centuries raw edges sufficed
much more, since cloth-finishing processes ren-
dered many wool fabrics less likely to fray.

The evidence of the textiles from London suggests that on a woollen cloth a single hem was
usually considered adequate during the 14th century. This could be hem-stitched (Nos 235, 238,
Fig 127A), held with a running-stitch (Nos 219,
243, 244, Fig 127B) or top-stitched from the right
side (Fig 127C). The first method offers a protection to a raw edge and is appropriate to the hem of
a garment. The two other methods produce an
edge more capable of taking some stress and it is
not surprising to find them the preferred
methods for the tops of hose or the wrist edges of
sleeves.

A sleeve fragment from the deposit dating to
the second quarter of the 14th century at BC72
has 4–5mm folded back, held by back-stitching in
silk thread 2mm from the edge; a further two
fragments with edges treated in this way may be
suspected to have come from sleeves as well (Nos

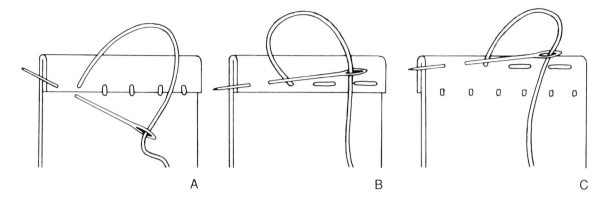

A   B   C

Fig 127   Single-folded hems: (A) hem-stitch, (B) running-stitch, (C) top-stitch

A   B

Fig 128   Double-folded hems: (A) hem-stitch, (B) with running-stitches along edge, No 330, from a late 14th-century deposit. Scale 1:1

34, 159). The same method may have been used on the top edges of hose; two examples of such hems on the edge of bias strips (Nos 245, 276) are more likely to be from hose than from any other part of a garment, whilst an almost complete lower leg section of hose has a straight, horizontal upper edge with a single hem and the remains of top-stitching in silk thread (No 235, Fig 167A).

Part of a coarse woollen garment patterned with coloured bands from an early 13th-century deposit seems to have been hemmed with running-stitches in linen thread (No 430). Traces of two hems which together form a corner are present. The side edge was folded back 8–9mm and stitched 5–6mm in from the edge. The lower edge was then folded back to a depth of 25mm resulting in a large hem allowance and also stitched 5–6mm in from the edge.

There are only two examples of double hems — one fold imposed upon the other — amongst the wool fragments. One small offcut of 60mm × 35mm (No 197), almost but not quite on the straight of the grain, has a preliminary fold of 5mm and a final hem depth of 9mm held by hem-stitching. The second and considerably larger fragment is probably from the hem of a mantle, a dress or supertunic made from a fine twilled wool (No 44, Fig 160). The finished depth of the hem is 5mm and it is held by hemming stitches at about 4mm intervals. Certainly in this instance a double fold was necessary because of the nature of the twilled cloth, and it is possible therefore that this was the edge of a trailing garment, such as a soft, flowing dress or cloak.

Because the cut edge of silk cloth is so much more likely to fray, and to fray rapidly, many more examples of double hems survive among the silk textiles from London. These hems reflect the quality of the cloth, ranging in depth from 6–9mm, with carefully executed hem-stitching in fine silk thread (Figs 66, 128, 138).

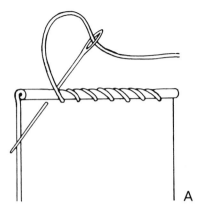

Fig 129   (A) Rolled hem, (B) No 333, from a late 14th-century deposit. Scale 2:1

Another form of hem particularly suited to fine silks is the rolled hem. This is less conspicuous than the double hem but demands more skill and manual dexterity as it cannot easily be pinned in place before sewing. The left hand rolls the raw edge and holds this in place whilst it is stitched by the right hand. The technique is used solely on the fine transparent silk veils of the late 14th-century (Nos 333, 334, Figs 68, 129) where it has proved most efficient as well as unobtrusive. The rolling and stitching — long diagonal hem-stitching which wraps itself around the roll — is especially finely executed, the roll being less than 1mm deep and with approximately 5–6 stitches per cm. These hems are clearly the work of a highly experienced and skilled worker and often seem to have been stitched with the material facing away from the sewer; today it is more usual for the material to be held the other way round.

Bindings and facings

Where a single or double hem was an inappropriate finishing for an edge, and particularly where some additional strength was required, strips of material could be applied as facings or bindings.

All surviving facings and bindings are of a fine tabby silk on the straight grain of the fabrics; no bias strip is known to have been used for this purpose on bias-cut or curving edges.

Three examples of bound edges survive, all from late 14th-century deposits. One is a short length of silk ribbon on the slightly curved edge of a fragment of cloth with eight small buttonhole slits (No 219). The function of this piece is puzzling. It may be the lower edge of a buttoned hood, perhaps a child's hood, as the buttonholes are so small (8mm): or it may be the wrist of a sleeve extended to cover the back of the hand. The ribbon was held by slanting hem-stitching on both sides, but only one stitch is now preserved. A second example (No 216, Fig 144) is almost certainly from the lower edge of a tightly buttoned sleeve which extended over part of the hand, similar to those portrayed in many effigies and monumental brasses dating to the second half of the 14th century (e.g. Fig 157). The third example is an unattached evenly-folded length of silk ribbon, 155mm long (No 386), which has a succession of small regularly-spaced stitching holes along each edge and may well have been used as a binding in a similar way, although folded ribbons of this type were also used to bind the edges of pouches, including examples made from leather (Fig 130)

Fig 130 Leather
pouch finished with a
silk ribbon binding, No
383, from a late 14th-cen-
tury deposit. Scale 1:1

Fig 131 Edge of a
neck or armhole with a
narrow silk facing, No 78
(both sides), from a
deposit dating to the
second quarter of the
14th century: (A) photo-
graph, scale 3:4, (B) line
drawing, scale 1:3

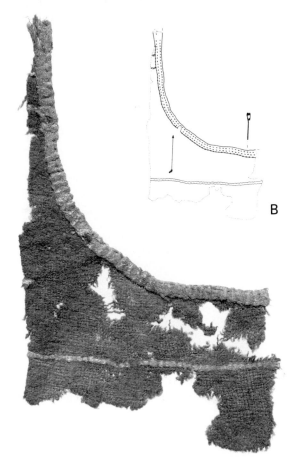

B

A

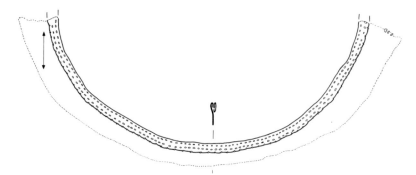

Fig 132   Neckline of a wool garment with a narrow silk facing, No 50, shown from the reverse, from a de-posit dating to the second quarter of the 14th century. Scale 1:2

Two fragments of curved edgings which were probably neck or armhole edges still retain their stitched facings (No 78, Fig 131, and No 50, Fig 132, Pl 2B); they come from the deposit at BC72 dating to the second quarter of the 14th century. In both instances a 3mm fold of the curved woollen edge has been turned inward and covered with a 5mm-wide strip of silk held firmly in place by two rows of tiny running-stitches which slightly puncture the upper, outer surface. The lower edge of each facing is additionally held in place by small slanted hem-stitches, approximately 3–4mm apart. Although in fact cut as a semi-circle, the tension of the stitching on No 50 seems to have made it form an almost complete circle so that it now, misleadingly, resembles a complete neck edge.

Facings attached to raw woollen edges also occur. A clothing fragment (No 57), perhaps the shoulder portion of a sleeveless overtunic, has two parallel edges with incomplete remains of facings composed of 9mm strips of fine silk. A single turning is firmly hemmed or overstitched to the raw edge of cloth and below this a row of tiny running-

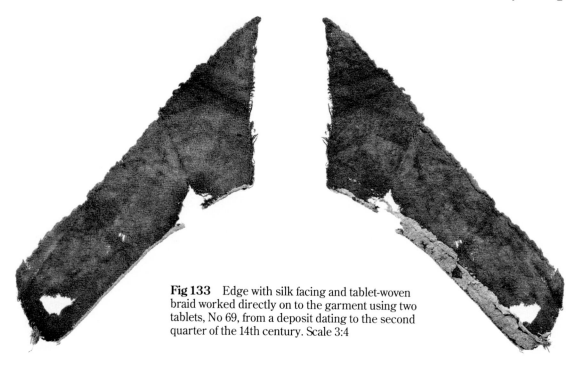

Fig 133   Edge with silk facing and tablet-woven braid worked directly on to the garment using two tablets, No 69, from a deposit dating to the second quarter of the 14th century. Scale 3:4

stitches holds the facing flat and gives additional strengthening to the edge. The inner edge of the facing has a hemmed single turning. In a few instances of this kind, all raw cut edges with narrow facings, the edges have been further strengthened by the addition of a directly applied narrow tablet-woven edging (Nos 36, 69, 137, Fig 133). The original use of these fragments is not known — perhaps they were neck edgings of overtunics — but just such an edge survives almost intact on the buttonhole edge of a sleeve cuff (No 64, Fig 142, Pl 1) discarded in the second quarter of the 14th century. Here such strengthening was vital since the buttonholes finish only 2–3mm from the edge of the sleeve opening and so narrow a channel could easily be torn by wear and tension. There are three other buttonhole strips finished with tablet-woven edges, one completely intact (No 67, Fig 135), another fragmentary where almost all the main woollen fabric has disappeared (No 32, Fig 136), and a third where the edging has

become very worn (No 159, Fig 163). Other examples of buttonholes lack such a refinement as this edging but on one strip, at least, stitching holes along the edge suggest that it was originally finished in a similar way, although probably with linen thread rather than with silk (No 34, Fig 137).

Buttonholes were normally backed by a facing to give overall strengthening, and in quite a number of instances this is now missing (e.g. Nos 173, 217, 218, 220–224, 246, 272, 273, Figs 164, 170). In these cases the missing facing, like the similarly absent stitching, was almost certainly of linen or perhaps bokeram (a cotton fabric). The facings usually extend well beyond the buttonhole at the inner edge to provide strength. This is not the case, however, on the best preserved sleeve fragment itself, where the facing only extends 2mm beyond the buttonholes. As with the neck and armhole bindings, the silk strip or facing was held in place by a series of running-stitches along the length of the inner edge, being hem-stitched into place.

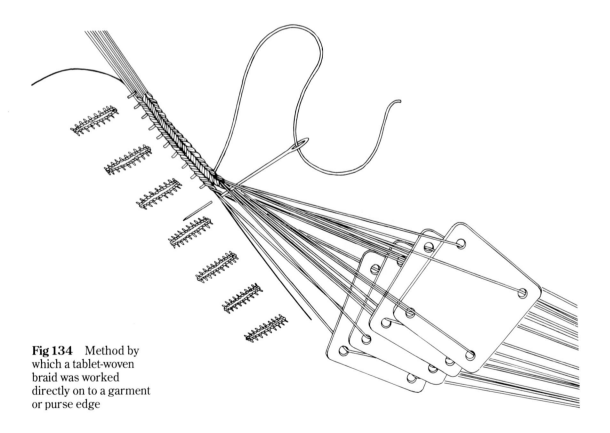

Fig 134 Method by which a tablet-woven braid was worked directly on to a garment or purse edge

Fig 135 Buttonhole edge finished with a tablet-woven silk braid worked with four tablets, No 67 (both sides), from a deposit dating to the second quarter of the 14th century. Scale 3:4

Fig 136 Buttonhole edge finished with a tablet-woven braid worked with two tablets, No 32, from a deposit dating to the second quarter of the 14th century. Very little of the woollen cloth of the garment is preserved so that the inside of the silk facing is visible. Scale 1:1

Fig 137 Buttonhole edge, No 34, from a deposit dating to the second quarter of the 14th century. This was originally finished with a tablet-woven edge but only the stitch holes of this are preserved. (A) Complete piece, scale 3:4, (B) and (C) details, scale 2:1

Fastening methods

The chief method of fastening among the remnants of garments is that of buttons and buttonholes, although lacing was almost certainly widely used, and perhaps predominant, at the time. The latter was a method of considerable antiquity, ultimately derived from the age of skin clothing.

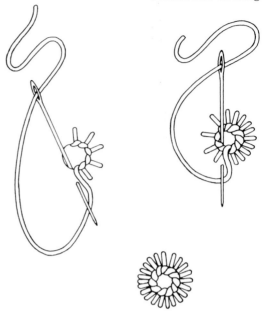

Fig 139   Diagram showing how the eyelets were stitched on No 329

Fig 138   Detail of eyelet holes on silk facing and associated strip of silk, No 329, from a deposit dating to the late 14th century: (A) front, note traces of the woollen cloth to which the facing was originally stitched are visible round the eyelet in the centre, (B) reverse, (C) associated strip with two rows of stitching holes down the centre. Scale 1:1

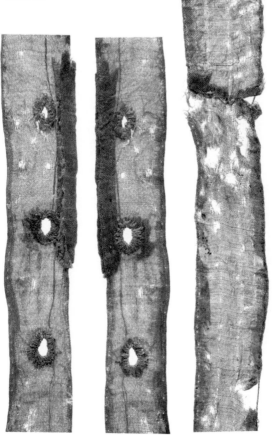

A   B   C

Only one example of eyelet holes for lacing is preserved among the textile finds from London. This is a strip of fine tabby-woven silk (No 329, Fig 138) from a deposit of the late 14th century. The now fragmentary strip is 186mm long and 17–20mm wide; it has narrow turnings along the long edges, to one of which is still attached a folded length of similar silk. A companion strip of silk facing 255mm long and 16–22mm wide has been held in place by running-stitches on three edges and by two equally spaced lines of stitching extending the full length of the strip. The eyelet strip has six eyelets still intact, evenly placed 22mm apart. They are worked in two-ply silk thread, the overstitching of each hole being achieved by two complete circuits of buttonhole-stitch (Fig 139). After the completion of each eyelet the sewing

Fig 140   Alabaster effigy of Catherine Beauchamp, Countess of Warwick, *c.*1370–75, St Mary's Church, Warwick. She wears a gown fastened at the front with lacing while the sleeves are buttoned to above the elbow. (Conway Library, Courtauld Institute of Art, reproduced by permission of Canon M H Ridgway)

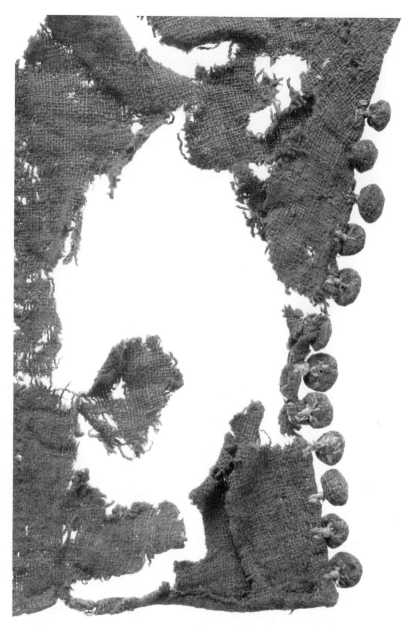

Fig 141 Details of sleeve, No 64 (both sides), showing buttons and silk stitching at wrist edge. Note the row of stitch holes visible on the reverse. Scale 1:1

thread was carried up the back of the work to the next eyelet hole. A sufficiently long sewing thread seems to have been used to complete all six sur-viving eyelets. The eyelets show no sign of wear, nor indeed does the strip itself appear to have been used or fastened under tension, but traces of a woollen fabric remain round one eyelet. This suggests that the strips come from a loose gar-ment, a supertunic for example.

Contemporary illuminations often depict lacing very clearly. Some tomb effigies show its use down the centre front of dresses and tunics to

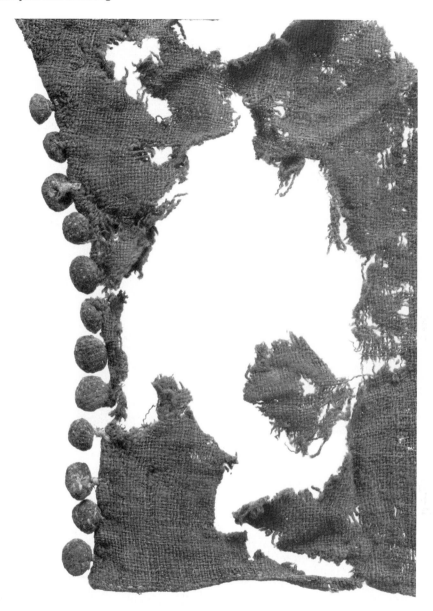

help achieve the close fit fashionable in the middle of the 14th century (Fig 140). Similar lacing could be placed in the side seams and this is illustrated as early as the middle of the 12th century in the Winchester Psalter (Wormald 1973, pl 21), although perhaps as a ridicule of a fairly new fashion. Wrist fastenings were, of course, also often laced. In addition, slip covers of rich silks were laced over pillows and cushions enabling them to

be quickly and easily removed. An alternative solution may be found in the practice of holding the metal shanks of buttons through eyelets by means of a lace at the back (see p. 172).

Two other examples of facings with eyelets have been recorded from medieval deposits in England; one from a pit fill dating to the last decade of the 13th century at Southampton (Crowfoot 1975, 335, no T2, fig 273) and the other

Fig 142 Details of buttonholes, silk facing and tablet-woven edging on sleeve No 64 (both sides). Scale 1:1

from a 14th-century deposit in Kingston upon Hull (Walton forthcoming), In both of these the silk cloth is similar to that of the London piece but in each the sewing thread has disappeared suggesting that the eyelets were worked in linen. In view of the widespread use of lacing it is not surprising that eyelet-stitch became part of the embroiderer's repertoire in England, as well as on the Continent, during the 13th and 14th centuries (Chandler & King 1960, 23; Alexander & Binski 1987, 279, no 206; Schuette & Müller-Christensen 1963, 306, nos 51–3; Geijer 1964, 46, no 38, pl 49; Ceulmans *et al.* 1988, 190–92, no 33). Here it seems was a utilitarian method of stitching that was adopted for decoration.

Buttons appear to have been introduced into north European clothing during the first half of the 13th century (White 1978, 238, 273), when they were worn more for ornament than for practical purposes. There seems no other good explanation for the way buttons gradually supplanted the brooch, itself an excellent vehicle for extravagance, as the preferred fastening at the neck. Perhaps the chief influence was the adoption of button fastenings for the wrist openings of sleeves in place of daily stitching of the openings or of lacing. By the early years of the 14th century buttons were being used in increasing numbers as a fashion feature. On the whole, the excesses of this fashion are not evident among the remains of 14th-century garments from London. A wrist fragment of a sleeve (No 64, Figs 141, 142, Pl 1), with its twelve small cloth buttons and buttonholes, is a conservative form of the fashion; far more buttons are used up the opening than is strictly necessary, but they do not reach up to the elbow in the manner demonstrated by contemporary effigies and

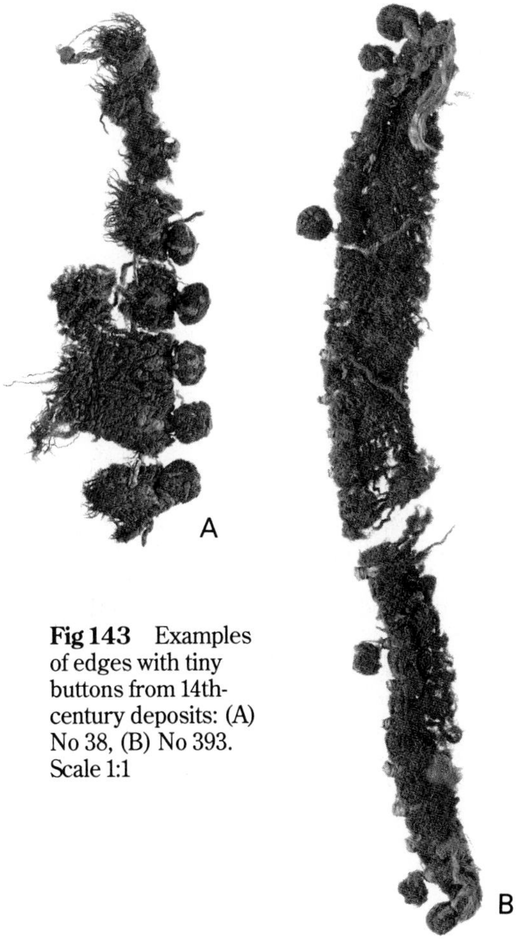

Fig 143 Examples of edges with tiny buttons from 14th-century deposits: (A) No 38, (B) No 393. Scale 1:1

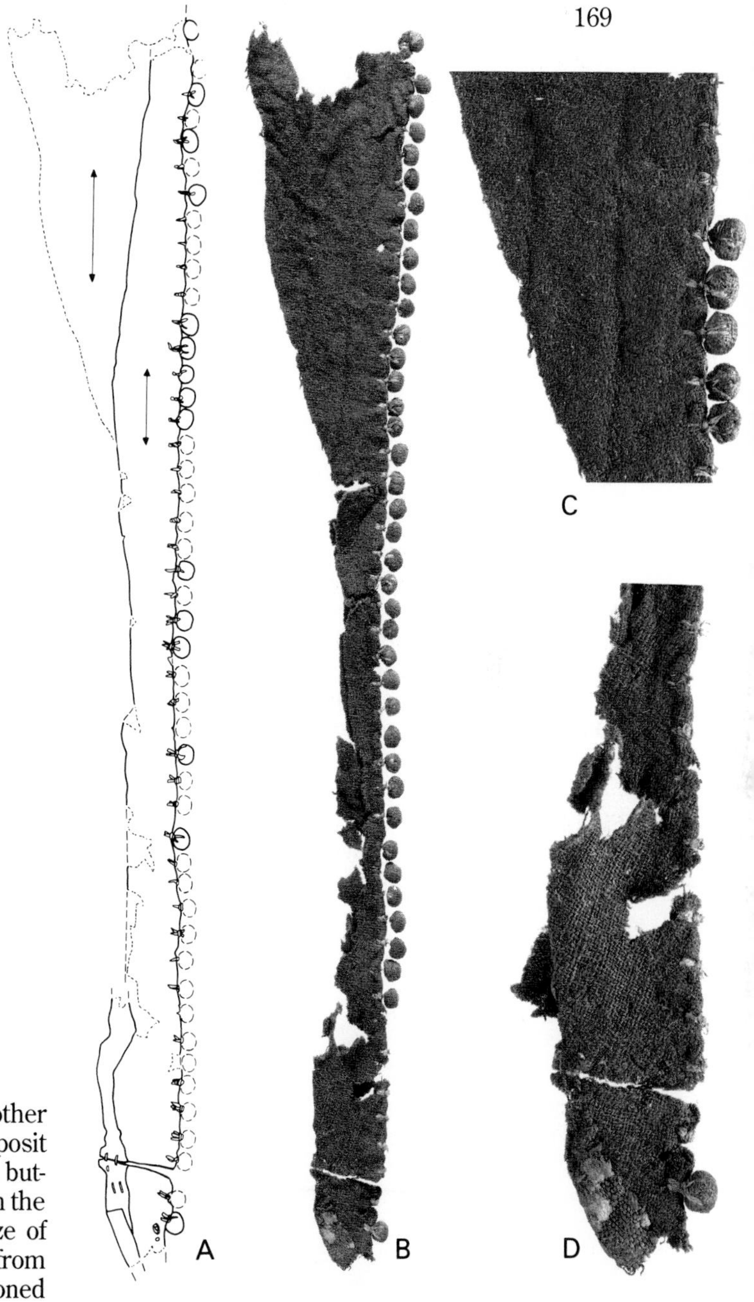

Fig 144 Edge of garment, No 216, with at least 46 cloth buttons, from late 14th-century London: (A) line drawing, scale 1:2, (B) complete piece, scale 1:2, (C) and (D) details, scale 1:1

manuscript illuminations (see Fig 140). Two other fragments of sleeve edges from the same deposit of *c.*1330–40 preserve a larger number of buttonholes, 16 on one (No 34, Fig 137) and 25 on the other (No 67, Fig 135), while the small size of some buttons by this date can be judged from other fragments (No 38, Fig 143A). A buttoned edging from the late 14th century, however, originally had as many as 46 cloth buttons in a stretch of only 315mm (No 216, Fig 144).

Whilst, of course, they served the practical purpose of holding two edges together, the essentially decorative nature of buttons in the 14th century is evident in the approach to the construction of the edges to be joined in this way. The edge to which the buttons themselves are at-

tached is merely a single fold of cloth and the stalks of the buttons are attached firmly to this fold (Figs 141, 144, 147). One edge, however, to

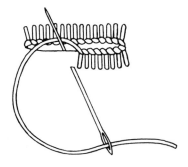

Fig 145   Method of sewing buttonholes

which very small buttons are stitched has a single fold only 3mm wide and here a silk facing was used only traces of which now remain (No 395, Fig 143B). On the buttonhole side of the opening the edge of the cloth was left raw and, once a silk facing had been applied to the underside, a tablet-woven silk braid was worked directly along the raw edge, giving it a neat but barely visible finish which would only be appreciated by the wearer of

Fig 146   Small buttonholes worked in silk thread on a garment made from a medium grade wool cloth, No 220 (both sides), from a deposit dating to the late 14th century. Scale 1:1

the garment and those in close proximity to him or her (Figs 135, 136, 142, 163).

Holes, in the form of slits at right angles to the opening edge, were cut for the buttonholes *before* they were worked; it is usual today to cut the holes *after* they have been worked with buttonhole-stitches. There is no visible evidence of a circuit of running-stitches round the hole to hold the two layers together and to strengthen the vulnerable cut slits. The 14th-century buttonholes examined here are all worked with a strong two-ply (Z-twisted, S-plied) silk thread in buttonhole-stitch (Fig 145). The direction in which the stitching was carried out seems to vary, for reasons that are not completely clear today. We can feel reasonably certain that the more recent uniform approach to sewing technique, taught and passed on by means of sewing sample books and, latterly, printed text-books, did not exist in the middle ages. Some disparity may be the result of left-handedness in the workers but it may equally be evidence for a less sophisticated stage in the evolution of the skills of tailors and seamstresses. Some of the buttonholes appear to have been worked in a clockwise fashion, whilst in others the direction of the stitching is clearly anti-clockwise. The sewing thread was carried up the back of the work from buttonhole to buttonhole (see Figs 136, 146) pro-viding simple, but clearly effective protection to

the raw edges. There is no evidence of special techniques to strengthen the weakest parts of the holes (the points at each end of the slit) by close radial stitching or by the addition of a plain or worked thread bar at one or both ends of the slit. Such techniques were certainly in use by the 16th century when the stress often placed on buttonholes by padded and tight-fitting fashionable clothing made such reinforcement imperative (see Arnold 1985, 33, fig 48). It seems unlikely that such strain was placed upon buttonholes on most 14th-century garments.

The size of the buttonholes varies considerably. Those on identifiable wrist openings of sleeves are 7–10mm, whilst others as large as 12–14mm (Nos 217, 272) are perhaps from the front edge of a garment. The buttonhole slits fastening the hood under the chin (No 246, Fig 170) are 11–14mm long. The depth of the buttonhole-stitching is usually not great, about 1–1.5mm. The stitches are mostly set apart about 0.5mm, and are not packed closely together to form a solid band as is normal today. These small stitches could be used on quite loosely-woven cloths, No 220 for example where the buttonholes are only 6–7mm long (Fig 146), but presumably sufficed for their purpose, in combination with the fine silk facings. On larger buttonholes large stitches can appear, being about 2mm deep.

This is only the third archaeological site in which cloth buttons of a 14th-century date have been found; the other sites are Herjolfsnes, Greenland (Nørlund 1924, fig 65), and Nieuwendijk, Amsterdam, The Netherlands (Vons-Comis 1982, 154), where they include buttons sewn to the wrist opening of a sleeve made from a patterned cloth very similar to No 64. The cloth buttons from London fall into a number of groups. Many are simply circles of well-fulled cloth manipulated to form well-condensed domes. They were probably gathered by one of several running-stitches close to the outside edge and tightly gathered up underneath (Fig 147). The whole was then strengthened by concentric rings of stitches stabbed vertically through all thicknesses. It is possible that at this stage further solidity may have been achieved by an additional fulling or shrinking process, for some buttons (e.g. those on sleeve No 64) are immensely compact. These particular buttons are 9mm in diameter and are attached to the folded diagonal sleeve opening by a 2–3mm stalk

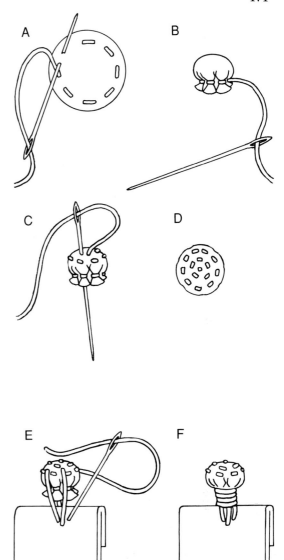

Fig 147 Method by which some of the buttons were made and attached

formed by silk threads.

Loose single buttons found in the late 14th-century deposit at BC72 are 14mm, 17mm, 18mm, 20mm and 35mm in diameter (Nos 225–228, 274, Fig 148). Unlike the earlier, smaller examples these form flattish buttons and have no additional stiffening inside them. The largest of the group (No 228, Fig 148B) may not have been used in the

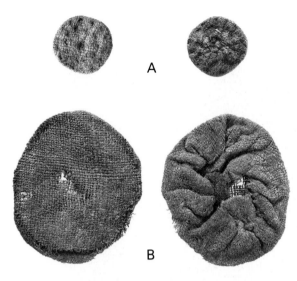

Fig 148 Buttons from a deposit dating to the late 14th century: (A) No 225, (B) No 228 (each button shown both sides). Scale 1:1

same way. It has no sign of stab stitching from front to back, and the gathered cloth at the back is not consolidated as on the other buttons. Its flatness and the way the upper surface and edges are very worn suggest that it may have contained a flat disc, perhaps made from wood or horn, like later buttons; alternatively it may simply have been used for decorative purposes.

Precisely how cloth was manipulated to make the smallest of the buttons is not altogether clear. There is no possibility of constricting the material in quite the same way as was done for the larger examples, but certainly a needle and silk thread once more played a vital role in forming and attaching them. Firm stitches pierced both the button and the folded edge, the silk thread extending between the fold of the cloth and linking one button to another (Fig 143A). These buttons are mostly 5–6mm in diameter (3–4mm on No 393, Fig 143B) and are placed at intervals of 5–8mm, 6mm being the most usual. Such buttons must have been the work of a highly skilled person. They would also have suffered fairly rapidly from the effects of wear and tear. No wonder, therefore, that these edges were removed and discarded while the rest of the garment was recycled.

Metal buttons made from tin, pewter, bronze and brass have also been recovered from 13th-and 14th-century deposits in London (Egan & Pritchard 1991) but, by contrast to cloth buttons, none now remain attached to any item of clothing. This is perhaps because they were attached in a different way; indeed, shanks at the back of the metal buttons suggest that they could have been moved from garment to garment by the simple expedient of setting the button shank through a worked eyelet hole and passing a lace down the back of the eyelets and through the shank, a technique well attested in surviving clothing of the 16th century and by earlier visual evidence. Indeed this may have been the purpose of the silk eyelets (Fig 138) and would explain why they show no stress-lines from tension. Like brooches before them, buttons in the 14th century became settings for precious jewels. In 1351, for instance, the Duke of Orleans had a set of 25 gold buttons each with a diamond surrounded by four pearls (Staniland 1980, 21) and no doubt these were attached to his clothing by this method. The type of buttons worn by the female weeper from Edward III's tomb (Fig 157) and by William of Hatfield (Fig 178) were probably also attached in this way.

Decorative features

Textiles often had patterns woven into them but in a few instances there are indications of decorative techniques applied after weaving as part of the construction of a garment.

Perhaps more functional than decorative is the single apparent evidence for gathering found at one end of a damaged strip of tabby-woven cloth (No 72). Most of the creasing suggests the possibility of a broad band of regular, shallow gathers, such as was later controlled by surface stitching (smocking). This fragment, together with several other small related fragments, would appear to have come from a garment of some kind, perhaps the neck edge of a cape or cloak. A rather similar piece of gathered cloth was recovered from a 15th-century deposit in Oslo where the cloth is a 2.1 twill and the sewing thread wool (Kjellberg 1979, 91, 103, fig 7). A further strip of cloth from London has stitching and folding evidence which suggest narrow tucks or ridges (No 233, Fig 149); these again may be decorative ways of controlling fullness. These gathers are very different from the pleats which have been

Fig 149 The gathered edge of a garment, No 233, from late 14th-century London. Scale 1:1

recorded on pieces of clothing from Scandinavia — Oslo, Bergen and Trondheim in Norway (Kjellberg 1979, 93, 104; Kjellberg 1982, 143–4, fig 3a; Bergli 1988, 222–3) and Gamla Lodose, Swe-

den (Nockert 1984, 191–4), where they range in date from the 11th to the 14th centuries. These narrow pleats, 7–23mm wide, were stitched on the wrong side of the garment with small running-stitches which held the pleats permanently in place.

A series of parallel rows of running stitches in silk thread on a very fine worsted cloth (No 171, Fig 150) also present evidence of decoration or a constructional technique which cannot for the moment be explained. The fragment, from a deposit dating to the late 14th century, is now in more than

Fig 150 Fine six-shed twill with rows of running-stitches in silk thread, No 171, from a deposit dating to the late 14th century. Scale 1:1

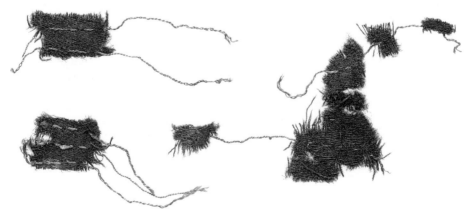

Fig 151 Three-shed twill with traces of a silk facing sewn to it with horizontal and diagonal rows of stitching, No 35, from a deposit dating to the second quarter of the 14th century. Scale 1:1

a dozen very small pieces with long trailing ends of silk thread; two rows of stitching with starting knots survive on one fragment 21mm x 13mm, with loose ends some 40mm long. This may have been decorative stitching of a darning type. An example from the second quarter of the 14th century gives a clearer impression of the decorative effect of this type of stitching (No 35, Fig 151). Here a woollen 2.1 twill is lined with a piece of silk tabby and they are held together with rows of

running stitches which form a triangular pattern.

A fragment of fine silk (No 136, Fig 152), now 140mm x 135mm, is punctured by a multitude of stitching holes although not a single stitch remains intact. This may have been a decorative square or label from a garment once ornamented with stitching in silk or linen thread in a darning stitch forming a linear geometrical design. The stitching may have served the purpose of holding layers of material together, as in quilting, but the

Fig 153 Two methods by which strips of cloth were applied as decoration and two silk trimmings of this type in satin weave from late 14th-century London: (A) and (B) No 345 (note the weft face is shown in (B) with its warp horizontal). Scale 1:1

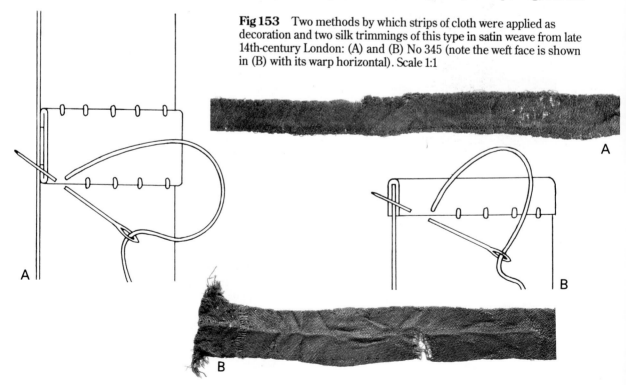

Fig 152 Silk tabby cloth covered with diagonal and horizontal rows of stitching holes, No 136, from a deposit dating to the second quarter of the 14th century. Scale 1:1

proximity of the stitches (perhaps prick-stitches, about 4mm apart) and rows (regularly 5mm in the upper right corner of the cloth as illustrated)

rather suggest that little thickness was involved and that this was a purely decorative addition to some other textile object.

Decoration could also be achieved by applying one material to another. A group of three strips of silk satin (Nos 345, 346, Figs 93, 153) 9–11mm and 13–14mm wide might be construed as just such ornamental additions to a garment. Each has narrow turnings along the length of the strip and stitching holes, and they appear to have been hemmed in place. One strip has a short end also turned under and displays evidence of many stitches, perhaps for holding a circular, disc-like ornament in place. Two strips of velvet (No 351, Fig 96) also appear to have been stitched to another fabric originally.

Whilst the elaborate, time-consuming and expensive embroidery of the middle ages was the prerogative of the church and royal circle, it is certain that less affluent citizens of London found ways to enliven their otherwise plain woollen clothing. Earlier chapters of this book have demonstrated the decorative effects which could be introduced into woollen cloths on the loom — stripes, checks and mottled effects — and which did not necessarily add exorbitantly to the price. Contrasting braids could be manipulated to produce a further decorative effect and this, coupled with a little of the top-stitching discussed above, was almost certainly the only decoration that most people wore. Silk cords and braids could also have served to ornament clothing as, of course, could jewelled brooches and girdles for those who could afford such luxuries. The medieval textiles from London, however, include none of the varied decorative techniques indicated in the accounts of the royal household (Staniland 1980; Staniland 1989).

Construction

There is still much speculation about the way in which clothing construction developed during the middle ages. Many well-established writers on the history of dress, working almost solely from visual sources, have highlighted a tailoring revolution in the decade 1330–40, supporting their argument by a few contemporary quotations criticising sartorial excesses (Laver 1963; Byrde 1979). It is highly unlikely that a radical change took place in such a short time, but rather that external pressures helped to speed up a process which had been developing for a considerable time.

The most important body of evidence for the shaping of medieval garments is to be found in neither visual nor literary sources, however, although the evidence from both is by no means negligible. The most reliable evidence for medieval cut and construction is to be found in the surviving garments themselves, many of which have been excavated in the Scandinavian countries during the last 100 years (Nørlund 1924; Hald 1980; Hägg 1983; Hägg 1984; Nockert 1985; Fentz 1987). These are supplemented by clothing from the tombs of rulers, nobles and churchmen, for example the Emperors Henry III and Henry IV, and Philip of Swabia at Speyer Cathedral, Germany (Müller-Christensen *et al.* 1972), the Castilian royal family at the abbey of San Salvador and later the convent of Las Huelgas, both in the province of Burgos, Spain (Gómez-Moreno 1946; Lopez 1970; Carretero 1988), and Cangrande della Scala in Verona, Italy (Magagnato 1983). The evidence which these garments can provide has yet to be explored fully or collated, whilst information about a number of recent finds is only just beginning to be available through publication. In addition, so far as is known, there has been no study in which the evidence provided by excavated clothing has been compared with that of garments which have survived above the ground. The latter, most notably the remarkable *pourpoint* associated with Charles de Blois (died 1364) (Evans 1952, 30, fig IV; Newton 1980, 108, pl 39) have similarly not been fully studied for the information they can provide about approaches to construction or sewing methods, and it is likely that this would add greatly to our very limited knowledge.

Interpretation of the clothing fragments from London is fraught with problems and uncertainties. Certain items or groups emerge with little difficulty, but there are quite a number of individual pieces which for the time being defy accurate indentification. Discussion of these pieces must be left for publication at a later date when a greater quantity of comparative material has emerged to throw more light on the problems involved.

Methods of shaping clothing in the early middle ages were unsophisticated in modern terms but nevertheless effective to the contemporary eye. Whilst it is true that there was an unwillingness to waste cloth by cutting into it, the increasing pressure to fit cloth closely to the human body, from the time of the Norman conquest at least, slowly produced increasingly inventive use of what were essentially geometrical shapes. For instance, triangular sections cut from sleeves

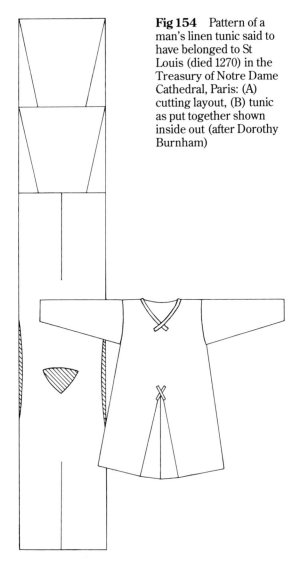

Fig 154 Pattern of a man's linen tunic said to have belonged to St Louis (died 1270) in the Treasury of Notre Dame Cathedral, Paris: (A) cutting layout, (B) tunic as put together shown inside out (after Dorothy Burnham)

fulling techniques, lent itself to this practice since smaller pieces could easily be joined together, patchwork-fashion, to create a larger piece. Any scraps still left over could be used to form smaller articles (purses, for instance, or seal bags) or cut up and applied as decorative bands. In fact most of the London fragments are themselves evidence for the use and reuse of cloth in medieval clothing: they are discarded offcuts from larger pieces (or whole garments) which were involved in the re-cycling process, at the very time the archaeological deposits were laid down.

On the whole these fragments from garments provide clues rather than complete evidence for the construction of the clothing of citizens of medieval London. By the 14th century a number of methods of cutting and shaping clothing ex-isted, or were in the process of being developed. The older dependence upon rectangles and tri-angles (gores) was to continue in fashionable dress for some centuries to come, particularly in underwear and shirts, and ultimately became fos-silised in some forms of national costume. A num-ber of the London fragments are related to this construction approach. Small triangular sections could be used at the sides of the heels of hose to help shape the cloth around the foot (Fig 168). A number of fragments from such triangular sec-tions also survive amongst the London textiles. Longer triangular sections may well be identified as inserted side gores from tunics or women's gowns, whilst short triangles helped the shaping of hoods (Fig 170). For shaping tunics, inserted gores served to provide fullness at the hem but not the waist. These required bulky seams, avoided when the gore was cut as an integral part of the main section. Some small remnants in the late 14th-century deposit at BC72 (Nos 229-231) suggest such an origin for themselves and proba-bly come from tunics or supertunics.

to fit them to the arm could easily be fitted into the lower part of a tunic to add to the fullness at the hem (Fig 154). Thus there need be no waste: off-cuts were capitalised upon by being used elsewhere in the garment. This approach to divid-ing a rectangle of cloth was well developed in the 12th century, for aristocratic dress at least, and was to be explored and developed to a much greater extent in the 13th century. For instance, the offcuts of circles or semi-circles could be eco-nomically deployed elsewhere on the same cloak or mantle, leaving little or no waste. The close texture of the cloth, aided by both weaving and

Tunics

A group of textile remains from the late 14th-cen-tury deposit at BC72 (No 233), generally the largest pieces from the assemblage, seem to be the lower section of a garment, probably a wo-man's dress (Fig 155). They can be compared with complete medieval garments excavated in Greenland (Fig 156A; Nørlund 1924). These Scan-dinavian finds demonstrate that the shaping of tunics in the middle ages was more developed and

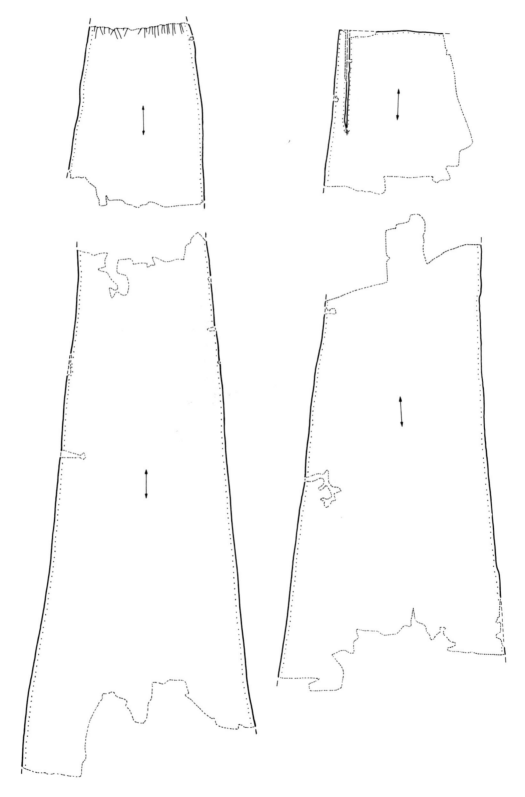

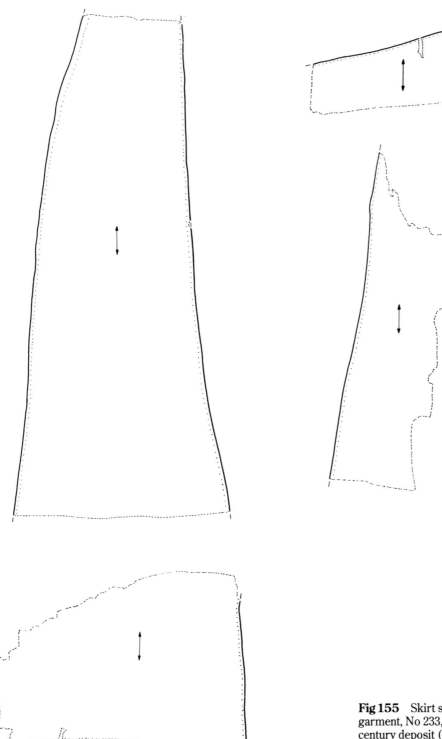

Fig 155 Skirt sections of a garment, No 233, from a late 14th-century deposit (see Fig 149 for gathered edge). Scale 1:4

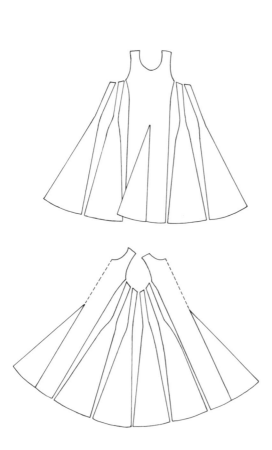

Fig 156   (A) Pattern of a woman's outer garment (omitting the sleeves) from Herjolfsnes, Greenland (after P Nørlund). The main pieces have a gore inserted in the centre front and centre back and in addition there is a series of side gores. (B) Reconstruction showing how such a dress might have looked

complex than pictorial sources have so far suggested. From a community very distant from the great medieval conurbations, these tunics were made of up to eight shaped sections, with some seams on the straight grain of the fabric and others on a partial bias. The juxtaposition of bias and straight edges would give an elegant movement to the garment in wear, which is evident even in the rather coarse twill cloths. Recent excavations in

Sweden seem likely to establish that this form of construction was known in Sweden in the second quarter of the 13th century at least (Margareta Nockert pers comm). This discovery, still awaiting conservation, study and report, suggests that a re-evaluation of medieval clothing construction will shortly be necessary.

The remnants of the London dress are of a fairly fine tabby, which would hang elegantly on a female figure. Though now a dark brown they were originally dyed blue with woad and probably were not heavily fulled. There are the remains of seven skirt panels, all incomplete. None have indications of a hem or of stitching along any lower edges. Little remains of the seams joining the panels, many apparently having broken away or perhaps been cut away. Some very narrow turnings (4mm wide) extant down the sides may be the remains of seams; normally one might have expected to find a broader seam allowance, as in the fragments of hose, for example. Narrow seams are also a feature of the London hoods and this may have been a method of economising on cloth. Of four tapering pieces from the tops of skirt panels, two can be satisfactorily matched to larger lower sections. Three of these sections measure 100mm at the waist edge, one seems to curve in to give a smooth fit over the hips, and another, the only one to show any indication of this, has evidence of single thread gathering along the upper (? waist) edge (Fig 149). A vertical break in another upper section may possibly be read as a slit giving access to a purse or pouch attached to a belt underneath, a detail that can be seen in the dress of a weeper from the tomb of Edward III (Fig 157).

The longest surviving section of a skirt panel measures 690mm (followed by others 650mm and 520mm). The original cut and arrangement of these panels is difficult to ascertain now. Each has one edge almost on the straight grain of the fabric. In only one instance, however, does the seam appear to be along the line of a warp thread; in all other cases there is a divergence of 10–20mm down the length of this edge, perhaps more indicative of a casual than of a sophisticated approach to cut. None of the skirt panels appears to have been of the rectangular form found in other excavated medieval dresses and usually associated with triangular gores in the skirt to give additional fullness at the hem. The Scandinavian dresses are mainly without a waist seam, but probably represent much older shaping traditions. Waist seams become noticeable in Italian paintings of the 1340s when clothing for men and women began to be moulded closely to the form

Fig 157 Joan de la Tour, weeper from the tomb of Edward III, 1377–86, (Conway Library, Courtauld Institute of Art)

of the body. Although tomb effigies and brasses of the late 14th century repeatedly show women wearing closely-fitting dresses (Fig 157), they do not include details of seams to indicate exactly how this shaping was achieved. It is clear, however, that a change in cut was necessary, a change which is exemplified in these fragments from London.

A single large piece from a different garment (No 71, Fig 158) is in a coarse, dark red tabby with an evenly spun warp and a rather irregular, overspun weft and was originally dyed with madder. This incorporates part of the neck and armhole of a dress, tunic or supertunic, probably of a young girl. All seams and hemmed edges have been cut away but the present measurements suggest a chest size of approximately 810–860mm (32–

Fig 158 Part of bodice of a garment, No 71, from a deposit dating to the second quarter of the 14th century. Scale 1:3

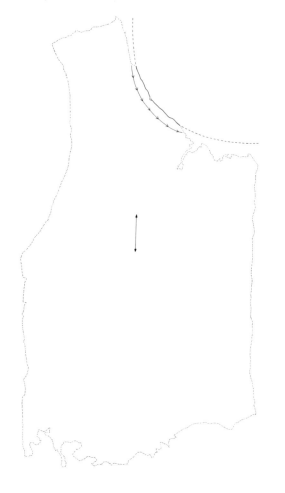

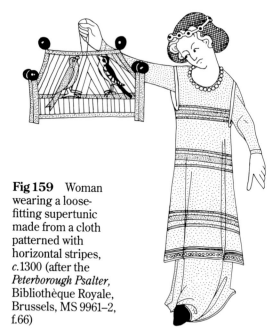

Fig 159 Woman wearing a loose-fitting supertunic made from a cloth patterned with horizontal stripes, *c.*1300 (after the *Peterborough Psalter,* Bibliothèque Royale, Brussels, MS 9961–2, f.66)

34ins). The neckline is wide and cut well away from the base of the neck. The present depth of the armhole is 170mm. The shaping of this bodice is well in accord with the Greenland dresses and shows the familiar shape of a semi-fitted garment to be seen in many contemporary manuscript illuminations and tomb effigies (Fig 159).

Cloaks

Very few examples of hems have been found amongst the fragments and it is likely that with well-fulled materials single or double fold hems were not as usual on clothing as they are today. One fragment from the hem of a garment cut in a curve (No 44, Fig 160) has a double fold of approximately 5mm with slanting hemming stitches. This is in a fine worsted 2.2 twill originally dyed with madder. Such a material would be inclined to fray and therefore would require the protection of a strengthened lower edge. The sweep of the curve suggests a semi-circular garment like a cloak, the hem of which, probably touching the ground, would be subject to a fair amount of wear.

Sleeves

Evidence for the cut of sleeves is mainly confined to a sleeve section recovered from a deposit of the second quarter of the 14th century (Fig 161, Pl 1).

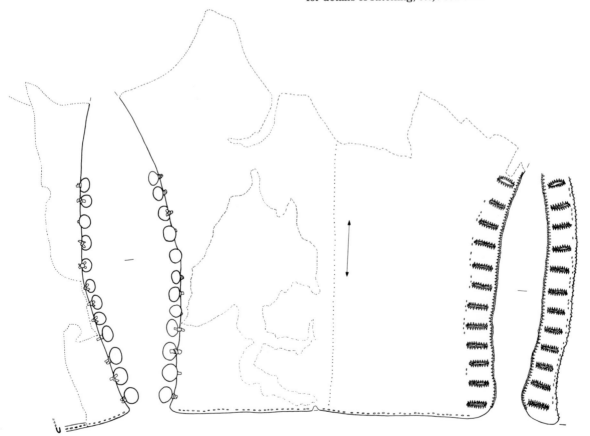

Fig 160 The lower edge of a garment, possibly a cloak, with a double-folded hem, No 44, from a late 14th-century deposit. Scale 1:3 (detail 1:1)

Fig 161 Lower edge of buttoned sleeve cut with a straight cuff, No 64, from a deposit dating to the second quarter of the 14th century (see Figs 141, 142 for details of stitching, etc). Scale 1:2

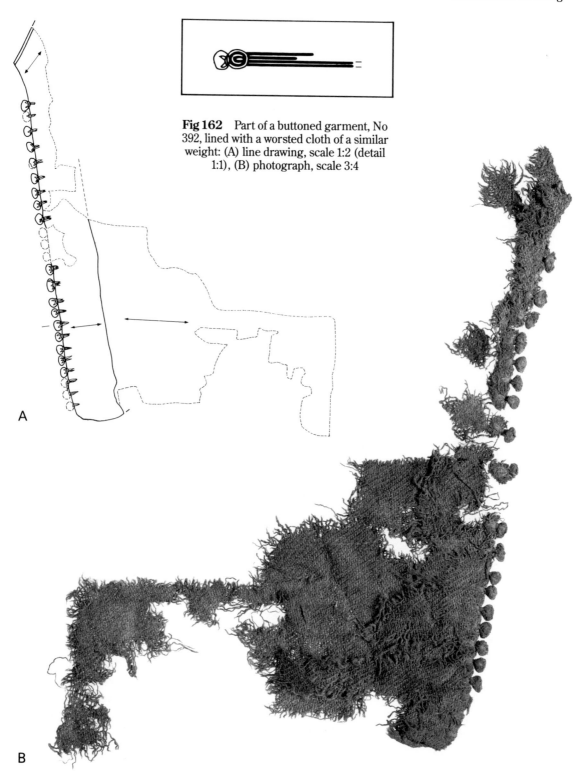

A

B

Fig 162 Part of a buttoned garment, No 392, lined with a worsted cloth of a similar weight: (A) line drawing, scale 1:2 (detail 1:1), (B) photograph, scale 3:4

It is of a medium weight tabby weave patterned with groups of red and white threads forming checks which are outlined in a third colour (see p. 50). The wrist edge of the sleeve is cut on the straight and neatened with a single top-stitched fold. The side seam edges slope outwards from the wrist to give fullness to the upper arm, but as only 205mm of the lower sleeve survives it is impossible to project the shape of the upper sleeve with any degree of accuracy. The measurement of the wrist is 167mm which suggests that this fragment came from a garment of a slender person. The buttonhole edge is neatly sewn with a carefully applied silk facing to strengthen the fine stitching of the buttonholes, and with a narrow tablet-woven braid worked directly on to the raw edge (Fig 142). No constructional attention was given to the edge to which the buttons are attached. Some 20mm to 25mm of cloth was turned back, and presumably continued up the arm as the seam allowance, and the cloth buttons were firmly attached through the folded edge (Fig 141). There are 12 buttons and buttonholes. A further row of stitch holes can be seen running down the centre of the sleeve and this stitching may have held a lining in place.

Linings are preserved on two edges with tiny buttons (No 38, Fig 143A, and No 392, Fig 162) and another with buttonholes (No 159, Fig 163). The lining of No 392 is a similar worsted fabric to the main garment. The other two examples, which are perhaps from the same tunic, have a red and ?yellow lining that contrasts with the woollen cloth of the garment. The buttonhole edging here has a narrow silk facing as well as a lining.

Other buttoned edges are fragmentary (see Figs 135–137, 144, 146, 164) but it is probable that many of them are from sleeves.

Bias cutting

There is not a great deal of evidence for the use of bias cutting in the middle ages and the evidence from the London textiles tends to support this finding. This way of achieving maximum effect from woven cloth by utilising the flexible qualities of the bias or diagonal is an eminently satisfactory way of smoothing cloth round the human form as well as achieving elegant and flowing drapes. The use of a circular cut, or of segments of circles (as for skirt gores), certainly demonstrates an appre-

Fig 163 Edge of garment, No 159, made from a woollen 2.1 twill. The buttonholes are faced with silk and finished with a tablet-woven edge very little of which is preserved. The garment is lined with a fine worsted 2.2 twill woven in contrasting red and yellow yarns. From late 14th-century London. Scale 1:1

ciation of the qualities of the bias. Contemporary pictorial evidence showing diagonal stripes and checks suggests that bias cutting was in use for parti-coloured clothing (Frontispiece), but in this sort of instance probably more for the novel visual effect than for body-fitting qualities so essential to 1930s fashionable female dress.

Hose

The main evidence for bias cutting found among the excavated textiles from London centres upon fragmentary pieces of leg coverings from 14th-century deposits. The elasticity which bias cutting offers makes it far superior as regards fit and, although wasteful of material, it was widely used for this reason in the middle ages. It has been

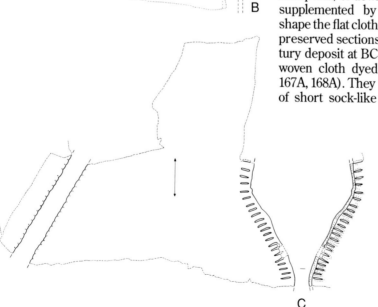

suggested that bias-cut legwear came into use by the 11th or 12th century since manuscript illuminations show diagonally striped legwear fitting closely to the contour of the leg.

For men the hose usually extended to the upper thigh and was attached by laces to a breech clout, the girdle which slotted through the top of men's linen underbreeches. These in turn were tucked inside the hose. Manuscript illuminations frequently reveal just such arrangements (Fig 165), and garters are sometimes represented holding hose in place below the knee (Figs 112, 166). The leg coverings of women did not normally extend so high up the leg, probably usually reaching only to below the knee and having to be held in place by garters. They were presumably shaped exactly like men's hose, but without the pointed upper edge. It is likely that men, too, sometimes wore shorter sock-like hose. Indeed contemporary illustrations reveal a number of variations shared by the sexes.

There are many fragmentary pieces of hose from 14th-century deposits in the City, some more readily identifiable than others. It is likely that there was no uniform approach to construction and this adds to the difficulties of identifying the origins of smaller fragments. Basically a strip of true bias cloth was fitted round the leg from thigh to ankle. Part of this strip might continue over the instep and/or down the sides of the ankles, and be supplemented by additional sections to help shape the flat cloth round the foot. A group of well-preserved sections of hose from the late 14th-century deposit at BC72 is of medium weight tabby-woven cloth dyed with madder (No 235, Figs 167A, 168A). They are perhaps remnants of a pair of short sock-like hose. The two larger pieces

Fig 164   Edges of garments with buttonholes from late 14th-century deposits: (A) and (B) No 221, (C) No 234. Scale 1:3

Fig 165 Two labourers threshing with flails, one man wears breeches and the other has his breeches tucked into his hose, *c.*1250 (after Pierpont Morgan MS Facs)

come from the leg sections. One shows the top edge of the hose, a single-fold horizontal hem which has been top-stitched with back-stitches; the width across this hem is 280mm, a small measurement which suggests that this hose may have belonged to a slim person, perhaps a young girl. The second fragment shows that the section covering the front of the foot was attached at the centre and had additional pieces at the sides. The constructional details contained in these two fragments are typical and help to identify yet smaller pieces. The back seam of the hose was joined by either running or back-stitches. It then appears that the seam allowance on each piece was held in place by tiny running-stitches, worked from the outside, 2–3mm from the seam. This approach to consolidating a seam does not appear to have been used elsewhere on medieval garments, to judge from the evidence of the London textiles. It

Fig 166 Man wearing a garter with his hose, *c.*1325–35 (after the *Luttrell Psalter*, BL Add MS 42130, f.60)

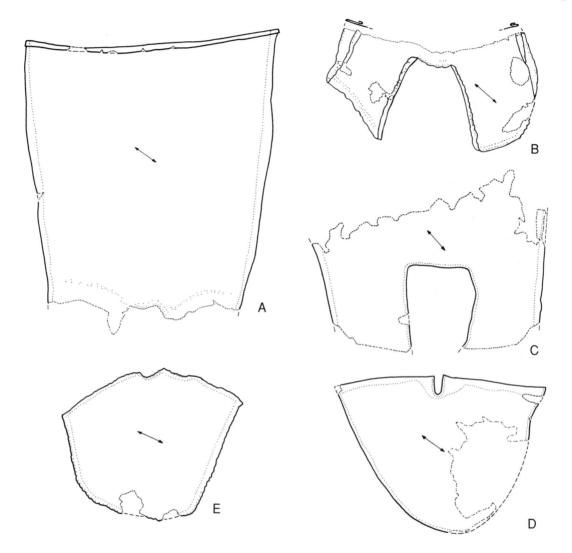

Fig 167   Leg and foot pieces of hose from late 14th-century deposits: (A) No 235, (B) No 236, (C) and (D) No 237, (E) No 238. Scale 1:3

does, however, appear on the seam of the dress associated with Queen Margareta in Uppsala Cathedral, Sweden (Geijer *et al.* 1985, pl 23a), which is variously ascribed to the 14th or 15th century. In this instance the method helps long skirt seams to lie flat. Sixteenth-century hose, excavated from City sites earlier this century and as yet unpublished, exhibit the same treatment of the back seam, although the stitching holes are

less evident in the worsted 2.2 twill from which they were made.

Whereas in these same 16th-century hose the shaping is found to be virtually uniform, cleverly cut in one piece to continue smoothly over the instep, supplemented by triangular sections below the instep and with a sole underneath (Fig 169), the very fragmentary evidence of the 14th-century hose from London seems to indicate that this constructional refinement had not yet been devised. Some 14th-century fragments demonstrate the continuation of wedge-shaped sections over the ankles and heel (e.g. Nos 236 and 237, Fig 167B and C), whilst others, resembling very

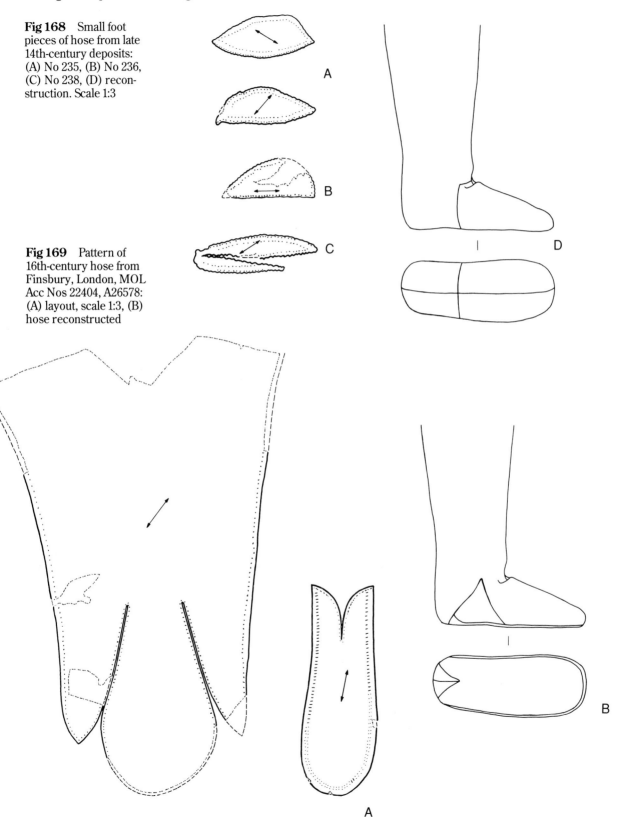

Fig 168 Small foot pieces of hose from late 14th-century deposits: (A) No 235, (B) No 236, (C) No 238, (D) reconstruction. Scale 1:3

Fig 169 Pattern of 16th-century hose from Finsbury, London, MOL Acc Nos 22404, A26578: (A) layout, scale 1:3, (B) hose reconstructed

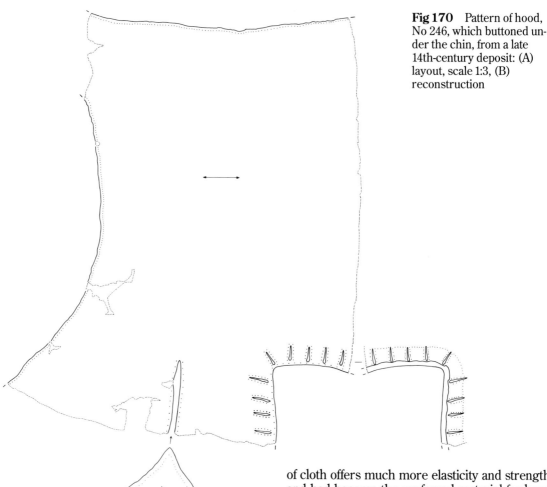

Fig 170   Pattern of hood, No 246, which buttoned under the chin, from a late 14th-century deposit: (A) layout, scale 1:3, (B) reconstruction

A

of cloth offers much more elasticity and strength and had become the preferred material for hose by the 16th century.

Hoods and headwear

The late 14th-century deposit at BC72 yielded a damaged but almost complete hood (No 246, Fig 170), now in six pieces. It is of medium weight tabby-woven cloth, stained a dark brownish-black, which has not been tested for dyes. The two largest fragments are head sections, each later having had a large finger-shaped piece torn away from the front edge. This edge shows no evidence for a hem and so a strip including the hem may have been cut away; this also seems to be the case with the lower neck edge. Extra fullness has been achieved at this edge by the insertion of two triangular sections (gussets) at each side, roughly below the ears. This form of construction is known from several excavated hoods dating to the

broad tongues, appear to have covered the instep and front of the foot (e.g. Nos 237 and 238, Fig 167D and E.) As already discussed (see p 153) the seams used on the foot sections — overlaps sewn along each raw edge to achieve a strong smooth finish — appear to be peculiar to this one clothing accessory. There were probably several variations at this time, and oval or elliptical sections found in association with hose fragments may be explained as strengthening at toes and heels (Fig 168), the first areas to become worn and replaced. All the hose fragments so far recognised from 14th-century London are made from tabby cloth rather than worsted four-shed twill. The latter type

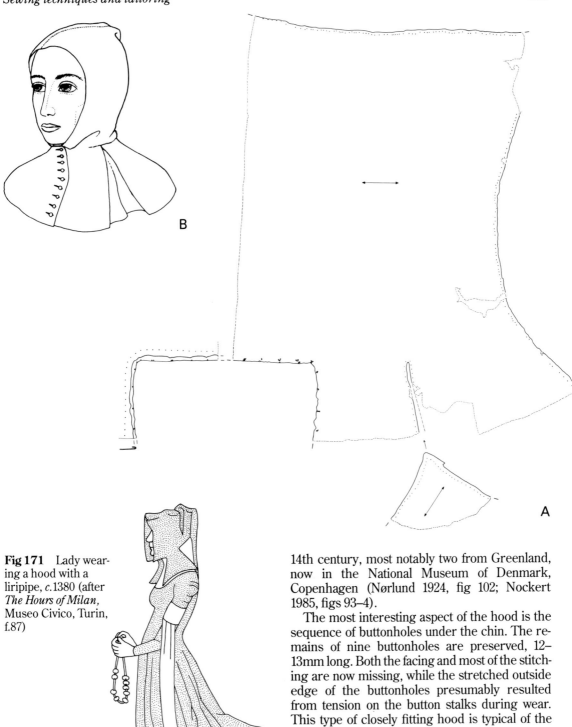

Fig 171 Lady wearing a hood with a liripipe, *c.*1380 (after *The Hours of Milan,* Museo Civico, Turin, f.87)

14th century, most notably two from Greenland, now in the National Museum of Denmark, Copenhagen (Nørlund 1924, fig 102; Nockert 1985, figs 93–4).

The most interesting aspect of the hood is the sequence of buttonholes under the chin. The remains of nine buttonholes are preserved, 12–13mm long. Both the facing and most of the stitching are now missing, while the stretched outside edge of the buttonholes presumably resulted from tension on the button stalks during wear. This type of closely fitting hood is typical of the late 14th century and is to be seen in many manuscript illuminations and sculptural figures (Fig 171). It was worn mainly by women and continued

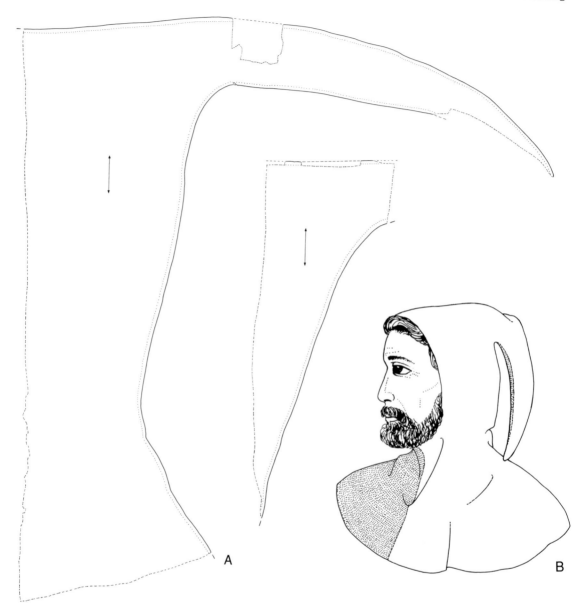

Fig 172 Part of hood with liripipe, No 174, from late 14th-century London: (A) layout – the smaller piece includes part of the backseam, scale 1:3, (B) reconstruction

in use, in varying guises, until well into the 16th century. There are no exactly similar hoods fastened with buttons among the remains of 14th-century clothing from Scandinavia, but part of the lower head and neck section of a buttoned hood was recovered from a deposit dating to *c.*1400 in Dordrecht, The Netherlands (Sandra Vons-Comis pers comm). This hood, which was similarly made from a tabby-woven cloth, originally had at least 17 buttons and, like the hood from London, has a slit for a gusset let into the lower edge at the side of the neck below the ears.

In London, there are also fragments of another buttoned hood made from a tabby-woven cloth of medium weight (No 247). It has four buttonholes

Fig 173 Gooseherd attempting to scare a hawk with his striped hood and stick, *c.*1325–35 (after the *Luttrell Psalter*, BL Add MS 42130, f.169b)

remaining, 13mm in length (the sewing thread and facing are again missing), and a gusset slit with traces of stitching. All these features are in almost exactly the same relationship to each other as on the more complete hood.

A third hood (No 174), which would have fitted a larger head, was also cut in two parts with a seam over the skull, a method which enabled hoods to be made up from two cloths of contrasting colours. Only the back of the head section is preserved, but from this various details of its pattern can be reconstructed (Fig 172). A special feature of this hood is its narrow tapering tail, called a liripipe, which survives to a length of 300mm and which was cut in one with the head-pieces. Six hoods similar to this were excavated at Herjolfsnes, Greenland, although some of the liripipes are considerably longer and required the addition of an extra strip of cloth (Nørlund 1924, 101; Nockert 1985, 91–2, 120, figs 90–92). Instead of gussets below the ears, a triangular gore was fitted to the centre front of these hoods at the throat to provide fullness round the shoulders. This hood, like the other London examples, is made from a firm tabby-woven cloth, which has

been fulled, shorn and napped. The seam allowances remaining are all extremely narrow, only 3–4mm wide.

Also very tentatively put forward as the remnants of headwear are two layers of a reddish-brown tabby cloth, which appear to have been moulded into the shape of an oval ridged crown with a flat top (No 175, Fig 175); the material appears to extend into a brim and is heavily folded at this point. Although a tempting solution, this hypothesis is weak; the moulding may have taken place during deposition, despite the fact that no

Fig 174 Mock wake showing men wearing hoods with exaggerated liripipes, *c.*1340 (after *The Romance of Alexander*, MS Bodl 264, f.129v)

Fig 175   Possibly a cloth hat, No 175, from a late 14th-century deposit. Diameter of crown 110mm. Scale 1:2

Fig 176   Labourer sowing seed, wearing a hat with an upturned brim, *c.*1325–35 (after the *Luttrell Psalter,* BL Add MS 42130, f.170b)

other textile fragment in the same late 14th-century deposit at BC72 seems to have had this experience. It is hoped that other excavations may yield similar material which will clarify the purpose and original form of this item.

Dagges

Since medieval cloth was often well fulled, indeed deliberately heavily fulled to exclude rain, cut edges could be left without protective over-stitching or binding. Thus grew up the practice of cutting cloth into shapes as ornamental edges or applications. The 14th-century deposits at BC72, particularly that of the late 14th century, have yielded a number of interesting examples of this simple yet decorative technique which was to be elaborated considerably in the three succeeding centuries. Only a few visual sources record the technique in the 13th century, when it was used to decorate the hems of knights' tabards or musicians' tunics. It seems to have blossomed in the 14th century, coming into use for all edges of garments and, eventually, headwear, as well as for ornamental horse trappings. These pendant ornaments were known as dagges. Decoration of this kind, an extravagant and wasteful fashion which demonstrated the tenet of conspicuous consumption, was even more widespread in the early 15th century.

One such dagge (No 70, Fig 177) from the deposit dating to the second quarter of the 14th century is of a well-fulled light brown tabby, a 6mm-long oak leaf, with a curved upper edge suggest-

Fig 177   Dagge, No 70, from a deposit dating to the second quarter of the 14th century. Scale 1:1

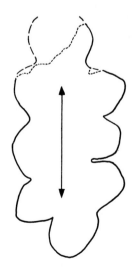

Fig 178 Alabaster effigy of William of Hatfield (died 1344) in York Minster. (Conway Library, Courtauld Institute)

ing that originally it may have hung from the sloping, or curved edge, of a cape or sleeve. Indeed, it has a close parallel in the long loose mantle shown on the virtually contemporary tomb effigy of Edward III's son, William of Hatfield (Fig 178), now in York Minster. The dagge comes from a group of seven fragments in the same material, all probably originating from the same garment.

The usual form of dagge found in 14th-century deposits in London was created from a straight strip of material with regular diagonal slits down each side. Two fragments from a deposit of the second quarter of the 14th century are cut not quite on the grain of the cloth to form a strip 43–44mm wide (No 51, Fig 179). They have narrow, shallow slits, approximately 10mm deep, cut somewhat erratically at intervals of 25–30mm.

Fig 179 Dagges, No 51, from a deposit dating to the second quarter of the 14th century: (A) photograph, scale 1:2, (B) line drawing, scale 1:3

A   B

these are shown in manuscript illuminations, particularly hanging down from the edges of short shoulder capes or from above the elbow on short tight sleeves. They also appear, though probably rather later than this deposit, as decorative additions to horse trappings. A further group of dagges from the late 14th century are narrower and are constructed with central vertical seams (Nos 249–251, Fig 182). These presumably demonstrate the economical use of older, recycled pieces of cloth.

An item in this late 14th-century assemblge of textiles which, in the absence of any more likely

Fig 180   Man wearing hood with dagged edge, *c.*1400 (after Chaucer, *Troilus and Criseyde*, Corpus Christi College, Cambridge, MS 61, f.1v)

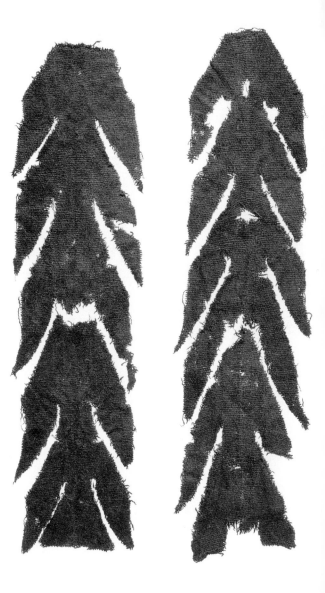

They may well have been cut from an old garment. Groups of stitch holes on each strip suggest that ornaments, probably made from metal, were once attached to them (see Fig 180).

The main outcry from contemporary commentators regarding dress seems to have come in the middle decades of the 14th century, perhaps as the fashionable excesses of the rich spread down through the social scale, eventually threatening to become ubiquitous. Dagges were certainly a distinctive use of new cloth, but also an excess easily created from an old garment and hence an attractive and attainable fashion lower in the social scale.

Dagges from the late 14th-century deposit at BC72 are, with one exception, constructed in the same manner as the earlier 14th-century examples. A group of six fragmentary dagges in a medium weight tabby, apparently dyed with woad, were created from 60mm wide strips cut on the straight of the grain (No 248, Fig 181). These are larger with slits 47mm deep at intervals of 50–55mm. Stitch holes suggest the possibility of metal ornaments, although this is not so certain as in the earlier examples. Ornamental strips like

Fig 182 Dagges from late 14th-century deposits: (A) No 249, (B) No 250, (C) No 251. Scale 1:3

Fig 181 Dagges, No 248, from a late 14th-century deposit: (A) photograph, scale 1:2, (B) line drawing, scale 1:3

A

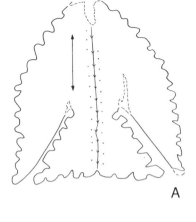

A

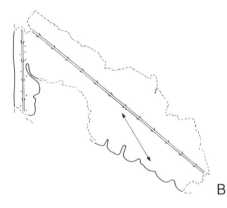

B

Fig 183   Dagges from late 14th-century deposits:
(A) No 252, photograph scale 1:1, line drawing scale
1:2, (B) No 253, scale 1:2

explanation is currently interpreted as being connected with dagges, is of a fine, fulled rich brown cloth (No 252, Fig 183A). It now resembles a headless bird and could have come from a strip of dagges like No 248. It is alone in having almost all of its edges scalloped or pinked, presumably snipped with shears or scissors. Whether this represents an idle doodling on an already discarded scrap or is the only evidence for the most elaborate decorative dagges, is now difficult to as-

sess. The piece would certainly have fluttered attractively in a breeze. Another fragment (No 253, Fig 183B), now far from complete, looks as though it may also be a discarded pendant leaf dagge from a garment or textile accessory. It appears to have some edges intentionally cut into scallops and to have a tiny section of another leaf attached. This dagge seems to be particularly akin to the cut leaf-like edges depicted on garments in manuscript illuminations and monumental effigies.

APPENDIX

The dyes

Penelope Walton

In 1975 Professor M C Whiting of the University of Bristol undertook a search for dyes in a small selected sample of textiles from BC72. This was the first time that modern techniques of dye analysis had been applied to the heavily soil-stained textiles which are generally recovered from wet archaeological sites. The work of the Bristol team was of great significance in establishing that small amounts of dye can be detected in such finds, even though the original colour has faded and been swamped by the brown of tannins and humic acids. In all, 15 of the 18 textiles in this preliminary study proved to contain detectable dye, enough to suggest that a systematic sampling of a larger group of finds would be worthwhile.

Over the next five years, further samples were tested by the Bristol team and this included samples selected at random rather than because they retained visible colour. By 1982, however, less time was available for the work and samples were sent to York, where the author carried out dye analyses, using the techniques developed by Professor Whiting. Thanks are due to him for providing details of his system of analysis, to G W Taylor for his adaptation of the Bristol methods (see Taylor 1983), and to York Archaeological Trust for the provision of laboratory facilities.

By the end of the study, in 1987, a total of 351 medieval samples from London sites had been examined and dye analysis had become firmly established as a routine part of the investigation of early textiles.

Method of extraction and identification

The procedure for the extraction of dyes has been described in detail elsewhere (Taylor 1983; Walton 1989B, 398–400). In brief, a small sample of the textile is treated in a strong solvent in order to extract dyes which have been applied directly to the fibre (e.g. woad, indigo and lichen purple). The sample is then treated in an acid-plus-alcohol mixture, which will remove dyes which have been applied after the fibre has been pretreated with a metal mordant (madder, kermes, brazilwood and several of the yellow dyes are of this sort).

The two liquid extracts are further refined and developed and then examined with the aid of a UV/Visible spectrophotometer. This machine draws up a graph of how light passing through the sample is absorbed at different wavelengths. The spectrophotometry graphs may then be compared with those of known dyestuffs. This often provides an immediate identification of the class of dye used.

For further information on the individual components that make up the dye, the extracts may also be used in chromatography. Samples of the dye extract are spotted on to Thin-Layer Chromatography plates. When the plate is up-ended in a small amount of solvent, the solvent will creep along the plate, taking parts of the dye with it. Since different components travel at different speeds, the chromatogram, once taken out and developed, will show spots at varying intervals along the plate. These spots indicate the constituents of the dye: for example, alizarin and purpurin, the main components of dyers' madder, *Rubia tinctorum* L., may be identified in this way.

Results

As described, a total of 351 samples, representing yarns from 311 medieval textiles, were tested for dye. Most (299 samples) were from BC72; the remainder were small groups from CUS73, SH74, TL74, DUK77, FRE78, BYD81, SWA81, and BWB83. Most come from deposits dated to the 14th century, although there are small numbers from the 12th, 13th and 15th centuries. The textiles sampled are indicated in the Concordance. A complete list of the results is stored in the Museum of London archive and copies may be obtained on written application to the Archive Assistant.

Of the 351 samples, 220 (63%) gave positive results. The dyes proved to be madder, kermes, woad/indigo, lichen purple, and a range of yellows including weld, a tentative identification of brazilwood, and a small number of dyes, mainly yellows or browns, which could not be firmly identified.

By far the most common dye was madder, which was present in 45% of the 1330–40 group and 62% of the late 14th-century group from BC72. There were no 12th- or 13th-century examples of the dye, but it represented 29% of the 14th- to mid-15th-century samples from the other sites. Alizarin was present in all the madder samples examined by chromatography. This indicates that the dye was almost certainly from the roots of dyers' madder, *Rubia tinctorum* L., rather than the native wild madder, *R. peregrina* L., or any of the British bedstraw dyes, all of which have been shown to lack any detectable alizarin (Taylor 1983, 158–9).

Madder is a versatile dye, usually used for a warm brick-red, although it can also produce peach, yellow, violet, brown and tan. It is also used to boost other colours such as greens and blues, and can give a golden tone to the yellow of weld. In seven cases (five from BC72, one from BYD81 and one from SWA81) the dye had been combined with blue to give purple or black; in three silks from BC72 it had been combined with a yellow; and in a wool cloth some madder-dyed threads in the selvedge had been overdyed with yellow, to form an orange or brown selvedge stripe in a yellow cloth.

It is probable that the plant, *R. tinctorum*, although not native to this country, had been introduced before the Norman conquest and was being cultivated in the Anglo-Saxon period (Walton 1989A, 400). Waranchiers, traders or dyers in madder, were resident at Winchester in 1148 (Biddle 1976, 430–32) and there are records of madder being grown in the Beverley area in 1331 (Hebditch 1946, 14–15), while legislation of the early 14th century forbade the export of the dye (EHD, 546–7). By the 15th century, additional

supplies were being brought in from the Low Countries, where madder growing was to become a speciality (Schaefer 1941, 1400). Both the Bristol and York tests showed that the proportions of the two major dye components, alizarin and purpurin, varied considerably from sample to sample, which Professor Whiting took to indicate a range of sources for the dye — although the possibility that the method of dyeing may alter the ratio is also worth considering.

Kermes, another red dye, was detected in ten of the better quality wool fabrics from BC72 and in three of the 13th- and 14th-century tabby-woven silks from SWA81 and CUS73. Kermes is derived from the kermes shield louse, *Kermes vermilio* (Planch.) Targ., a Mediterranean insect which was imported into this country under the name of grain. Kermes was expensive but much prized for the rich scarlet which it gave. It was always associated with rank and has been found in several ecclesiastical burials of the medieval period (Walton 1984, 31).

A third red dye which might be expected in any large group of medieval textiles is brazilwood, obtained from the heartwood of trees of the *Caesalpinia* family. This dye seems to have been imported into Europe from at least the late 12th century (Brunello 1973, 130–31, 137), but there is only one tentative identification among the textiles sampled from London (No 51). It is also rare in other excavated textiles, although it has been encountered in larger numbers in textiles surviving above ground (Hofenk de Graaff & Roelefs 1976, 32, 34). It may be that the dye decomposes in the soil in such a way as to be undetectable.

A purple dye derived from lichens was found in a silk and a half-silk fabrics from late 14th-century London (Nos 340, 351). This dye has previously been identified in a small number of pre-Norman and medieval textiles, generally of good quality (Taylor & Walton 1983, 15). The dye may be obtained from a number of different lichens, some of which can be found growing in north-west England and Scotland. Such lichens appear in the 13th-century *Consuetudinary of Winchester* under the name of cork (Smirke 1852, 74, 80, 86), and as lacmus were imported from Norway in the 14th century (Kok 1966, 252). A similar dye, derived from eastern Mediterranean lichens, probably species of *Rocella* and *Lecanora*, began to be traded as a Florentine monopoly under the name of orchil around 1300 (Kok 1966, 252–3). The two textiles from BC72, presumably dyed near their place of manufacture, are most likely to represent examples of the Florentine orchil.

Historians may be surprised to discover that indigotin, the blue colorant derived from woad and indigo (the two sources are as yet indistinguishable), was rare among the medieval London textiles. It occurs in only 16 examples, less than 5% of the total number. Woad is so commonly mentioned in trade documents of the period (Hurry 1930) that it might be expected in a larger number of textiles. The explanation may be that weak dyeings with woad fade and are difficult to detect after long-term burial. Plunkets, popular light blue cloths, much paler than azures and blues (Salzman 1923, 210), have perhaps remained undetected in this survey.

Yellow and brown dyes are even more difficult to find in archaeological samples, as they are masked by staining from the earth-matrix in which they have been buried. Traces of a yellow dye were found in 11 samples, ten from BC72 and one from SWA81. A relatively new technique, High-Pressure Liquid Chromatography (HPLC), was applied by the Bristol team to two of the yellows from BC72 (M C Whiting pers comm) and by this means individual dye components were identified: luteolin plus kaempferol and quercitin in No 210, and luteolin alone in No 254. Luteolin is the main constituent of weld, from *Reseda luteola* L. (although luteolin is also found combined with genistein in dyeings from dyer's greenweed, *Genista tinctoria* L.); kaempferol and quercitin suggest the presence of an additional dye in No 210. If it had been possible to apply the sensitive technique of HPLC to a greater number of samples, many more yellows may well have been detected and identified. At any rate, the present work has shown that yellow dyes were in use and, on occasion, combined with woad/indigo for green (one

definite example) or with madder for orange, gold or brown (five examples).

Two dyes were yellow on extraction but behaved in a similar manner to tannins, which suggests that they were brown or black when applied to the fibre. The tannin dyes — barks, nuts and oak galls — are notoriously difficult to separate from naturally occurring tannins acquired during burial, and the number identified may well not represent the true number of brown/black textiles. Naturally pigmented wool (brown/grey/black) was also noted, overdyed with madder in one example.

When the London textiles are divided according to fibre, the silks show a slightly different range of dyes from the wool fabrics. Reds are again common, but yellows and purples are better represented than in the wool textiles. There was also a greater number of unidentified dyes in the silks, reflecting their more exotic origin.

In summary, the dyes in the textiles show a predominance of reds. Purples and blues are present in small numbers and also yellows and browns and possibly black. However, there remains the 37% in which no dye was detected. It is possible, of course, that these were originally white and undyed, yet it seems more likely that some at least were once dyed, perhaps with brazilwood or one of the yellow dyes, or even with woad. Refinements to the analytical system are still being developed and it is possible that in the future the numbers of negative results will begin to be reduced. Meanwhile the work has already demonstrated that the rich, warm tones of madder were among the most popular colours worn in medieval London.

Based on the work of M C Whiting, A Harvey, J Harvey, T Sugiura, M J K Thomas, University of Bristol, and P Walton, Textile Research Associates.

Concordance

This chapter lists all the numbered items discussed in this book, under the sites in which they were excavated, and according to date and fibre/weave/twist of yarn.

Where an item consists of more than one textile, the same catalogue number is assigned to each component. Thus part of a buttoned garment which is cut from a woollen cloth woven in 2.1 twill, lined with a 2.2 twill and faced along the button holes with a strip of tabby-woven silk, is listed here three times under the same number (No 159) with an asterisk * placed next to it each time.

The excavated textiles have been catalogued and stored by site, so that up to three items of information are required to identify a piece: the *site code* (BC72, CUS73, etc., given in the site heading), the *archaeological context number* (in square brackets), and the *accession number* (in angular brackets: a continuous sequence of numbers unique within each site).

An additional number is listed for the textiles from BC72: the prefix TA signifies that a textile came from a deposit dating to the second quarter of the 14th century, TB signifies that a textile came from a deposit of the late 14th century, while textiles with the prefix TBX are contemporary with TB, the X indicating that they were conserved at the British Museum; these numbers are used in the MOL's archive catalogue.

The Roman numerals placed immediately before the archaeological context number under site code CUS73 represent the trench number of the context. Table, Fig and Pl references are to tables/illustrations in this book; a Roman numeral following these references identifies the Selected Catalogue in which a full description of the weave can be found. Finally, where dye testing has taken place, this is indicated at the end of the relevant entries (see also Appendix).

Baynard's Castle (BC72)

Dock construction, second quarter 14th century
NB: Nos 1–153 all have the archaeological context number [250].

Wool textiles: 2.1 twills (Z-spun yarn)

1	<3573/2>	TA225,	Table 2.
2	<3423/33>	TA214,	Table 2, Fig 11A.
3	<3423/61>	TA218,	Table 2, Fig 11B.
4	<3423/12>	TA213, Table 2, Fig 11C.	
5	<3517/98/159/163>	TA48,	Table 2, Fig 12.

Plus 15 others, 4 dye tested.

Wool textiles: 2.1 twills (mixed spinning)

6	<4085/3>	TA211,	dye tested.
7	<3517/121>	TA107,	Fig 14A.
8	<3424/37b>	TA106,	Fig 14B.
9	<3656/52>	TA108,	Fig 14C, dye tested.
10	<3517/120>	TA109,	Fig 15A.
11	<3656/63>	TA110,	Fig 15B.
12	<3656/38/85>	TA111,	Fig 15C.
13	<3517/104>	TA164,	Table 3, Fig 17C.
14	<3423/34>	TA117,	Table 3.
15	<3517/94>	TA62,	Table 3.
16	<3656/39>	TA197,	Table 3, dye tested.
17	<3424/29>	TA113,	Table 3, Fig 17A.
18	<3424/31>	TA29,	Table 3.
19	<3656/106>	TA114,	Table 3, Figs 17B, 18, dye tested.
20	<3517/126>	TA168,	Table 3.
21	<3517/99>	TA162,	Table 3.
22	<3823/10>	TA7,	Table 3, dye tested.
23	<3423/43>	TA61B,	Table 3.
24	<3517/75>	TA160,	Table 3, Fig 17D.
25	<3517/156>	TA187, Table 3.	
26	<3656/59>	TA208, Table 3.	
27	<3656/60>	TA209,	Table 3, Fig 17E, dye tested.
28	<3517/22>	TA158,	Table 3.
29	<3423/41>	TA61D,	Table 3.
30	<3424/10>	TA133,	Table 3, Fig 17F.
31	<3423/88>	TA20,	dye tested.
32	<3424/1b>	TA3,	Fig 136.
*33	<3424/1c>	TA4,	dye tested
*34	<3517/3>	TA6,	Fig 137.
*35	<3424/21>	TA10,	Fig 151, dye tested.
*36	<3517/35>	TA12,	dye tested.
37	<3424/23>	TA21,	dye tested.
*38	<3517/4>	TA22, Fig 143A, dye tested.	

Plus 99 others, 18 dye tested.

Wool textiles: 2.1 twills (S-spun yarn)

4 examples.

Wool textiles: 2.2 twills (Z-spun yarn)

*38	<3517/4>	TA22,	Figs 21, 143A, dye tested.
39	<4909/4>	TA98,	Table 4, Fig. 22.
40	<3424/39>	TA32,	Table 4, dye tested.
41	<4710/5>	TA95,	Table 4, dye tested.
42	<3424/36>	TA80,	Table 4, dye tested.
43	<3512.124>	TA85,	Table 4.
44	<4710/6>	TA58,	Fig 160, dye tested.

Plus 19 others,   3 dye tested.

Wool textiles: 2.2 twills (mixed spinning)

45	<3517/9>	TA101,	Fig 27.

Plus 4 others.

Wool textiles: 2.2 twills (S-spun yarn)

1 example.

Wool textiles: 3.3 twills (Z-spun yarn)

46	<3424/27>	TA73,	Table 5, dye tested.
47	<4909/5>	TA74,	Table 5, dye tested.
48	<4909/6>	TA75,	Table 5, Fig 28A, dye tested.

Wool textiles: 3.3 twill with patterned band (Z-spun yarn)

49	<4710/7>; and <3656/107>	TA72,	Table 5, Fig 29, Pl 2A, dye tested.

Wool textiles: tabbies (Z-spun yarn)

3 examples.

Wool textiles: tabbies (mixed spinning)

*50	<3517/5>	TA11,	Fig 132, Pl 2B, dye tested.
51	<3517/49>	TA18,	Fig 179, dye tested.
52	<3517/2>	TA347,	Table 6.
53	<3517/69>	TA368,	Table 6.
54	<3656/30/67>; and <3423/72>	TA237,	Table 6, Fig 34A, Pl 6A.
55	<3517/66>	TA367,	Table 6.
56	<3656/76>	TA25d,	Table 6.
*57	<3423/71>	TA8,	Table 6, dye tested.
58	<3656/87>	TA393,	Table 6.
59	<3423/104>	TA318,	Table 6.
60	<3517/33>	TA351,	Table 6.
61	<3423/13>	TA296,	Table 6.
62	<3517/95>	TA23,	Fig 36B, dye tested
63	<3423/30>	TA19,	Fig 37B, dye tested.
*64	<3573/1>	TA1,	Figs 38A, 141, 142, 161, Pl 1, dye tested.
65	<3423/77>	TA238,	dye tested.
66	<3423/68>	TA236,	dye tested.
*67	<3424/1a>	TA2,	Fig 135, dye tested.

*68	<3517/2>	TA5,	dye tested.
*69	<3656/2>	TA13,	Fig 133, dye tested.
70	<3423/82/83a>	TA17,	Fig 177.
71	<3656/15>	TA55,	Fig 158, dye tested.
72	<3656/76>	TA25b,	
73	<3423/21>	TA26.	
74	<3424/58>	TA37.	
75	<3656/105>; and <3517/40>	TA41.	
76	<3656/16>	TA56.	
77	<3517/76/81>	TA45,	dye tested.

Plus 116 others,   15 dye tested.

Wool textiles: tabbies (S-spun yarn)

2 examples,   2 dye tested.

Wool textiles: tabbies with weft-faced bands

*78	<3424/9>	TA9,	Fig 131, I, dye tested.
79	<3656/98>	TA247,	Fig 40A, I.
80	<3656/97>	TA246,	Fig 40B, I.
81	<3423/15>	TA248,	I.
82	<3423/17>	TA250,	I.
83	<3423/22>	TA253,	I, dye tested.
84	<3423/24>	TA254,	I.
85	<3423/26>	TA256,	I.
86	<3423/63>	TA258,	I.
87	<3424/6>	TA262,	I.
88	<3517/11/53>	TA268,	I, dye tested.
89	<3656/92a>	TA270,	I.
90	<3656/75>	TA272,	I.
91	<3517/68>	TA273,	I.
92	<3517/111>	TA274,	Pl 7A, I, dye tested.
93	<3517/115>	TA277,	I, dye tested.
94	<3517/119b>	TA280A,	I.
95	<3656/32>	TA281,	I.
96	<3656/94>	TA282,	I, dye tested.
97	<3656/33>	TA283,	I.
98	<3656/92b>	TA284,	I.
99	<3656/96>	TA286,	I, dye tested.
100	<3656/103>	TA289,	I.
101	<3423/16>	TA249,	I, dye tested.
102	<3423/18>	TA251,	I.
103	<3423/25>	TA255,	I.
104	<3423/29>	TA257,	I.
105	<3424/4>	TA260A,	I.
106	<3424/5>	TA261,	I.
107	<3424/8>	TA264,	Pl 7B, I.
108	<3424/11>	TA265,	I.
109	<3424/41c>	TA266,	I.
110	<3424/50aa>	TA267,	I.
111	<3656/104>	TA269,	I.
112	<3517/110>	TA271,	Fig 42, I, dye tested.
113	<3517/113>	TA275,	I.
114	<3517/119b>	TA280B,	I.
115	<3656/95>	TA285,	Pl 4B, I, dye tested.

116   <3656/102>   TA288,   I.
117   <3423/19>   TA25,   I,   dye tested.
118   <3423/20>   TA252,   I.
119   <3424/3/4>   TA260B,   I.
120   <3424/7>   TA263,   I.
121   <3517/116>   TA278,   I.
122   <3656/101>   TA287,   I,   dye tested.
123   <3424/2>   TA259, Pl 9A,   I,   dye tested.
124   <3517/117>   TA279,   I.
125   <3423/3>; and
      <3517/112>   TA234, Fig 41, Pl 6B,   I,   dye
      tested.
126   <3423/28>   TA235,   I,   dye tested.
127   <3656/69>   TA240,   I.
128   <3656/11/100>   TA245,   I,   dye tested.
129   <3517/118>; and <3656/9>   TA243,   I.
130   <3517/32>   TA242,   I.
131   <3517/122>   TA244,   I.
132   <3423/27>   TA241,   I.

Wool textiles: felt
      133   <4085.2945>   TA426a,   Fig 50.
      Plus 1 other.

Silk textiles: tabbies (Z/-)
      *33   <3424/1c>   TA4,   Table 10,   dye tested.
      *69   <3656/2>   TA13,   Table 10.
      134   <4909/7>   TA69,   Table 10.
      135   <4909/8>   TA70,   Table 10,   dye tested.
      *78   <3424/9>   TA9,   Fig 131.
      *50   <3517/5>   TA11,   Fig 132, Pl 2B.
      *57   <3423/71>   TA8.
      *36   <3517/35>   TA12.
      *67   <3424/1a>   TA2, Fig 135,   dye tested.
      *68   <3517/2>   TA5.
      *32   <3424/1b>   TA3, Fig 136.
      *34   <3517/3>   TA6,   Fig 137.
      *35   <3424/21>   TA10,   Fig 151.
      136   <4088/4>   TA16,   Fig 152.
      *64   <3573/1>   TA1,   Fig 142, Pl 1B.
      137   <4085/1a>   TA15.
      Plus 5 others,   2 dye tested.

Silk textiles: patterned cloths
      138   <4909/12>   TA65,   Fig 72, VI,   dye tested.
      139   <4909/11>   TA64,   Fig 74,   VII,   dye
      tested.
      140   <4909/10>   TA63,   Fig 75, Pl
      15A,   VII,   dye tested.

Narrow wares: raw silk
      141   <4094.3026>   TA425,   Fig 43,   dye tested.

Narrow wares: tablet-woven braids
      142   <3695>   TA60, Fig 99,   XII,   dye tested.
      143   <3515.5673>   TA59,   Fig 100A, XII,   dye
      tested.
      144   <3517/1>   TA402,   Table 11.

Narrow wares: fingerloop braids
      *145   <3665>   TA400,   Table 12, Fig 121.
      146   <3516>   TA403,   Table 12.
      147   <4091/1>   TA404,   Table 12.
      148   <4091/1>   TA405,   Table 12.
      149   <4093/2a>   TA408A,   Table 12.

Narrow wares: plaited braids
      150   <4091/4>   TA406,   Table 13,   dye tested.
      151   <4093/1>   TA407,   Table 13.
      152   <4093/2c>   TA408B,   Table 13,   dye
      tested.

Narrow wares: hairnets
      *145   <3665>   TA400,   Fig 121,   XIV.
      153   <3665>   TA400,   Fig 122,   XIV.

Dock infilling, late 14th century
Wool textiles: Z-spun yarn
      154   [83]   <1907/4>   TB619,   Fig 1.

Wool textiles: S-spun yarn
      155   [79]   <2221>   TB607,   Fig 2.

Wool textiles: 2.1 twills (Z-spun yarn)
      156   [88]   <3362>   TB66.
      Plus 8 others,   1 dye tested.

Wool textiles: 2.1 twills (mixed spinning)
      157   [150]   <4011/107>   TB167,   Table 3.
      158   [150]   <3401/17>   TB165,   Table 3.
      *159   [150] <3234/1>   TB8, Fig 163,   dye tested.
      Plus 2 others.

Wool textiles: 2.1 twills (S-spun yarn)
      160   [79]   <1830/26>   TB168,   Fig 19.
      Plus 2 others.

Wool textiles: 2.2 twills (Z-spun yarn)
      *159   [150]   <3234/1>   TB8,   Figs 21, 163.
      161   [79]   <2701>   TB133.
      162   [55]   <1713>   TB157,   Fig 23,   dye
      tested.
      163   [89]   4099/14   TB35,   Table 4, Fig
      25,   dye tested.
      164   [150]   <3400/2>   TB160,   dye tested.
      165   [83]   <2374/4>   TB136,   Table 4.

166 [55] <T.7> TB155, Table 4, Fig 24B.
167 [55] <1557> TBX5, Table 4, dye tested.
Plus 28 others, 8 dye tested.

Wool textiles: 2.2 twills (mixed spinning)
168 [88] <4098/4> TB162, Table 4.
169 [150] <3234/9> TB163, Fig 26, dye tested.
Plus 1 other, dye tested.

Wool textiles: 3.3 twills (Z-spun yarn)
170 [88] <2949/58> TB129, Table 5, Fig 30, dye tested.
171 [83] <2145> TB130, Table 5, Fig 150, dye tested.

Wool textiles: tabbies (Z-spun yarn)
172 [150] <3596> TB183, Fig 38C, Pl 3B, dye tested.
173 [150] <3613> TB13, dye tested.
174 [150] <3401/34> TB76, Fig 172.
175 [88] <3144> TB85, Fig 175.
Plus 29 others, 2 dye tested.

Wool textiles: tabbies (mixed spinning)
176 [150] <4011/46/12> TB242, Table 6, 34B.
177 [79] <1749/7> TB235, Table 6, dye tested.
178 [150] <3400/4> TB245, Table 6.
179 [79] <1749/3> TB229, Table 6.
180 [79] <1749/5> TB232, Table 6, dye tested.
181 [79] <2700/4> TB244, Table 6, dye tested.
182 [88] <4098/36> TB225, Table 6, dye tested.
183 [83] <1907/1/34> TB222, Table 6.
184 [79] <1830/11> TB23B, Table 6, dye tested.
185 [89] <4099/36> TB228, Table 6, dye tested.
186 [150] <3403/3b> TB248, Table 6.
187 [150] <4011/84> TB240, Table 6, dye tested.
188 [79] <1748/4> TB226, Table 6.
189 [150] <3401/21> TB75, Table 6.
190 [150] <3611/3> TB234, Table 6.
191 [25] <92a> TB243, Table 6.
192 [150] <3400/15> TB319, Table 6.
193 [150] <3641/27> TB237, Table 6
194 [150] <3401/13> TB230, Table 6.
195 [55] <1645/9> TB28, Table 6, Pl 5A, dye tested.
196 [79] <2700/16> TB221, Table 6.

197 [150] <4011/102> TB241, Table 6.
198 [55] <1557> TBX29, Table 6, dye tested.
199 [88] <4098/59> TB247, Table 6.
200 [150] <3611/36> TB236, Table 6.
201 [79] <1830/22> TB36, Table 6, Fig 37C, dye tested.
202 [55] <1557> TBX20, Table 6, dye tested.
203 [88] <3092/37> TB223, Table 6.
204 [150] <3401/14> TB231, Table 6.
205 [88] <4098/20> TB224, Table 6.
206 [88] <3902.14> TB246, Table 6.
207 [88] <4098/39> TB227, Table 6.
208 [55] <1557> TBX6, Table 6.
209 [150] <3401/16> TB233, Table 6.
210 [79] <1830/36> TB32, Fig 36A, dye tested.
211 [89] <4099/44> TB34, Fig 37A.
212 [55] <T.3> TB218, dye tested.
213 [55] <T.4> TB219.
214 [83] <1907/1/9> TB220, dye tested.
215 [150] <3611/8> TB75B, Fig 125B.
*216 [79] <1789> TB29, Fig 144 dye tested.
217 [25] <204>; and [83] <2374/22> TB1.
218 [79] <2700/10> TB2, dye tested.
*219 [88] <4098/1> TB4, dye tested.
220 [83] <1374> TB5, Fig 146.
221 [83] <2374/33> TB7, Fig 164A and B.
222 [150] <3403/1> TB9, dye tested.
223 [150] <3401/26> TB11, dye tested.
224 [79] <1830/12> TB14, dye tested.
225 [55] <1558> TB15, Fig 148A.
226 [150] <3597> TB16.
227 [150] <3403/3> TB17.
228 [25] <36a> TB18, Fig 148B.
229 [55] <1645/2A> TB40.
230 [79] <1748/9> TB45.
231 [79] <1750> TB50.
232 [79] <1830/18> TB55.
233 [79] <1738/1>; and
        [55] <T.2> TB44, Figs 149, 155, dye tested.
234 [55] <1557> TBX21, Fig 164C, dye tested.
235 [79] <1830/4> TB51, Figs 167A, 168A, dye tested.
236 [55] <1645/2B> TB41, Figs 167B, 168B.
237 [150] <3612.1> TB78, Fig 167C and D, dye tested.
238 [55] <1645/5> TB42, Figs 167E, 168C.
239 [55] <1645/14> TB43.
240 [150] <3401/39> TB77.
241 [79] <1830/10> TB455.
242 [55] <1557> TBX24, dye tested.

243 [150] <3401/44> TB413.
244 [150] <3641/44> TB428.
245 [150] <3234/11> TB74.
246 [55] <1645/1> TB39, Fig 170.
247 [55] <1645/3A> TB79.
248 [88] <3110/1> TB20, Fig 181, dye tested.
249 [150] <4011/68> TB21, Fig 182A, dye tested.
250 [150] <4011/103> TB22, Fig 182B, dye tested.
251 [83] <2374> TB25, Fig 182C.
252 [55] <1643/1k> TB24, Fig 183A.
253 [89] <4099/24> TB23, Fig 183B.
254 [79] <1830/6> TB52, dye tested.
Plus 248 others, 48 dye tested.

Wool textiles: tabbies (S-spun yarn)
255 [150] <4011/44> TB260, Table 7.
256 [79] <2519/8> TB249, Table 7.
257 [150] <4011/32> TB31, Table 7.
258 [150] <3611/20> TB256, Table 7.
259 [150] <3234/5> TB254, Table 7.
260 [150] <3641/53> TB258, Table 7.
261 [88] <2949/16> TB252, Table 7.
262 [88] <3902/41> TB251, Table 7.
263 [88] <3902/41> TB250, Table 7.
264 [88] <4098/37> TB253, Table 7.
265 [79] <2519/7> TB263, Table 7.
266 [150] <4011/78> TB261, Table 7, dye tested.
267 [150] <4011/41> TB259, Table 7.
268 [150] <4011/104> TB264, Table 7.
269 [150] <3401/15> TB255, Table 7.
270 [150] <3461/50> TB257, Table 7.
271 [79] <1830/28> TB262, Table 7.
272 [83] <2374/12> TB6
273 [150] <3611/1> TB10, dye tested.
274 [150] <3183> TB19.
275 [150] <4011/40> TB184, Fig 38B, Pl 3A, dye tested.
276 [79] <1749/4> TB47.
Plus 80 others, 12 dye tested.

Wool textiles: tabbies with weft-faced bands
277 [79] <1830/27> TB37, Pl 5B, I.
278 [150] <4011/34> TB201, I.
279 [150] <4011/35> TB202, I, dye tested.
280 [150] <4011/76> TB205, I, dye tested.
281 [83] <2374/8> TB212, I.
282 [89] <4099/34> TB195, I.
283 [150] <3641/23> TB199, I.
284 [150] <3641/33> TB200, I.
285 [150] <4011/39> TB204, I.
286 [55] <1481> TB207, I, dye tested.

287 [83] <1907/1/1> TB210, Pl 8A, I.
288 [88] <3902.13> TB213, I.
289 [88] <4098/50> TB215, I.
290 [88] <3902.15> TB216, I, dye tested.
291 [88] <3902.16> TB217, I.
292 [150] <4011/38> TB203, I.
293 [88] <4098/65> TB217A, I, dye tested.
294 [89] <4099/33> TB194, Pl 12A, I, dye tested.
295 [88] <4098/41> TB209, I.
296 [150] <3611/38> TB188, I.
297 [89] <4099/45> TB186, I.
298 [150] <3234/27> TB187, Pl 10A, I, dye tested.
299 [150] <4011/31> TB189, Pl 10B, I, dye tested.
300 [150] <4011/33> TB190, I.
301 [150] <4011/37> TB191, I.
302 [150] <3401/25> TB196, I.
303 [150] <4011/77> TB206, I.
304 [79] <2700/5> TB185, I.
305 [55] <1645/8> TB208, Pl 9B, I, dye tested.
306 [150] <3641/12> TB197, I.
307 [150] <3641/13> TB198, I.
308 [83] <1945> TB211, Pl 12B, I, dye tested.
309 [83] <1907/1> TB192, Pl 11A, I.
310 [150] <3400/3> TB193, Pl 11B, I.
311 [88] <3902.14> TB214, dye tested.

Wool textiles: tapestries
312 [150] <3401/18> TB180, Fig 44, II, dye tested.
313 [150] <3641/20> TB181, Fig 45, II.
314 [150] <4011/66> TB182A, Fig 46A, II, dye tested.
315 [150] <4011/66> TB182B, Fig 46B, II.

Wool textiles: knitting
316 [150] <3234/14> TB563, Pl 13A, dye tested.
317 [88] <311> TB562, Fig 47, dye tested.

Wool textiles: felt
318 [83] <2704a> TB631, Fig 51.
Plus 4 others, dye tested.

Goathair cloth
319 [89] <4099/6> TB557, Table 8.

Silk textiles: tabbies (yarn lacking in any appreciable twist)

320   [55]   <1523/1>   TB124,   Fig 62,   dye tested.
321   [79]   <1747/2>   TB120.

Silk textiles: tabbies (Z/-)

322   [88]   <3903/2>   TB105,   Table 10.
323   [83]   <1907/28>   TB103,   Table 10, Pl 14A,   dye tested.
324   [150]   <4005/8>   TB117,   Table 10.
325   [83]   <1907/87>   TB126,   Table 10, Fig 65.
326   [150]   <4005/1/2>   TB114,   Table 10, Figs 63, 124A.
327   [150]   <4005/1/2>   TB113,   Table 10, Figs.63, 124A.
328   [150]   <4005/3>   TB115,   Table 10,   dye tested.
329   [83]   <2705/1>   TB84,   Fig 138.
*159   [150]   <3234/1>   TB8,   Fig 163.
330   [83]   <1907/2a>   TB125,   Fig 128B.
Plus 11 others,   3 dye tested.

Silk textiles: tabbies (Z-twisted yarn)

331   [83]   <2705/2>   TB104,   Fig 66.
Plus 7 others,   1 dye tested.

Silk textiles: tabbies with weft-faced bands

332   [79]   <1747/1>   TB100,   Fig 67,   III.
333   [150]   <3903/1>   TB101,   Figs 68A, 129, III.
334   [150]   <4908/1>   TB102,   Fig 68B and C,   III.
335   [79]   <1747/4>   TB99,   Fig 69,   Pl 14B, IV.

Silk textiles: patterned cloths

336   [88]   <3903/9>   TB94,   Fig 76,   VII.
337   [150]   <4005/4>   TB93,   Fig 82,   IX.
338   [150]   <4908/2>   TB93,   Fig 83,   IX.
*339   [150]   <2822> TB88,   Fig 84,   IX.
340   [55]   <1645/15>   TB91,   Fig 85, IX,   dye tested.
341   [88]   <3903/10>   TB90B,   Fig 86,   IX.
342   [79]   <1747/67>   TB90A,   Fig 88,   IX.
343   [83]   <2705/3>   TB92,   Fig 90,   IX, dye tested.
344   [55]   <1523/2>   TB89,   Fig 91,   IX.

Silk textiles: satin weave

345   [55]   <1643/2a>   TB95,   Fig 153A and B,   X,   dye tested.
346   [55]   <1643/2b>   TB96,   Fig 93,   X.

347   [88]   <3903/8>   TB98,   Fig 124B,   X.
348   [55]   <1646>   TB97,   Pl 16A,   X,   dye tested.

Mixed cloths: half-silk velvets

349   [55]   <1849/1>   TB86,   Pl 16B.
350   [150]   <3684>   TB87,   dye tested.
351   [89]   <2363>   TB127,   Fig 96,   dye tested.
352   [88]   <2979>   TB128,   dye tested.

Mixed cloths: wool and linen

353   [88]   <2949/39>   TB559.
354   [88]   <3902.19>   TB560, Fig 97A.
355   [55]   <1522>   TB561,   Fig 97B,   dye tested.

Narrow wares: tablet-woven braids

356   [150]   <4005/9>   TB591,   Pl 13B, XII.
357   [150]   <2859>   Table 11, Fig 101,   XII.
358   [79]   <1836>   Table 11, Fig 106.
359   [88]   <3067>   TB587,   Table 11, Fig 105A.
360   [88]   <3068>   Table 11.
361   [83]   <1977>   TB586,   Table 11.
362   [88]   <3906>   TB589,   Table 11, Fig 105B.

Narrow wares: fingerloop braids

*339   [150]   <2822>   TB88,   Table 12, Fig 84A.
363   [150]   <3231>   TB585,   Table 12.
364   [89]   <2368>   TB575,   Table 12.
365   [55]   <1849/2>   TB584,   Table 12.
366   [55]   <1557>   TBX3,   Table 12, • dye tested.
367   [89]   <4099/2>   TB576,   Table 12.
368   [55]   <1659>   TB572,   Table 12.
369   [55]   <1867>   TB573,   Table 12,   dye tested.
370   [55]   <3753>   TB574,   Table 12, Fig 108B.
371   [55]   <1643/1>   TB571,   Table 12, Fig 108C.

Narrow wares: plaited braids

372   [150]   <4007/3>   TB578,   Table 13.
373   [55]   <1787>   TB579,   Table 13.
374   [83]   <1915>   TB580,   Table 13.
375   [150]   <3615>   TB581,   Table 13.
376   [150]   <4007/1>   TB582,   Table 13.
377   [150]   <4007/2>   TB583,   Table 13.
378   [150]   <2822>   TB588,   Table 13.
379   [150]   <4011/2>   TB577,   Table 13.

Narrow wares: tabby-woven braids
 *216 [79] <1789> TB29, Table 14, Fig 144.
 380 [150] <4005/5> TB569, Table 14, Fig
   111A.
 381 [88] <4098/30> TB566, Table 14.
 *219 [88] <4098/1> TB4, Table 14.
 382 [89] <4099/1> TB570, Table 14.
 383 [150] <3617> Table 14, Fig 130.
 384 [150] <4006> TB568, Table 14.
 385 [88/1] <2832> TB564, Table 14.
 386 [150] <3401/2> TB567, Table 14, Fig
   111B.
 387 [88] <3995> TB565, Table 14, Fig IIIC.

Narrow wares: garters
 388 [55] <1748> TB26, Fig 113, XIII.
 389 [55] <1643/1> TB27, XIII, dye
   tested.
 390 [55] <1557> TBX22, Fig 114, XIII.

Narrow wares: hairnet
 391 [89] <2367> TB592, XIV.

Unstratified

Wool textiles: 2.1 twills (mixed spinning)
 2 examples

Wool textile: 2.2 twill (Z-spun yarn)
 392 <4919/1> TA249, Table 4, Fig 162.

Wool textile: tabby (mixed spinning)
 393 <4919/2> TA430, Fig 143B.

Wool textile: tabby with weft-faced band
 394 <2706/2> TA432, Pl 8B, I, dye tested.

Silk textile: tabby (Z/-)
 395 <4919/2> TA430, Table 10, Fig 143B.

Baynard's Castle (BYD81)
First half 15th century

Wool textiles: 2.2 twill (mixed spinning)
 1 example, dye tested.

Wool textiles: 2.2 twill (S-spun yarn)
 1 example, dye tested.

Wool textiles: tabbies (mixed spinning)
 396 [80] <24>, Table 6, dye tested.
 Plus 2 others, dye tested.

Wool textiles: tabby (Z/?)
 1 example.

Trig Lane (TL74)
Revetment dump G2, late 13th century

Wool textiles: 2.2 twill (Z-spun yarn)
 1 example, dye tested.

Wool textiles: tabby (Z-spun yarn)
 397 [2542] <3033>, Fig 31, dye tested.

Silk textiles: patterned cloth
 *398 [2532] <2434>, Fig 77, VIII, dye
   tested.

Narrow wares: fingerloop braids
 *399 [2532] <3035>, Table 12, Fig 120.
 400 [2532] <2435>, Table 12, Fig 108A.

Narrow wares: plaited braids
 *398 [2532] <2434>, Table 13.
 401 [2542] <3032>, Table 13.

Narrow wares: hairnet
 *399 [2532] <3035>, Figs 119, 120, XIV.

Revetment dump, G10, late 14th century

Silk textiles: tabby (Z/-)
 1 example, dye tested.

Revetment dump, G15, first half 15th century

Wool textiles: tabby (Z-spun yarn)
 1 example, dye tested.

Wool textiles: tabby (mixed spinning)
 1 example.

Wool textiles: tabby (S-spun yarn)
 4 examples, 3 dye tested.

Wool textiles: tabby with weft-faced band
 402 [453] <1984>, I, dye tested.

Linen textile: tabby (Z-spun yarn)
 403 [275] <1077>, Table 9, Fig 54.

Narrow wares: tablet-woven braid
 *404 [364] <991>, Fig 104, XII, dye tested.

Narrow wares: fingerloop braid
    405 [275] <1154>, Table 12,   dye tested.

Narrow wares: tabby-woven braid
    406 [364] <431>, Table 14,   dye tested.

Milk Street (MLK76)
Late 12th-century pit fill

Narrow wares: fingerloop braids
    407 [1082] <373>, Table 12,   dye tested.
    408 [1145A] <1085>, Table 12.

Late 13th-century fill of garderobe

Linen textile: tabby (Z-spun yarn)
    409 [3061] <345>, Table 9.

Late 14th or early 15th-century fill of garderobe

Wool textile: 3.3 twill (Z-spun yarn)
    410 [1003] <1542>, Table 5.

Wool textile: tabby (Z-spun yarn)
    1 example,   dye tested.

Wool textiles: tabbies (mixed spinning)
    411 [1003] <45>, Table 6, Figs 34C, 35.
    412 [1003] <46>, Table 6,   dye tested.
    Plus 3 others,   2 dye tested.

Wool textiles: tabbies (S-spun yarn)
    2 examples,   1 dye tested.

Linen textile: tabby (Z-spun yarn)
    413 [25] <26>, Table 9.

Guildhall Car Park
12th-century fill of robber trench

Linen textile: patterned cloth
    414 ER1069 <15>, Table 9, Fig 56.

Public Cleansing Depot
Late 12th and early 13th-century Thames foreshore

Goathair cloth
    415 ER556 <15>, Table 8.

Swan Lane (SWA81)
Late 13th-century waterfront revetment dumps

Wool textiles: 2.1 twills (mixed spinning)
    2 examples,   dye tested.

Wool textiles: 2.2 twills (Z-spun yarn)
    2 examples,   1 dye tested.

Goathair cloth
    416 [2261] <2171>, Table 8.

 Silk textiles: tabbies (Z/-)
    417 [2042] <742>, Table 10, dye tested.
    418 [2042] <744>, Table 10, dye tested.
    419 [2056] <1034>, Table 10, dye tested.
    Plus 1 other.

Narrow wares: tablet-woven braid
    420 [2061] <4668>, Fig 98, XII, dye tested.

Narrow wares: plaited braid
    421 [2137] <4655>, Table 13, Fig 110A, dye tested.

Early 15th-century waterfront revetment dumps

Wool textiles: tabby with weft-faced bands
    422 [873] <2083>, I, dye tested.

Narrow wares: tablet-woven braid
    423 [2084] <2971>, Fig 103, XII.

Unstratified

Silk textiles: patterned cloth
    424 [2019] <1717>, Fig 94, XI, dye tested.

Narrow wares: plaited braid
    425 [+] <3920>, Table 13.

Seal House (SH74)
Early 13th-century waterfront revetment dump

Silk textiles: tabby (yarn lacking in any appreciable twist)
    426 [467] <721>, Fig 61, dye tested.

Narrow wares: fingerloop braid
   427 [467] <508>, Table 12

New Fresh Wharf (FRE78)
14th-century waterfront revetment dump

Wool textiles: tabby (mixed spinning)
   428 [2001] <2>, Table 6.

Wool textiles: knitting
   429 [2001] <82>, Fig 49, dye tested.

Billingsgate (BIG82)
Late 12th-century waterfront revetment dump

Wool textiles: 2.1 twill (S-spun yarn)
   1 example.

Early 13th-century waterfront revetment dump

Wool textiles: tabby (mixed spinning)
   430 [4080] <6008>, Fig 39.

Goathair cloths
   431 [5999] <3081>, Table 8.
   432 [3363] <2414>; and
               <2419>, Table 8.

   433 [3984] <2481>, Table 8.
   434 [4010] <5876>, Table 8.

Mid-13th-century waterfront revetment dump

Wool textiles: 2.1 twill (mixed spinning)
   1 example.

Goathair cloths
   435 [1668] <2334>, Table 8.
   436 [1914] <2055>, Table 8.

Late 13th-century waterfront revetment dump

Goathair cloth
   437 [3089] <2085>, Table 8.

Billingsgate watching brief (BWB83)
Late 14th-century waterfront revetment dump

Wool textiles: 2.2 twill (Z-spun yarn)
   1 example.

Wool textiles: tabby (S-spun yarn)
   1 example.

Wool textiles: knitting
   438 [330] <295>.

Goathair cloth
   439 [330] <190>, Table 8.

Silk textiles: tabby (yarn lacking in any appreciable twist)
   440 [150] <44>.

Narrow wares: tablet-woven braid
   441 [142] <34>; and
         [369] <350>, Fig 102, XII, dye tested.

Custom House (CUS73)
Waterfront revetment dump, first half 14th century

Wool textiles: 2.1 twills (mixed spinning)
   442 XIV[7] <781>, Fig 16.
   Plus three others, 1 dye tested.

Wool textiles: 2.2 twills (mixed spinning)
   443 XV[18] <775>, Table 4, Fig 24A, dye tested.
   444 XII[3] <686>, Fig 27B, Pl 4A.

Wool textiles: tabby (Z-spun yarn)
   1 example, dye tested.

Goathair cloths
   445 XIV[5] <823>, Table 8, Fig 53.
   446 XIV[3] <776>, Table 8.

Silk textiles: tabby (Z/–)
   447 I[12] <585>, Table 10, dye tested.
   448 III[16] <536>, Table 10, dye tested.
   Plus 1 other, dye tested.

Narrow wares: tablet-woven braids
   449 I[12] <109>, Fig 100C, XII.
   450 III[10] <594>, Fig 100B, XII,   dye tested.
   451 III[10] <598>, Table 11.

Narrow wares: fingerloop braids
   452 I[12] <602/3>, Table 12.
   453 I[12] <1245>, Table 12.
   454 I[12] <592>, Table 12.

Narrow wares: plaited braids
   455 I[12] <602/1>, Table 13, dye tested.
   456 I[12] <602/2>, Table 13.
   457 I[12] <602/4>, Table 13.

Dukes Place (DUK77)
Fill of cesspit, second half 14th century

Silk textiles: patterned cloths
   458 [494] <208>, Figs 70, 71, V, dye tested.
   459 [494] <133>, Figs 79–81, IX, dye tested.

Glossary

For more detailed definitions see CIETA 1964 and Burnham 1980.

Band	Transverse stripe in the weft
Binding warp	A secondary warp that binds weft floats
Brocading weft	An additional weft introduced into a ground weave and limited to the area where it is required by the pattern. It does not travel from selvedge to selvedge
Chevron twill	Any form of twill in which the direction of the diagonal lines is reversed over groups of picks (weft chevron), or over groups of ends (warp chevron)
Damask	A figured textile with one warp and one weft in which the pattern is formed by a contrast of binding systems
Decoupure	The smallest number of warp ends (warp decoupure), or the smallest number of picks or passes (weft decoupure) that forms one step in the outline of a design
End	An individual warp thread
Entering	The order in which warp ends are threaded through the heddles or leashes on a loom
Extended tabby	Tabby in which the weft picks pass under and over the warp ends in groups of two or more
Filé	A smooth thread composed of a lamella (often gilded membrane) wound around a core of another material (for example, silk or linen thread)
Heddle	A loop through which a warp end is passed so that it may be raised or lowered to open the shed to permit the passage of the weft
Huckaback	A self-patterned weave with a tabby ground and small all-over motifs in offset rows formed by warp floats on one face and weft floats on the other
Lampas	A figured weave in which a pattern, composed of weft floats bound by a binding warp, is added to a ground weave formed by a main warp and a main weft
Main warp	The principal, or only, warp in a textile
Pattern unit	Unit composed of one or more motifs which, by its repetition, constitutes the pattern of a textile
Pattern weft	Weft, auxilary to the main weft, passed from selvedge to selvedge to enrich the ground or to form a pattern
Point repeat	A reverse repeat in a woven pattern

Pick	A single passage of a weft thread, or group of weft threads, through the shed
Pick and pick selvedge	A selvedge where two shuttles of weft cross one another (Figs 11A & B, 17C & D, 34A)
Reeled silk	Thread produced by unwinding the baves (twin filaments) of several silkworm cocoons
Samite	See weft-faced compound twill
Satin	A weave based on a unit of five or more ends, and a number of picks equal to, or a multiple of, the number of ends. Each end either passes over or under four or more adjacent picks and under or over the next one. The binding points are set over two or more ends on successive picks and are distributed in an unobtrusive manner to give a smooth appearance
Selvedge	The longitudinal edge of a textile closed by weft loops
Shaft	A group of heddles fixed side by side in order that they may be moved together at the same time
Shed	The opening in the warp that permits the passage of each weft thread
S-spun, Z-spun	The letters S and Z are used to denote a yarn's direction of twist. The central stroke of the letter matches the direction in which the twisted fibres lie
S/S, Z/Z	The yarn has a similar direction of twist in both warp and weft
Straight repeat	The repetition of pattern units side by side without variation
Stripe	Vertical band in the warp
Tabby	Weave based on a unit of two ends and two picks in which each end passes over one and under one pick
Tablet weaving	A type of twined-warp weaving in which the sheds are formed by tablets with holes through which the warp ends are threaded. If the tablets are rotated, either in groups or singly, sheds are created for the passage of the weft
Tapestry	Weave with one warp, and a weft composed of threads of different colours, each of which is interwoven only with that part of the warp where it is required by the pattern
Thrown silk	The silk threads that result from the twisting of reeled filaments
Twill	A weave based on a unit of three or more ends and three or more picks, in which each end passes over or under two or more adjacent picks and under or over the next one or more. The binding points form diagonal lines
Velvet	A warp pile weave in which the pile is produced by a pile warp that is raised in loops above a ground weave through the introduction of rods during the weaving
Warp	The longitudinal threads of a textile; those that are arranged on a loom

Warp face	The side of a textile on which the warp predominates
Weft	The transverse threads of a textile; those that are passed through the sheds
Weft face	The side of a textile on which the weft predominates
Weft-faced compound twill	A weft-patterned weave with complementary wefts in two or more series, usually of different colours, and a main warp and a binding warp. Through the action of the main warp ends, only one weft thread appears on the face, while the other or others are kept to the reverse. The ends of the binding warp bind the weft in passes, and the ground and the pattern are formed simultaneously. The entire surface is covered by weft floats that hide the main warp ends
Weft-patterned	A textile in which a pattern is formed, or the ground enriched, by the use of more than one series of weft threads
Woollen	A yarn made from carded wool fibres
Worsted	A smooth thread spun from wool fibres which have been laid parallel by combing
Z/S	The yarn is Z-twisted in one system, usually the warp, and S-twisted in the other. The term mixed spinning is sometimes used in the text
Z/S-ply, S/Z-ply	The first letter is the direction of twist of the yarn and the second letter is the direction of ply

Bibliography

ALEXANDER, J & BINSKI, P (eds), 1987 *Age of Chivalry. Art in Plantagenet England*, London

ARNOLD, J, 1980 *'Lost from Her Majesties Back'*, The Costume Society

——, 1985 *Patterns of Fashion: The Cut and Construction of Clothes for Men and Women c. 1560–1620*, New York

AYLOFFE, J, 1786 'An account of the body of King Edward the First as it appeared on opening his tomb in the year 1774', *Archaeologia*, **3**, 376–413

BAART, J M *et al.*, 1977 *Opgravingen in Amsterdam*, Amsterdam

BAILDON, W P, 1911 'A wardrobe account of 16–17 Richard II, 1393–4', *Archaeologia*, **62/2**, 497–514

BAINES, P, 1977 *Spinning Wheels, Spinners and Spinning*, New York

BATTISCOMBE, C F (ed), 1956 *The Relics of St Cuthbert*, Oxford

BECKER, J, 1987 *Pattern and Loom: A Practical Study of the Development of Weaving Techniques in China, Western Asia and Europe*, Copenhagen

BENDER JØRGENSEN, L & TIDOW, K (eds), 1982 *Textilsymposium Neumünster Archäologische Textilfunde*, Neumünster

——, 1984 'North European textile production and trade in the first millenium AD', *J Danish Archaeol*, **3**, 124–34

——, 1986 *Forhistoriske Textiler i Skandinavien: Prehistoric Scandinavian Textiles*, Nordiske Fortidsminder Ser B, Bind **9**, Copenhagen

——, 1987 'A survey of north European textiles', *Studien zur Sachsenforschung*, **6**, 99–121

——, 1988 'Textilfunde aus dem Mittelelbe-Saale-Gebiet (Eisenzeit bis frühes Mittelalter)', *Jahresschrift für mitteldeutsche Vorgeschichte*, **71**, 91–123

——, MAGNUS, B & MUNKSGAARD, E (eds), 1988 *Archaeological Textiles: Report from the 2nd NESAT Symposium*, Arkaeologiske Skrifter **2**, Copenhagen

BENNETT, H, 1987 'Textiles', in Holdsworth (ed), 159–74

——, forthcoming 'The textiles', in *The Perth High Street Excavations*, Scottish Development Department

BERGLI, A, 1988 'Medieval textiles from the Finnegården excavation at Bryggen, Bergen', in Bender Jørgensen, Magnus & Munksgaard (eds), 221–7

BIDDLE, M (ed), 1976 *Winchester in the Early Middle Ages*, Winchester Studies, **1**, Oxford

—— (ed), 1990 *Object and Economy in Medieval Winchester*, Winchester Studies **7/2**, Oxford

BINSKI, P, forthcoming 'Aspects of the imagery of St Edward', in *England in the Thirteenth Century*, Proceedings of the Sixth Harlaxton Symposium

BLACKLEY, F D & HERMANSEN, G (eds), 1971 *The Household Book of Queen Isabella of England for the fifth regnal year of Edward II*, The University of Alberta Classical and Historical Studies 1, Edmonton

BONNER, G, ROLLASON, D & STANCLIFFE, C (eds), 1989 *St Cuthbert: His Cult and Community to 1200*, Woodbridge

BORN, W, 1939 'The twisting mill – the first step towards mechanized spinning', *CIBA Review*, **28**, 994–5

BOWDEN, P J, 1956 'Wool supply and the woollen industry', *Econ Hist Rev*, 2nd ser, **9**, 44–56

BRIDBURY, A R, 1982 *Medieval English Clothmaking: An Economic Survey*, London

BROWN, D, 1990 'Weaving tools', in Biddle (ed), 225–32

BRUNELLO, F, 1973 *The Art of Dyeing in the History of Mankind*, Vicenza

BUDNY, M, 1984 'The Anglo-Saxon embroideries at Maaseik: their historical and art-historical context', *Academiae Analecta, Medelingen van de Koninklijke Academie voor Wetenschappen, Letteren en Schone Kunsten van België, Klasse der Schone Kunsten*, **45/2**, 55–133

—— & TWEDDLE, D, 1984 'The Maaseik embroideries', *Anglo-Saxon England*, **13**, 65–96

—— & ——, 1985 'The early medieval textiles at Maaseik, Belgium', *Antiq J*, **65**, 353–89

BURKETT, M E, 1979 *The Art of the Felt Maker*, Kendal

BURNHAM, D K, 1980 *A Textile Terminology: Warp and Weft*, Royal Ontario Museum

BUYSE, L J, 1956 'The market for Flemish and Brabantine cloth in England from the XIIth to the XIVth century', MA thesis, London University

BYRDE, P, 1979 *The Male Image*, London

CAL WILLS, Sharpe, R (ed), *Calendar of Wills Proved Enrolled in the Court of Husting, London, Part I (1258–1358) and Part II (1358–1688)*, 1889 and 1890

CARRETERO, C H, 1988 *Museo de Telas Medievales Monasterio de Santa María la Real de Huelgas*, Patrimonio Nacional, Madrid

CARTER, H B & HENSHALL, A S, 1957 'The fabric from burial Q', in Robertson-Mackay, R, 'Recent excavations at the Cluniac priory of St Mary, Thetford, Norfolk', *Medieval Archaeol*, **1**, 102–3

CARUS-WILSON, E, 1944 'The English cloth industry in the late twelfth and early thirteenth centuries', *Econ Hist Rev*, 1st ser, **14**, 32–50

——— 1953 'La guède française en Angleterre: un grand commerce du moyen age', *Revue du Nord*, **35**, 89–105

———, 1954 *Medieval Merchant Venturers*, London

———, 1957 'The significance of the secular sculptures in the Lane Chapel, Cullompton', *Medieval Archaeol*, **1**, 104–17

———, 1969 'Haberget: a medieval textile conundrum', *Medieval Archaeol*, **13**, 148–66

——— & COLEMAN, O, 1963 *England's Export Trade, 1275–1547*, Oxford

CAWLEY, A C (ed), 1975 *G Chaucer, Canterbury Tales*, London

CCR, *Calendar of Close Rolls, 1288–1296*, London 1892

CEULMANS, C, DECONINCK, E & HELSEN, J (eds), 1988 *Tongeren Basiliek van O.-L.-Vrouw Geboorte I: Textiel*, Louvain

CHANDLER, M J & KING, D B, 1960 'Two charters and seal-bags of 12 Edward II', *The Guildhall Miscellany*, **211**, 20–3

CHARTRAIRE, E, 1911 'Les tissus anciens du trésor de la Cathédrale de Sens', *Revue de l'Art Chretién*, **61**, 261–80

CHILDS, W R, 1978 *Anglo-Castilian Trade in the Later Middle Ages*, Manchester

CHORLEY, P, 1987 'The cloth exports of Flanders and northern France during the thirteenth century: a luxury trade?', *Econ Hist Rev*, 2nd ser, **40**, 349–79

CHRISTIE, A G, 1938 *English Medieval Embroidery*, Oxford

CIETA, 1964 *Vocabulary of Technical Terms: Fabrics*, 2nd edn, Lyon

CIGGAAR, K, 1982 'England and Byzantium on the eve of the Norman Conquest (the reign of Edward the Confessor)', *Anglo-Norman Studies*, **5**, 78–96

CLARK, J, 1988 'Some medieval smith's marks', *Tools and Trades*, **5**, 11–22

———, ELLIS, B & GRIFFITHS, N, forthcoming *Medieval Finds from Excavations in London: The Medieval Horse*, London

CLR *Calendar of Liberate Rolls, 1226–1288*, 2 vols, London 1961

COLLIN, B, 1956 *The Riddle of a 13th century Sword-belt*, Heraldry Society

COLLINGWOOD, P, 1982 *The Technique of Tablet Weaving*, London

CONSITT, F, 1933 *The London Weavers' Company*, Vol I, Oxford

COOKE, B, 1990 'Fibre damage in archaeological textiles', in O'Connor, S A & Brooks, M M, *Archaeological Textiles*, UKIC Occasional Papers **10**, 5–14

CROWFOOT, E, 1966 'Fragment of braid from bronze belt link', in Tebbutt, C F, 'St Neots Priory', *Proc Cambs Ant Soc*, **59**, 54

———, 1975 'The textiles', in Platt, C & Coleman-Smith, R, *Excavations in Medieval Southampton 1953–69, Vol 2: The Finds*, Leicester, 334–9

———, 1976 'The textiles', in Hassall, T G, 'Excavations at Oxford Castle, 1965–73', *Oxoniensia*, **41**, 271–4

———, 1977 'Textiles', in Clarke, H & Carter, A, *Excavations in King's Lynn 1963–1970*, Soc Medieval Archaeol Monograph Ser, **7**, 374–7

———, 1978 'The textiles', in Green, B & Rogerson, A, *The Anglo-Saxon Cemetery at Bergh Apton, Norfolk*, East Anglian Archaeol Rep **7**, 98–106

———, 1979 'Textiles', in Carver, M O H, 'Three Saxo-Norman tenements in Durham City', *Medieval Archaeol*, **23**, 36–9

———, 1980 'The textiles', in Hill, Millett & Blagg, 112–15

———, 1981 'The textiles', in Cook, A M, *The Anglo-Saxon Cemetery at Fonaby, Lincolnshire*, Occasional Papers in Lincolnshire History and Archaeol **6**, 89–101

———, 1983 'The textiles', in Bruce-Mitford, R, *The Sutton Hoo Ship Burial*, Vol 3, I, 409–62

———, 1987 'The textiles', in Green, B, Rogerson, A & White, S G, *The Anglo-Saxon Cemetery at Morning Thorpe, Norfolk*, East Anglian Archaeol Rep, **36/1**, 171–88

———, 1990 'Textiles', in Biddle (ed), 467–88

———, forthcoming A Textile report, in Finglesham

———, forthcoming B Textile report, in Tattersall Thorpe

———, forthcoming C Textile report, in Snape

——— & HAWKES, S C, 1967 'Early Anglo-Saxon gold braids', *Medieval Archaeol*, **11**, 42–86

CROWFOOT, G M, 1939 'The tablet-woven braids from the vestments of St Cuthbert at Durham', *Antiq J*, **19**, 57–80

———, 1954 'Tablet-woven braid from a thirteenth century site' in Musson, R C, 'A thirteenth century bronze buckle with attached braid from Bramble Bottom, near Eastbourne', *Antiq J*, **34**, 234–5

———, 1956 'The braids', in Battiscombe (ed), 433–63

CUNNINGTON, C & CUNNINGTON, P, 1952 *Handbook of English Medieval Costume*, London

CUTBY, H, 1952 'St Gall, the linen town', *CIBA Review*, **91**, 3271–7

DALE, M K, 1928 'Women in the textile industries and trade of fifteenth-century England,' MA thesis, London University

———, 1932–4 'The London silkwomen of the fifteenth century', *Econ Hist Rev*, 1st ser, **4**, 324–35

DAVIS, N (ed), 1971 *Paston Letters and Papers*, 2 vols, Oxford

DEDEKAM, H, 1924–5 'To tekstilfund frå folkevandringstiden', *Bergen Museums Årbok*, 1–57

DEPPING, G D (ed), 1837 *Règlements sur les Arts et Métiers de Paris rédigés au XIIIe siècle et connus sous le nom du Livre des Métiers d'Etienne Boileau*, Collection des documents inedits sur l'histoire de France Ser 1, Paris

DESROSIERS, S, VIAL, G & JONGHE, D DE, 1989 'Cloth of Aresta. A preliminary study of its definition, classification, and method of weaving', *Textile History*, **20/2**, 199–233

DIGBY, G F W, 1939 'Sixteenth-century silk damasks: a Spanish group', *Burlington Magazine*, **74**, 222–8

DILLON, VISCOUNT & ST JOHN HOPE, W H, 1897 'Inventory of the goods and chattels belonging to Thomas, Duke of Gloucester, and seized in his castle at Pleshy, Co Essex, 21 Richard II', *Archaeol J*, **54**, 276–308

DODWELL, C R, 1982 *Anglo-Saxon Art: A New Perspective*, Manchester

DUNNING, G C, 1959 'Anglo-Saxon pottery — a symposium', *Medieval Archaeol*, **3**, 31–78

DYSON, T, 1989 *Documents and Archaeology: The Medieval London Waterfront*, Annual Archaeology Lecture, Museum of London

EGAN, G, 1979 'A shearman's hook from London', *Trans London and Middlesex Archaeol Soc*, **30**, 190–2

——— & PRITCHARD, F, 1991 *Medieval Finds from Excavations in London: 3 Dress Accessories*, London

EHD, Rothwell, H (ed), *English Historical Documents III (1189–1327)*, London 1975

ENDREI, W, 1983 'The productivity of weavers in late medieval Flanders', in Harte & Ponting (eds), 108–19

ERRERA, I, 1927 *Catalogues d'Etoffes Anciennes et Modernes*, 3rd edn, Brussels

EVANS, J, 1952 *Dress in Medieval France*, Oxford

FALKE, O von, 1913 *Kunstgeschichte der Seidenweberei*, 2 vols, Berlin

FENTZ, M, 1987 'En hørskjorte fra 1000-årenes Viborg', *Kuml*, 23–45

FINGERLIN, I, 1971 *Gürtel des Hohen und Späten Mittelalters*, Kunstwissenschaftliche Studien Band **46**, Munich & Berlin

FITCH, M, 1976 'The London makers of Opus Anglicanum', *Trans London and Middlesex Archaeol Soc*, **27**, 288–96

FLANAGAN, J F, 1956 'The figured silks', in Battiscombe (ed), 484–525

FLURY-LEMBERG, M, 1988 *Textile Conservation and Research*, Schriften der Abegg-Stiftung, Band **7**, Bern

——— & STOLLEIS, K (eds), 1981 *Documenta Textilia: Festschrift fur Sigrid Müller-Christensen*, Munich

FORBES, J, 1956 *Studies in Ancient Technology*, Vol 4, Leiden

FORD, D W, 1983 'Textiles', in Mayes, P & Butler, L A S, *Sandal Castle Excavations 1964–1973*, Wakefield, 335–6

FRANCE-LANORD, A & FLEURY, M, 1962 'Das Grab der Arnegundis in Saint-Denis', *Germania*, **40**, 341–59

FRANZÉN, A M & GEIJER, A, 1968 'Textile finds from excavations in Swedish towns, 1960–66', *Res Medievales*, **3**, 129–34

FUJIAN SHENG BOWUGUAN, 1982 *Fuzhou Nan Song Huangsheng mu*, Beijing

GADDUM, P W, 1979 *Silk, How and where it is produced*, Macclesfield

GEIJER, A, 1938 *Birka III: Die Textilfunde aus den Gräbern*, Uppsala

———, 1951 *Oriental Textiles in Sweden*, Copenhagen

———, 1964 *Textile Treasures of Uppsala Cathedral from Eight Centuries*, Stockholm

———, 1979 *A History of Textile Art*, Stockholm & London

———, FRANZÉN A M & NOCKERT, M, 1985 *Drottning Margaretas Gyllene Kjortel i Uppsala Domkyrka* (The Golden Gown of Queen Margareta in Uppsala Cathedral), Uppsala

GODDARD, E R, 1927 *Women's Costume in French Texts of the eleventh and twelfth centuries: The John Hopkins Studies in Romance Literatures and Languages Vol VII*, Baltimore & Paris

GÓMEZ-MORENO, M, 1946 *El Panteon Real de las Huelgas de Burgos*, Madrid

GOODRIDGE, J F (trans), 1966 *Piers the Ploughman*, revised edn, Harmondsworth

GRANGER-TAYLOR, H, 1989A 'The weft-patterned silks and their braid: the remains of an Anglo-Saxon dalmatic of *c.*800 ?', in Bonner, Rollason & Stancliffe (eds), 303–27

——, 1989B 'The Inscription on the Nature Goddess Silk', in Bonner, Rollason & Stancliffe (eds), 339–41

——, 1989C 'The Earth and Ocean Silk from the tomb of St Cuthbert at Durham', *Textile History*, **20/2**, 151–66

GREIG, J, 1981 'The investigation of a medieval barrel-latrine from Worcester', *J Archaeol Science*, **8**, 265–82

GREW, F & NEERGAARD, M DE, 1988 *Medieval Finds from Excavations in London: 2 Shoes and Pattens*, London

GUICHERD, F, 1963 'Lampas Bouyides', *Bull de Liaison CIETA*, **18**, 18–28

GIUSEPPI, M S, 1920 'The wardrobe and household accounts of Bogo de Clare, AD 1284–6', *Archaeologia*, **70**, 1–56

GUTTMANN, A L, 1938 'Technical peculiarities of Flemish cloth-making and dyeing', *CIBA Review*, **14**, 484–7

HÄGG, I, 1983 'Viking women's dress at Birka: a reconstruction by archaeological methods', in Harte & Ponting (eds), 316–50

——, 1984 *Die Textilfunde aus dem Hafen von Haithabu*, Berichte über die Ausgrabungen in Haithabu, **20**, Neumünster

HALD, M, 1980 *Ancient Danish Textiles from Bogs and Burials*, Copenhagen

——, 1981 'Spinning goat's hair', in Flury-Lemberg & Stolleis (eds), 19–22

HALL, A R, TOMLINSON, P, HALL, R A, TAYLOR, G W & WALTON, P, 1984 'Dyeplants from Viking York', *Antiquity*, **58**, 58–60

HAMPE, T, 1901 *Katalog der Gewebesammlung des Germanischen Nationalmuseums, Vol 2; Stickeren, Spitzen und Posamentierarbeiten*, Nuremberg

HARDING, V A, 1987 'Some documentary sources for the import and distribution of foreign textiles in later medieval England', *Textile History*, **18/2**, 205–18

HARTE, N B & PONTING, K G (eds), 1983 *Cloth and Clothing in Medieval Europe*, Pasold Studies in Textile History **2**, London

HAYNES, A E, 1975 'Twill weaving on the warp-weighted loom: some technical considerations', *Textile History*, **6**, 156–64

HEBDITCH, M J (ed), 1946 *Yorkshire Deeds, IX*, Yorkshire Archaeological Society Record Series, **111**

HECKETT, E, 1987 'Some Hiberno Norse Headcoverings from Fishamble Street and St John's Lane, Dublin', *Textile History*, **18/2**, 159–73

HEDGES, J W, 1979 'The textiles and textile equipment', in Heighway, C M, Garrod, A P & Vince, A G, 'Excavations at 1, Westgate Street, 1975', *Medieval Archaeol*, **23**, 190–93

——, 1982 'Textiles', in MacGregor, A, *Anglo-Scandinavian Finds from Lloyds Bank, Pavement, and Other Sites*, The Archaeology of York **17/3**, 102–79

HENSHALL, A S, 1950 'Textile and weaving appliances in prehistoric Britain', *Proc Prehist Soc*, new ser, **16**, 130–62

——, 1964 'Five tablet-woven seal tags', *Archaeol J*, **121**, 154–62

HERALD, J, 1980 *Renaissance Dress in Italy, 1400–1500*, The History of Dress Series, London

HERRMANN, H & LANGENSTEIN, Y (eds), 1987 *Textile Grabfunde aus der Sepultur des Bamberger Domkapitels*, Munich

HIGGINS, C, 1989 'Some new thoughts on the Nature Goddess silk', in Bonner, Rollason & Stancliffe (eds), 329–37

HILL, C, MILLETT, M & BLAGG, T, 1980 *The Roman Riverside Wall and Monumental Arch in London*, London and Middlesex Archaeol Soc Special Paper **3**

HODGETT, G A J (ed), 1971 *Cartulary of Holy Trinity Aldgate*, London

HOFENK DE GRAAFF, J H & ROELEFS, W G T, 1976 'Occurrence of textile red dyes 1450–1600', *American Dyestuff Reporter*, **65**, 32–4

HOFFMANN, M, 1964 *The Warp-weighted Loom*, Oslo

HOLDSWORTH, P (ed), *Excavations in the Medieval Burgh of Perth 1979–1981*, Soc Antiq Scotland Monograph Ser, **5**, Edinburgh

HORNSTEIN, L H, 1941 'The historical background of the King of Tars', *Speculum*, **16**, 404–14

HOUGEN, B, 1935 'Snartemofunnene', *Norsk Oldfunn*, **7**, 58–97

HUNDT, H-J, 1980 'Textilreste aus dem frühgeschichtlichen Kriegergrab von Sievern, Kr Wesermunde, 1954', *Studien zur Sachsenforschung*, **2**, 151–60

——, 1983 'Ein Textilfund aus Grab 8 von Dorverden, Kr Verden (Aller), Niedersachsen', *Studien zur Sachsenforschung*, **4**, 207–11

HURRY, J B, 1930 *The Woad Plant and its Dye*, Oxford

INGSTAD, A S, 1982 'The functional textiles from the Oseberg ship', in Bender Jørgensen & Tidow (eds), 85–94

———, 1988 'Textiles from Oseberg, Gokstad and Kaupang', in Bender Jørgensen, Magnus & Munksgaard (eds), 133–48

JONGHE, D DE & TAVERNIER, M, 1978 'Met selectieroeden geweven Koptische weefels', *Bull van de Koninklijke Musea voor Kunst en Geschiedenis, 50*, 75–106

——— & ———, 1982 'Die textielresten uit graf 6', in *Maria van Bourgondië*, Bruges, 212–34

JOYCE, J G, 1869 'On the opening and removal of a tomb in Winchester Cathedral, reputed to be that of King William Rufus', *Archaeologia, 42*, 309–21

KAMINSKA, J & NAHLIK, A, 1960 'Etudes sur l'industrie textile du haut Moyen Age en Pologne', *Archaeologia Polona, 3*, 89–119

KEENE, D, 1990 'The textile industry', in Biddle (ed), 200–14

KENDRICK, A F, 1924 *A Catalogue of Tapestries*, Victoria and Albert Museum, London

———, 1925 *Catalogue of Early Medieval Woven Fabrics*, Victoria and Albert Museum, London

KERRIDGE, E, 1985 *Textile Manufactures in Early Modern England*, Manchester

KING, D, 1960 'Sur la signification de "Diasprum"', *Bull de Liaison du CIETA, 11*, 42–7

———, 1963 *Opus Anglicanum: English Medieval Embroidery*, Arts Council of Great Britain, London

———, 1968 'Two medieval textile terms: "draps d'ache", "draps de l'arrest"', *Bull de Liaison du CIETA, 27*, 26–9

———, 1969 'Some unrecognised Venetian woven fabrics', *Victoria and Albert Yearbook, 1*, 53–63

———, 1971 'The textiles', in H G Ramm, 'The tombs of Archbishops Walter de Gray (1216–55) and Godfrey de Ludham (1258–65) in York Minster, and their contents', *Archaeologia, 103*, 127–31, 136

———, 1977 'How many Apocalypse tapestries?', in V Gervers (ed), *Studies in Textile History in Memory of Harold B Burnham*, Toronto, 160–7

———, 1981 'Early textiles with hunting subjects, in the Keir collection', in Flury-Lemberg & Stolleis (eds), 95–104

———, 1984 'Textiles and embroideries', in Zarnecki, G, Holt, J & Holland, T (eds), *English Romanesque Art 1066–1200*, Arts Council of Great Britain, London, 356–9

———, 1987 'Embroidery and textiles', in Alexander & Binski (eds), 157–61

——— & KING, M, 1988 'Silk weaves of Lucca in 1376',
in Estham, I & Nockert, M (eds), *Opera Textilia variorum Temporum*, The Museum of National Antiquities, Stockholm Studies *8*, 67–76

KJELLBERG, A, 1979 'Tekstilmaterialet fra "Oslogate 7"', *De Arkeologiske Utgravninger i Gamlebyen, Oslo*, Bind *2*, 83–104

———, 1982 'Medieval textiles from the excavations in the old town of Oslo', in Bender Jørgensen & Tidow (eds), 136–49

KOK, A, 1966 'A short history of orchil dyes', *The Lichenologist, 3*, 248–72

LACEY, K, 1987 'The production of "narrow ware" by silkwomen in fourteenth and fifteenth century England', *Textile History, 18/2*, 187–204

LAPORTE, J-P, 1988 *Le Trésor des Saints de Chelles*, Societé Archaeologique et Historique de Chelles

LAVER, J, 1963 *Costume*, London

LEGG, J W, 1890 'On an inventory of the vestry in Westminster Abbey, taken in 1388', *Archaeologia, 52/1*, 197–228

LEMON, H, 1968 'The development of hand spinning wheels', *Textile History, 1*, 83–91

LENNARD, R V, 1947 'An early fulling-mill: a note', *Econ Hist Rev, 17*, 150

LESSING, J, 1913 *Die Gewebe–Sammlung des Königlichen Kunstgewerbe–Museums Berlin*, 5 vols, Berlin

LINDSTRÖM, M, 1976 Textilier, in Mårtensson, A W, 'Uppgrävt forflutet för PK-banken i Lund', *Archaeologica Lundensia, 7*, 279–91

LOPEZ, R A L, 1970 'Découverte de deux riches étoffes dans l'Eglise paroissiale d'Ona', *Bull de Liaison du CIETA, 31*, 21–5

LOPEZ, R S, 1943 'European merchants in the Medieval Indies: the evidence of commercial documents', *J Economic Hist, 3*, No 2, 164–84

———, 1952 'China silk in Europe in the Yuan period', *J American Oriental Soc, 81*, 72–6

LYSONS, S, 1812 'Copy of a roll of the expenses of King Edward I at Rhuddlan Castle, in Wales, in the 10th and 11th years of his reign remaining among the records in the Tower', *Archaeologia, 16*, 32–79

———, 1814 'Copy of a roll of purchases made for the tournament of Windsor Park, in the sixth year of King Edward I, preserved in the Record Office at the Tower', *Archaeologia, 17*, 297–310

MCDONNELL, K, 1978 *Medieval London Suburbs*, London

MAGAGNATO, L (ed), 1983 *Le Stoffe di Cangrande*, Florence

MAGNUS, B, 1984 'How was he dressed? New light on the garments at Evebø/Eide in Gloppen Norway', *Studien zur Sachsenforsung*, **4**, 293–313

MAIK, J, 1988 *Wyroby Włókiennicze na Pomorzu z Okresu Rzymskiego i ze Średniowiecza*, Acta Archaeologica Lodziensia, **34**

MALANIMA, P, 1986 'The first European textile machine', *Textile History*, **17/2**, 115–27

MALDONADO, B P, 1978 *Tudela, Cuidad Medieval: Arte Islamica y Mudejar*, Madrid

MANNING, W H, 1972 'The method of manufacture of Romano-British wool combs', *Antiq J*, **52**, 333–5

MANNOWSKY, W, 1931–38 *Der Danziger Paramentenschatz*, 5 vols, Berlin & Leipzig

MARTINIANI-REBER, M, 1986 *Lyon, Musée historique des tissus soieries, sassanides, coptes et byzantines V–XI siècles*, Inventaires des collections publiques françaises, Paris

MAY, F L, 1957 *Silk Textiles of Spain: Eighth to Fifteenth Centuries*, New York

MAZZAOUI, M F, 1981 *The Italian Cotton Industry in the Later Middle Ages 1100–1600*, Cambridge

MEAD, V K, 1977 'Evidence for the manufacture of amber beads in London in 14–15th century', *Trans London and Middlesex Archaeol Soc*, **28**, 211–14

MILNE, G & MILNE, C, 1982, *Medieval Waterfront Development at Trig Lane, London*, London and Middlesex Archaeol Soc Special Paper **5**

MONNAS, L, 1986 'Developments in figured velvet weaving in Italy during the 14th century', *Bull de Liaison du CIETA*, **63/64**, 63–100

——, 1987 'The artists and the weavers: The design of woven silks in Italy 1350–1550', *Apollo*, **125**, No 304, 416–24

——, 1988 'Loomwidths and selvedges prescribed by Italian silk weaving statutes 1265–1512: A preliminary investigation', *Bull de Liaison du CIETA*, **66**, 35–44

——, 1989 'Silk cloths purchased for the Great Wardrobe of the Kings of England 1325–1462', *Textile History*, **20/2**, 283–307

MÜLLER-CHRISTENSEN, S, 1960 *Das Grab des Papstes Clemens II im Dom zu Bamberg*, Munich

——, 1983–4, 'En persisk brokade fra Domkirken i Augsberg', in By og Bygd: Festskrift til Marta Hoffmann, *Norsk Folkemuseums Årbok*, **30**, 185–94

——, KUBACH, H E & STEIN, G, 1972 'Die Graber im Konigschor', in Kubach, H E & Haas, W, *Der Dom zu Speyer*, Munich, 923–1024

MUNRO, J H, 1978 'Wool-price schedules and the qualities of English wools in the later middle ages *c*.1270–1499', *Textile History*, **9**, 118–69

——, 1979 'The 1357 wool-price schedule and the decline of Yorkshire wool values', *Textile History*, **10**, 211–19

——, 1983 'The medieval scarlet and the economics of sartorial splendour', in Harte & Ponting (eds), 13–70

MUSEO DE SANTA CRUZ, 1984 *Alfonso X*, Toledo

MUTHESIUS, A M, 1982A 'The silk textiles from the tomb', in Stratford, N, Tudor-Craig, P & Muthesius, A M, 'Archbishop Hubert Walter's tomb and its furnishings', *Medieval Art and Architecture at Canterbury*, Brit Archaeol Assoc Conference V 1979, 71–89

——, 1982B 'The silk fragment from 5 Coppergate', in MacGregor, A, *Anglo-Scandinavian Finds from Lloyds Bank, Pavement and Other Sites*, The Archaeology of York **17/3**, 132–6

——, 1984 'A practical approach to the history of Byzantine silk weaving', *Jahrbuch der Osterreichischen Byzantinistik*, **34**, 235–54

——, 1987 'Silk' in Holdsworth (ed), 169–71

——, forthcoming *Catalogue of the Silk Textiles in the Treasury of St Servatius, Maastricht*

NAHLIK, A, 1963 'Textiles from the excavation' in Artsikhovsky, A V & Kolchin, B A (eds), *Dwellings of Ancient Novgorod*, Excavation Reports **4**, 228–313

NEVINSON, J L, 1977 'Buttons and buttonholes in the fourteenth century', *Costume*, **11**, 38–44

NEWTON, S M, 1980 *Fashion in the Age of the Black Prince*, Bury St Edmunds

NICOLAS, N H, 1846 'Observations on the Institution of the Order of the Garter', *Archaeologia*, **31**, 1–163

NOCKERT, M, 1984 'Medeltida drakt i bild och verklighet', in *Den Ljusa Medeltiden, studier tillagnade Aron Anderson*, The Museum of National Antiquities, Stockholm, Studies **4**, 191–6

——, 1985 *Bockstensmannen och Hans Drakt*, Falkenberg, Sweden

—— & LUNDWALL, E, 1986 *Ärkebiskoparna fran Bremen*, Statens Historiska Museum, Stockholm

—— & POSSNERT, G, 1989 'När levde Bockstensmannen? Drakthistorisk och Kol —14 datering av fyndet', *Varbergs Museum Årsbok*, 55–74

NORDLAND, O, 1961 *Primitive Scandinavian Textiles in Knotless Netting*, Studia Norvegica **10**, Oslo

NØRLUND, P, 1924 *Buried Norsemen at Herjolfsnes*, Copenhagen

NYBERG, G G, 1984 'Eine Schaftrolle aus Haithabu als Teil eines Trittwebstuhls mit waagerecht gespannter Kette', *Berichte über die Ausgrabungen in Haithabu*, **19**, 145–50

ØSTERGÅRD, E, 1982 'The medieval everyday costumes of the Norsemen in Greenland', in Bender Jørgensen & Tidow (eds), 267–76

OWEN-CROCKER, G, 1986 *Dress in Anglo-Saxon England*, Manchester

ØYE, I, 1988 *Textile Equipment and its Working Environment, Bryggen in Bergen, c.1150–1500*, The Bryggen Papers Main Ser **2**, Bergen

PARSONS, J C (ed), 1977 *The Court and Household of Eleanor of Castile in 1290*, Toronto

PATTERSON, R, 1956 'Spinning and weaving', in Singer, C, Holmyard, E J, Hall, A R & Williams, T I, *A History of Technology, II*, Oxford, 191–220

POERCK, G de, 1951 *La Draperie médiévale en Flandre et Artois: technique et terminologie*, 3 vols, Bruges

PRITCHARD, F A, 1982 'Textiles from recent excavations in the City of London', in Bender Jørgensen & Tidow (eds), 193–208

——, 1984 'Late Saxon textiles from the City of London', *Medieval Archaeol*, **28**, 46–76

——, 1985 'Traces of vanished splendour — medieval textiles from London', *Popular Archaeol*, **6/12**, 28–33

——, 1988 'Silk braids and textiles of the Viking Age from Dublin', in Bender Jørgensen, Magnus & Munksgaard (eds), 149–61

——, 1991 'Small finds', in Vince, A G, (ed), *Aspects of Saxo-Norman London: 2. The Finds and Environmental Evidence*, London and Middlesex Archaeol Soc Special Paper **12**, 120–278

PRO, 1968 *Guide to Seals in the Public Record Office*, London

RAWSON, J, 1984 *Chinese Ornament: The Lotus and the Dragon*, The British Museum, London

RIGOLD, S, 1982 'Jettons and tokens', in Milne & Milne, 99–106

RILEY, H T (ed), 1868 *Memorials of London and London Life in the XIII, XIV and XV centuries*, London

ROBINSON, G & URQUHART, H, 1934 'Seal bags in the treasury of the cathedral church of Canterbury', *Archaeologia*, **84**, 163–211

ROBINSON, J A (ed), 1909 *The History of Westminster Abbey by John Flete*, Cambridge

ROOVER, F E DE, 1950 Lucchese Silks, *CIBA Review*, **80**, 2902–30

——, 1966 'Andrea Banchi, Florentine silk manufacturer and merchant in the fifteenth century', *Studies in Medieval and Renaissance History*, **3**, 223–85

ROSKAMS, S & SCHOFIELD, J, 1978 'Milk Street excavations: 2', *London Archaeol*, **3**, 227–34

ROTH, H LING, 1909 *Hand Woolcombing*, Bankfield Museum Notes No 6, Halifax

RUDDOCK, A A, 1951 *Italian Merchants and Shipping in Southampton*, 1270–1600, Southampton

RUTT, R, 1987 *A History of Hand Knitting*, London

RYDER, M L, 1966 'Coat structure and seasonal shedding in goats', *Animal Production*, **8**, 289–302

——, 1981 'British medieval sheep and their wool types', in Crossley, D W, (ed), *Medieval Industry*, CBA Res Rep, **40**, 16–20

——, 1983 *Sheep and Man*, London

SAFFORD, E W, 1928 'An account of the expenses of Eleanor, sister of Edward III, on the occasion of her marriage to Reynald, Count of Guelders', *Archaeologia*, **77**, 111–40

ST JOHN HOPE, W H, 1891–3 'Some remains of early vestments found in a bishop's coffin at Worcester', *Proc Soc Antiq*, **14**, 196–200

SALZMAN, L F, 1923 *English Industries of the Middle Ages*, Oxford

SANCTUARY, A, 1980 *Rope, Twine and Net Making*, Shire Album **51**, Princes Risborough

SANTANGELO, A, 1964 *The Development of Italian Textile Design*, English edn, London

SCHAEFER, G, 1941 'The cultivation of madder', *CIBA Review*, **39**, 1398–1406

SCHJØLBERG, E, 1984 *The Hair Products*, The Bryggen Papers Supplementary Ser **1**, Bergen

SCHLABOW, K, 1956 'Spätmittelalterliche Textilfunde aus der Lübecker Altstadtgrabung 1952', *Zeitschrift des Vereins für Lubeckische und Altertumskunde*, **36**, 133–53

SCHMEDDING, B, 1978 *Mittelalterliche Textilien in Kirchen und Klöstern der Schweiz*, Schriften der Abegg-Stiftung Band **3**, Bern

SCHOFIELD, J (ed), 1986 *Museum of London: Department of Urban Archaeology Archive Catalogue*, Museum of London

——, ALLEN, P & TAYLOR, C, forthcoming *Medieval Buildings and Property Development in the Area of Cheapside*, London and Middlesex Archaeol Soc Special Paper

SCHUETTE, M & MÜLLER-CHRISTENSEN, S, 1963 *The Art of Embroidery*, English edn, London

SCOTT, M, 1980 *Late Gothic Europe, 1400–1500*, The History of Dress Series, London

——, 1986 *A Visual History of Costume: the Fourteenth and Fifteenth Centuries*, London

SERJEANT, R B, 1972 Islamic Textiles: *Material for a History up to the Mongol Conquest*, Beirut

SHARPE, R R (ed), 1899–1912 *Calendar of Letterbooks of the City of London*, 12 vols, London

SHEPHERD, D G, 1951 'Another silk from the tomb of Saint Bernard Calvo', *Bull of Cleveland Museum of Art*, **38**, 74–5

——, 1954 'A Persian textile of the Buyid period', *Bull of Cleveland Museum of Art*, **41**, 53–5

——, 1957 A dated Hispano–Islamic silk, *Ars Orientalis*, **2**, 373–82

——, 1967 'Technical aspects of the Buyid silks', in Pope, A U & Ackerman, P (eds), *A Survey of Persian Art from Prehistoric Times to the Present, Vol 14, New Studies 1938–1960. Proc 4th International Congress of Iranian Art and Archaeology, Part A*, London & New York, 3090–99

——, 1974 'Medieval Persian silks in fact and fancy. (A refutation of the Riggisberg Report)', *Bull de Liaison du CIETA*, **39/40**, 1–239

——, 1981 'Zandanījī revisited', in Flury-Lemberg & Stolleis (eds), 105–22

SHERLEY-PRICE, L (trans), 1955 *Bede: A History of the English Church and People*, Harmondsworth

SMIRKE, E (ed), 1852 'Ancient consuetudinary of the city of Winchester', *Archaeol J*, **9**, 69–89

SMITH, J T, 1807 *Antiquities of Westminster*, London

SMITH, R, 1976 'Marble and Stucco', in *The Arts of Islam*, The Arts Council of Great Britain, 295–308

SPARROW SIMPSON, W (ed), 1887 'Two inventories of the cathedral church of St Paul, London', *Archaeologia*, **50/2**, 439–524

SPEISER, N, 1983 *The Manual of Braiding*, Basle

STALEY, E, 1906 *The Guilds of Florence*, London

STANILAND, K, 1975 'The excavated textiles', in Tatton Brown, 167

——, 1978 'Clothing and textiles at the court of Edward III, 1342–1352', in Bird, J, Chapman, H & Clark, J (eds), *Collectanea Londiniensia. Studies presented to Ralph Merrifield*, London and Middlesex Archaeological Society Special Paper **2**, 223–34

——, 1980 'Medieval courtly splendour', *Costume*, **14**, 7–23

——, 1989 'The Great Wardrobe accounts as a source for historians of fourteenth-century clothing and textiles', *Textile History*, **20/2**, 275–81

STAPLETON, T, 1836 'A brief summary of the wardrobe accounts of the 10th, 11th and 14th years of King Edward the Second', *Archaeologia*, **26**, 318–45

STATUES OF THE REALM, VOL 2, 1826, London

STEIN, A, 1921 *Serindia*, Oxford

SUTTON, A F, 1989 'The early linen and worsted industry of Norfolk and the evolution of the London Mercers'

Company', *Norfolk Archaeol*, **40**, 201–25

TALBOT-RICE, D, 1975 *Islamic Art*, revised edn, London

TATTON BROWN, T, 1974 'Excavations at the Custom House Site, City of London', 1973, *Trans London and Middlesex Archaeol Soc*, **25**, 117–219

——, 1975 'Excavations at the Custom House Site, City of London, 1973 — Part 2', *Trans London and Middlesex Archaeol Soc*, **26**, 103–70

TAYLOR, G W, 1983 'Detection and identification of dyes on Anglo–Saxon textiles', *Studies in Conservation*, **28**, 153–60

—— & WALTON, P, 1983 'Lichen purples', *Dyes on Historical and Archaeological Textiles*, **2**, 14–19

THIRSK, J, 1978 *Economic Policy and Projects: The Development of a Consumer Society in Early Modern England*, Oxford

THOMPSON, M W, 1968 The horizontal loom at Novgorod, *Medieval Archaeol*, **12**, 146–7

THOMSON, W G, 1973 *A History of Tapestry*, 3rd edn, Wakefield

TIDOW, K, 1982 'Untersuchungen an Wollgeweben aus Schleswig und Lübeck', in Bender Jørgensen & Tidow (eds), 163–77

——, 1987 'Gewebefunde aus Ausgrabungen in mittelalterlichen Siedlungen und Kirchen — ein vergleich der Webtechniken einfacher Gewebe', in Herrmann & Langenstein (eds), 91–8

——, 1990 'Spätmittelalterliche und frühneuzeitliche Textilfunde aus Lübeck und ihre früheren Verwendungen', in Walton, P & Wild, J P (eds), *Textiles in Northern Archaeology NESAT III: Textile Symposium in York 6–9 May 1987*, Institute of Archaeology, London, 165–74

TIETZEL, B, 1984 *Italienische Seidengewebe des 13, 14 und 15 Jahrhunderts*, Kataloge des Deutschen Textilmuseums Krefeld, Band **1**, Cologne

TOMLINSON, P, 1985 'Use of vegetative remains in the identification of dyeplants from waterlogged 9th–10th century AD deposits at York', *J Archaeol Science*, **12**, 269–83

TOUT, T F, 1920–33 *Chapters in the Administrative History of Medieval England*, 6 vols, Manchester

TURNAU, I, 1983 'The diffusion of knitting in medieval Europe', in Harte & Ponting (eds), 368–89

TYMMS, S (ed), 1850 *Wills and Inventories from the Registers of the Commissary of Bury St Edmunds*, Camden Society, **49**

VEALE, E M, 1966 *The English Fur Trade in the Later Middle Ages*, Oxford

VERHECKEN, A, & WOUTERS, J, 1988/9 'The coccid insect dyes. Historical, geographical and technical data' *Bull Institut Royal du Patrimoine Artistique/Koninklijk Institut Voor Let Kunstpatrimonium,* **22**, 207–39

VIAL, G, 1963 'La chasuble de Brauweiler, *Bull de Liaison du CIETA,* **18**, 29–38

——, 1971 'Un ruban de velours tissé "aux cartons"', *Bulletin de liaison du CIETA,* **34**, 54–74

VISSER, W J A, 1935 'Een reliek "de vestimentis" van den H Lebuinus', *Het Gildeboek,* **18**, 3–8

VONS-COMIS, S Y, 1982 'Medieval textile finds from The Netherlands', in Bender Jørgensen & Tidow (eds), 151–62

——, 1983 'Een veertiende eeuwse textielsnipper uit het kasteel Voorst te Westenholte (gem Zwolle)', in *Het Kasteel Voorst Macht en val van een Overijsselse burcht circa 1280–1362 naar aanleiding van een opgraving,* 85–6

WAATERINGE, W G-VAN, 1984, *Die Lederfunde von Haithabu,* Berichte über Ausgrabungen in Haithabu, **21**, Neumünster

WALTON, P, 1982 'Old sock', *Interim,* **8/2**, 5–8

——, 1984 'Dyes on medieval textiles', **3**, 30–4

——, 1986 Dyes in early Scandinavian textiles, *Dyes on Historical and Archaeol Textiles,* **5**, 38–41

——, 1988 'Caulking, cordage and textiles', in O'Brien, C, Brown, L, Dixon, S & Nicholson, R *The Origins of the Newcastle Quayside Excavations at Queen Street and Dog Bank,* Soc of Antiq Newcastle upon Tyne Monograph Ser **3**, 78–85

——, 1989A *Textiles, Cordage and Raw Fibre from 16–22 Coppergate,* The Archaeology of York **17/5**

——, 1989B 'Dyes of the Viking Age: a summary of recent work', *Dyes in History and Archaeology,* **7**, 14–24

——, forthcoming 'Textile Report', in Armstrong, P, 'Excavations in High Street, Blackfriargate, Hull', *East Riding Archaeologist,* **8**

WARD PERKINS, J B, 1940 *London Museum Medieval Catalogue,* London

WARDWELL, A E, 1976–7 'The stylistic development of 14th- and 15th-century Italian silk design', *Aachener Kunstblatter,* **47**, 177–226

——, 1989 'Recently discovered textiles woven in the western part of Central Asia before AD1220, *Textile History,* **20/2**, 175–84

WATKIN, D M (ed), 1947/8 *Inventory of Church Goods temp Edward III,* 2 vols, Norwich

WATSON, A M, 1967 'Back to gold — and silver', *Econ Hist Rev,* 2nd ser, **20**, 1–34

WEBSTER, L & CHERRY, J, 1973 'Medieval Britain in 1972', *Medieval Archaeol,* **17**, 138–88

—— & ——, 1978 'Medieval Britain in 1977', *Medieval Archaeol,* **22**, 142–83

WEIBEL, A C, 1951 *Two Thousand Years of Tapestry Weaving: A Loan Exhibition,* Wadsworth Atheneum, Hartford/Baltimore Museum of Art

——, 1952 *Two Thousand Years of Textiles: The Figured Textiles of Europe and the Near East,* New York

WEIGERT, R-A, 1962 *French Tapestry,* English edn, London

WERNER, J, 1964 'Frankish royal tombs in the cathedrals of Cologne and Saint-Denis', *Antiquity,* **38**, 201–16

WHITE, L, 1978 *Medieval Religion and Technology (collected essays),* London

WHITEHOUSE, D, 1972 'Chinese porcelain in Medieval Europe', *Medieval Archaeol,* **16**, 63–78

WILCKENS, L von, 1958 *Aus dem Danziger Paramentenschatz und dem Schatz der Schwarzhaupter zu Riga,* Nuremberg

——, 1981 'Seidengewebe in Zusammenhang mit der heiligen Elisabeth', in *Sankt Elisabeth Fürstin Dienerin Heilige,* Sigmaringen

——, 1987 'Zur kunstgeschichtlichen Einordnung der Bamberger Textilfunde', in Herrmann & Langenstein (eds), 62–79

WILD, J P, 1964 'The textile term *scutulatus*', *The Classical Quarterley,* new ser, **14/2**, 263–6

——, 1965 'A Roman silk damask from Kent', *Arch Cantiana,* **80**, 246–50

——, 1970 *Textile Manufacture in the Northern Roman Provinces,* Cambridge

——, 1977 *Vindolanda III: The Textiles from Vindolanda 1973–1975,* Vindolanda Trust

——, 1984 'Some early silk finds in north–west Europe', *The Textile Museum Journal,* **23**, 17–23

WOLFF, P, 1983 'Three samples of English fifteenth-century cloth', in Harte & Ponting (eds), 120–5

WORMALD, F, 1973 *The Winchester Psalter,* London

WOUTERS, J, 1988 'Dye analyse van de Kleurstoffen', in Ceulmans, Deconinck & Helsen (eds), 100–6

WYLIE, J H, 1898 *History of England under Henry IV, Vol 4,* London

WYSS, R L, 1973 'Die Handarbeiten der Maria (Eine ikonographische studie unter Berucksichtigung der Textilen techniken)', in Stettler, H von M & Lemberg, M (eds), *Artes Minores: Dank an Werner Abegg,* Bern, 113–88

YOUNGS, S M, CLARK, J, & BARRY, T B, 1983 'Medieval Britain in 1982', *Medieval Archaeol,* **27**, 191–5